More Essential Than Ever

More Essential Than Ever

Community College Pathways to Educational and Career Success

DAVIS JENKINS
HANA LAHR
JOHN FINK
SERENA C. KLEMPIN
MAGGIE P. FAY

HARVARD EDUCATION PRESS
CAMBRIDGE, MASSACHUSETTS

Paperback ISBN 9781682539910

Library of Congress Cataloging-in-Publication Data is on file.

Published by Harvard Education Press,
an imprint of the Harvard Education Publishing Group

Harvard Education Press
8 Story Street
Cambridge, MA 02138

Cover Design: Patrick Ciano
Cover Images: merovingian and Greg Paprocki via Getty Images

The typefaces in this book are Adobe Garamond Pro and Myriad Pro.

Contents

Foreword

There are times when it is useful to pause and consider what we have learned from the hard work of community college redesign—and then to reach again for improvement, for equity, for the future. That is the opportunity provided by Jenkins, Lahr, Fink, Klempin, and Fay in this timely volume, *More Essential Than Ever: Community College Pathways to Educational and Career Success.*

It was a decade ago that community college educators began to discover the impactful book by Bailey, Jaggars, and Jenkins, *Redesigning America's Community Colleges: A Clearer Path to Student Success* (2015). That book brought to the field an inescapable picture painted by data on community college student progress and success; a depiction of the ways that institutional practice can impede successful college entry, progress, and completion; an insistence on moving from disparate practices to structured pathways; and a clearly articulated guided pathways framework, with available evidence marshaled to support it. The challenge was to scale an integrated set of practices comprising a redesigned educational experience for *all* students, with a fierce commitment to equity infused across every design decision.

The Book, as it came to be known, was chosen for campuswide reads; prompted on-campus, state-level, and national discussions; and ultimately served as a motivator and guide for hundreds of community colleges to engage in collegewide redesign in accord with the guided pathways model.

Notably, from the early 2000s, a lot of action in the community college field was prompted both by the recognition of the invaluable role these institutions play in serving a large and wildly diverse student population and by accumulating and often alarming data about student progress and college completion. *Redesigning* (2015) came, for example, after the founding of the Community College Survey of Student Engagement (2001), Achieving the Dream (2004), Complete College America (2009), Dana Center Mathematics Pathways and Carnegie Math Pathways (2009–2010), the Community College Completion

Agenda (2010), the California Acceleration Project (2010), Completion by Design (2011), the Aspen Prize for Community College Excellence (first awarded in 2011), the American Association of Community Colleges' report "Reclaiming the American Dream: Community Colleges and the Nation's Future" (2012), the National Center for Inquiry and Improvement (2013), and the "Core Principles for Transforming Remedial Education Within a Comprehensive Student Success Strategy" (2012, 2015, 2020)—foundation for the work of Strong Start to Finish (2018)—and a host of other institution-initiated, state-based, and foundation-supported initiatives.

Even as *Redesigning* acknowledged the extant body of work focused on student success, it added transformative value by articulating the shortcomings of the predominant "cafeteria college," in which a collection of disparate and unconnected strategies, practices, and courses—although they might produce good results for small numbers of students—would not move the big needles on success for all students. The authors also took seriously Judith Scott-Clayton's 2011 assertion that a lack of structure and systematic support made the community college student journey akin to "navigating a shapeless river on a dark night."[1] Thus, the book described the need for more structure for students and more intentional support for career choices and educational planning. More important, it advocated an alternative: the guided pathways model, which included mapping programs to student end goals, thus helping students choose and enter a path, keeping students on their path, and ensuring student learning.

The ensuing work in the community college field—as colleges increasingly committed to consider, design, and implement guided pathways for students—propelled a major reform movement. Looking backward now, we of course see that the timing of that early momentum was just before the global COVID-19 pandemic; before the ensuing losses of community college enrollment, exacerbating losses over the previous decade; before the necessary and dramatic pivot to online learning. It was before a surge of explicit public and policy attacks on ideas and action related to diversity, equity, and inclusion, even as that work was elevated to the center of reform efforts in some places and actively erased in others. It was before a renewed set of questions was raised about the value of college degrees and who should have them. It was before artificial intelligence became a significant force, for better and for worse, in higher education and the broader society.

College leaders find themselves now in a maelstrom of change, with an imperative to prepare their students to thrive and prosper in a future not fully foreseeable.

NOW COMES FRESH INSIGHT AND PRACTICAL ADVICE

In *More Essential Than Ever*, the authors celebrate the continuing work of community colleges committed to redesigning students' educational experiences. They summarize the key messages from *Redesigning*, briefly explicating the guided pathways model. They articulate important lessons learned from research on implementation of the model; they illuminate pertinent examples from a variety of colleges; and extremely helpfully, they elaborate on actions colleges can take to achieve the next important steps for improvement of results and equity across groups.

Among the most important insights from the early years of work on guided pathways reform is one gained both individually and collectively by the Community College Research Center and partner organizations that have collaborated in the work. That is, that colleges must be focused on and accountable not just for successful and equitable student outcomes from their community college experience but also for *postcompletion outcomes*. The most important outcomes of a student's community college experience are *what comes after it*. Whether that means seamless transfer to a chosen major in a transfer institution, or a clear path to postbaccalaureate credentials, or direct transition to employment, the student outcome most central to the mission of US community colleges is a career providing family-supporting income, which promotes economic upward mobility and disrupts the intergenerational poverty cycle. *More Essential Than Ever* focuses strongly on strategies to achieve that mission.

Based on evaluation research, Jenkins et al. raise the bar on established elements of guided pathways work—for example, by pushing for embedding advisors within students' meta-majors, strengthening processes for monitoring students' progress on their educational plans, and ensuring that class scheduling is aligned with students' plans—a dramatic change for most colleges.

Raising the bar yet again, the authors advocate development of much deeper partnerships between community colleges and their K–12 systems, emphasizing the potential for pathways to upward mobility to begin long before students arrive at the community college and calling for the diminishment of "random acts of course-taking" that have long characterized dual enrollment programs. The partnership imperative, of course, extends not just to K–12 but also to transfer institutions and employers.

A deeply concerning finding from the evaluation research is that although colleges implementing guided pathways practices at scale show improvements in certain leading indicators of success across all student groups, stubborn equity gaps persist. Next-step work described in the book includes key strategies for addressing those gaps; but achieving equity remains a critical challenge, and as the authors assert, it demands more attention.

THE HARD STUFF

Unsurprisingly, the work of whole-college transformation—using the guided pathways model to redesign the educational experience at scale—for *all students*—is exceedingly challenging. It challenges institutional norms, structures, biases, fondly held traditions, independent operations of individuals and organizational units, and faculty and staff convenience. It takes a long time—three, five, ten years, depending on the starting point and available support. It requires a comprehensive vision and a plan. It needs broad faculty, staff, and midlevel administration involvement. It is propelled by faculty senates and unions that choose to lead. It needs governing board understanding and support, along with the development of external partnerships and coalitions, with K–12 systems, transfer institutions, employer communities, and policy makers.

It requires leadership—at the CEO level and distributed throughout the organization—that rises to the challenges of major change. After a lot of work in the field with diverse community colleges committed to the work, observations regarding continuing issues include the following:

- Whole-college change is countercultural. Community colleges have long excelled at development of small-scale initiatives that benefit a few fortunate students; overhauling the entire student experience is an entirely different and far more challenging undertaking.
- Long-term commitments to sustained change work are rare. As noted, scaled implementation of guided pathways can take as much as a decade. Sustaining that focus is a formidable challenge but is aided through an annual planning process that identifies a small set of priorities for important next steps and connects them to resource allocation.

- Collaboration across within-institution silos is not the collegiate tradition; however, its importance and effectiveness are widely celebrated in colleges that have made substantial progress on whole-college redesign.
- The real test of commitment often comes when newly designed practices that benefit students require significant structural changes to support institutionalization and sustainability of the work—for example, modifications in resource allocation, roles and job descriptions, collective bargaining agreements, program mix, organizational structure, governance processes, class scheduling, and so on.
- Creating "versatile learners," as strongly advocated in chapter 3, requires creating versatile institutions. Agility, future focus, alacrity in decision-making, and leaning into change rather than resisting it are defining characteristics of institutions effectively stepping up to this challenge.

Changing practices, although difficult, is easier than changing cultures. Throughout *More Essential Than Ever*, the authors describe changes in mindsets—about students, about institutional policies, and about practices—that are crucial to the work moving forward.

None of this is easy. If it were not so urgently important, we wouldn't do it. Yet scores of community colleges across the United States have risen to the challenge. With the learning shared and the practical advice proffered, this book lifts up again the promise of community colleges. If the colleges and the people who support them will focus on the strategies that help them meet this new moment, then we can surely create together the colleges that communities need for the future. The colleges that all students deserve.

Kay M. McClenney
Senior Advisor to the President, American Association of Community Colleges
Past Director, Center for Community College Student Engagement (CCCSE)

Introduction

Now more than ever, America's community colleges are essential for advancing the social mobility of their students and supplying talent to support economic growth in communities and states across the nation. These institutions, which number nearly one thousand, offer broad access to a mix of programs, including workforce education that prepares students for careers in technical fields and upskills employed workers, academic programs for students who want to transfer to a four-year college, and dual enrollment courses for high school students seeking to get a jump on college.

No other institution—not K–12 schools, four-year institutions, or trade schools—offers such programs at anywhere near the scope and scale of public two-year colleges. Despite recent enrollment declines, community colleges still educate nearly 40 percent of undergraduates in the United States, including a majority of Hispanic and Native American college students and the largest share of students from low-income families. They also serve hundreds of thousands of students annually in noncredit workforce and adult basic education programs. About 10 percent of the colleges are located in rural communities, compared with only 2 percent of public four-year colleges.

Yet community colleges face unprecedented challenges that threaten their ability to advance economic mobility for residents of their communities and to support workforce development for their regional economies. Enrollment declines in recent years are perhaps their most pressing challenge. As a result of the COVID-19 pandemic, community colleges nationally lost nearly three-quarters of a million students; their enrollments fell by more than 14 percent between fall 2019 and fall 2022, with sharp declines among students of color, older working adults, and students from low-income families.[1] By contrast, public four-year colleges lost just over two hundred thousand students (or 3 percent) during that time. Equally concerning, community colleges experienced a marked drop in students entering immediately after high school, particularly among students from low-income families and communities of color. Although enrollment has begun to recover, it is still well below prepandemic levels at most community colleges.[2]

While the recent declines are alarming, community college enrollment was declining for a decade before COVID-19. Following a surge in enrollment after the Great Recession of 2008, community colleges nationally lost one million students, or about 13 percent of their enrollments, between fall 2011 and fall 2019.[3] Declines were steep among men, Black and white students, and older students. Enrollment of working adults in career-technical education programs outside of healthcare fell to historic lows, and community colleges also lost market share of traditional college students (ages eighteen to twenty-four) to public four-year colleges.

These declines stem from a complex set of circumstances in the past and present, some of which are beyond the control of community colleges:

- *Tight labor markets have increased the opportunity costs of returning to school.* Since the end of the Great Recession, community colleges have struggled to recruit working adults who can afford to focus on long-term earnings potential rather than on the immediate needs of their families as pay for relatively unskilled work has risen well above the federal minimum wage in many areas.[4]
- *Degree requirements have increased for good jobs.* Most jobs that pay living wages are increasingly held by workers with a bachelor's degree or higher.[5] Many of the remaining good jobs typically require at least a career-technical associate degree or apprenticeship. Skills training by itself, such as that provided in short-term certificate programs, is generally insufficient for students to get a good job.[6] Thus, it is a steeper climb education-wise from jobs that pay subsistence wages to those that can support an individual, much less sustain a family.

- *Competition from public and private four-year colleges has grown.* Because of the increased financial returns to workers who hold at least a bachelor's degree and heightened competition from higher education institutions for a shrinking pool of high school graduates, traditional college-age students who previously might have started at a community college and transferred to a four-year institution are entering them directly.[7]
- *Changing consumer preferences have generated more desire for easy-to-use systems and online programs.* Many community colleges have yet to adopt the "service-at-a-click" experience for registration, advising, and similar processes that students expect from other service providers.[8] Community colleges have expanded online offerings to respond to the increased demand, although they face competition from online universities and programs that specialize in remote learning and have resources to market and support these offerings.[9]

COVID-19 exacerbated these pressures. In the early stages of the pandemic, hundreds of thousands of community college students and their family members lost jobs in the service sector, giving them little choice but to forgo the expense of school.[10] The pandemic also set back many lower-income families that were finally recovering from the Great Recession. At the same time, it created new challenges for community colleges responding to their students' needs. They had to transition quickly from in-person to online teaching and advising, compete with higher-paying private sector jobs to attract and retain qualified faculty and staff, and deal with financial uncertainties after exhausting much-needed federal pandemic relief funding.[11]

Even so, the enrollment challenges community colleges have experienced are by no means completely outside their control. Only one-third of students who started at a community college in fall 2017 earned a certificate or degree at their original institution within six years, while an additional 11 percent earned an award at another two- or four-year institution.[12] Eleven percent were still enrolled in college, and 45 percent were no longer enrolled with no credential. That means more than half of community college starters (56 percent) did not earn any postsecondary credential in six years, with even higher noncompletion rates for Hispanic (62 percent) and Black (69 percent) students. Poor outcomes at community colleges often start early in the student experience. Nearly

40 percent of all community college starters, and higher proportions of Black and low-income students, do not return to any college for their second year.[13]

Increasing the rates at which community college students persist and complete programs would help replenish enrollment and provide needed revenue to keep these important institutions healthy and solvent. Equally important, increasing student success rates would demonstrate the value of a community college education and thus encourage more students to enroll.

REDESIGNING COMMUNITY COLLEGES FOR ACCESS *AND* SUCCESS

Community colleges were working to improve student retention and completion rates long before enrollments fell nationally after the Great Recession. When the federal government began reporting outcome data for higher education institutions in the early 2000s, community colleges stepped up efforts to improve what were widely seen as unacceptable retention and graduation numbers through what was often referred to in the field as the "completion agenda." A notable early effort was Achieving the Dream (ATD), an ambitious national initiative launched in 2004 by the Lumina Foundation to improve community college outcomes, particularly for low-income students and students of color. ATD provided institutes for participating college teams and hired coaches to guide colleges to implement reforms and leverage data to improve student outcomes.

A 2011 evaluation of reforms at the original twenty-six ATD colleges by the nonprofit antipoverty research organization MDRC and our organization, the Community College Research Center (CCRC), found that although some students benefited, the reforms either affected too few students or were focused on too narrow of a slice of their overall experience to increase completion rates.[14]

In the 2015 book *Redesigning America's Community Colleges: A Clearer Path to Student Success*, three researchers from CCRC (including an author of this volume) examined why, despite over a decade of completion agenda reforms, community colleges had neither achieved substantial gains in completion rates for all students nor reduced persistent achievement gaps among students by race/ethnicity, family income, age, and other factors.[15] The authors argued that to improve outcomes for large groups of students, colleges needed to rethink their larger education model instead of scaling discrete interventions. The authors presented a blueprint for redesigning the "cafeteria-style" community college model that evolved during the 1960s and 1970s, when community colleges were integral to the national effort to dramatically expand access to higher education. That model was well suited for low-cost enrollment in college courses but was less effective in helping students choose and complete affordable programs that prepared them for further education and employment.

Redesigning called on colleges to start with students' end goals, and then backward-design programs, onboarding, and supports to help them explore, choose, plan, and complete a program that would prepare them for jobs and transfer to bachelor's programs. As we describe in chapter 1, CCRC researchers and partners later formalized this "guided pathways" model in what became a widely used framework for implementing reforms and measuring adoption rates. The framework provided guidance for rethinking college practice under what in the field have become known as the four pillars of guided pathways: (1) clarifying paths to student end goals, (2) helping students get on a path, (3) keeping students on path, and (4) ensuring that students are learning across their programs.

LEARNING FROM THE GUIDED PATHWAYS MOVEMENT

Redesigning helped catalyze what became the largest community college reform movement in decades. The book's ideas provided the framework for the American Association of Community College (AACC) Pathways Project involving thirty colleges and for statewide guided pathways scaling initiatives in nineteen states. Teams from hundreds of colleges nationally have since participated in institutes, workshops, coaching, and other activities designed to help these institutions redesign programs and practices following the guided pathways model. Many other colleges have initiated guided pathways reforms on their own. Community colleges in California and Washington received state funding for guided pathways efforts, but most have pursued these reforms without new funds.

Since *Redesigning* was published, CCRC has occupied a front-row seat studying the community college guided pathways reform movement through research projects funded by private foundations and federal agencies. CCRC has investigated how early adopter colleges approached guided pathways reforms, how leaders in these colleges managed the large-scale changes involved, and how colleges funded and sustained these reforms. On the basis of this research, CCRC provided these and other colleges with guidance on implementation, producing more than three dozen reports and practitioner guides with accompanying inquiry and action guides, data tools, and other resources. CCRC researchers have given hundreds of presentations and led scores of in-person and online workshops to share findings and guide practitioners and state agency staff on executing and evaluating guided pathways reforms.

CCRC's studies since *Redesigning* include two multiyear evaluations of the adoption of guided pathways practices and their effects on student progress and success in more than ninety colleges nationally. The first, funded by the Bill & Melinda Gates Foundation, examined the thirty colleges that participated in the AACC Pathways Project in seventeen states. The second, funded by the National Science Foundation (NSF), examined guided pathways adoption and effects across all community and technical colleges in Ohio, Tennessee, and Washington, where statewide initiatives helped colleges implement large-scale reforms based on the guided pathways model.

As we describe in chapter 1, both studies found evidence of a positive relationship between the scaled implementation of guided pathways practices and at least some leading indicators of longer-term success for students. In colleges and states that made less progress, however, this association was weak or nonexistent. Both studies provided evidence consistent with the theory that to improve student success, colleges must implement a complementary set of practices that align to change how students enroll, enter programs, and progress toward achieving their goals.

Like other CCRC research on guided pathways implementation, both studies also found that adopting these reforms at scale is a heavy lift, requiring dedicated and consistent leadership, broad collegewide involvement, and skilled implementation over multiple years. Some colleges in both studies implemented at scale—that is, for all or nearly all entering students—a full set of practices that research suggests is essential for improving outcomes, but implementation typically took at least five years. Many more colleges were on track to enact guided pathways at scale by fall 2020 or 2021, but their efforts stalled when COVID-19 hit. Even so, early adopters reported that they were better able to weather the pandemic because of their guided pathways reforms. Moreover, most colleges from both studies that delayed these projects have resumed their efforts, indicating in interviews that doing so is even more important to attract and retain students in the post-COVID-19 environment.

While promising, neither study's findings were conclusive. Certain metrics showed little evidence of progress in either study. Notably, the AACC Pathways Project study found that measures of student progression increased for all groups at a higher rate at colleges that scaled a fuller set of guided pathways practices, but equity gaps remained, particularly among students by race/ethnicity.

It is important to note that *Redesigning*'s prescriptions for reform reflected a *theory* of change grounded not in specific tested interventions per se, but rather in research-based principles (often borrowed from reforms undertaken by public universities rather than community colleges) for redesigning practice at scale to improve student outcomes. Work on the guided pathways model since *Redesigning* was published has involved rethinking and revamping decades-old practices. Despite the longer-than-anticipated pace of adoption and the lack of progress on some key student success metrics, education reformers learned a great deal from these early endeavors. Thanks to prodigious efforts by early adopter colleges—and research by CCRC and others—our understanding has evolved considerably about what it takes to substantially improve student success and close equity gaps.

One of the overarching lessons from early guided pathways reform efforts is that although students are ultimately responsible for putting in the time and effort to succeed, college practices create barriers to student success. This insight has motivated colleges to commit to the hard work of implementing guided pathways reforms. "A student should never fail because of a barrier we overlooked or unintentionally created" became a rallying cry for guided pathways reforms at San Jacinto College in Texas, an early adopter college that has been a finalist for the Aspen Prize for Community College Excellence in every cycle since 2019.[16]

To remove barriers that colleges unwittingly create and to strengthen paths to success, early guided pathways adopters paid a great deal of attention to improving program information and strengthening advising so that students could more easily plan and navigate programs. These early adopters also worked to better enable students to enter programs by helping them pass college-level gateway courses in math and English composition. CCRC's guided pathways evaluations indicated that reforms on these fronts were associated with improvements in at least some key measures of student success.

At the same time, our studies of the effects of guided pathways reforms on student outcomes raise questions about the rising-tide assumption implicit in *Redesigning*: improving guidance and supports for students generally in community colleges, which enroll disproportionate numbers from underserved groups, may help to improve outcomes for students across groups, but it is insufficient to close equity gaps by race/ethnicity, income, and age.

More recent research has revealed other areas for improvement that were not well addressed in *Redesigning* and in early college reforms. Although strengthening support for students to enter and navigate programs is an important advancement, it will take further changes in college practices to achieve more marked improvements in learning and success by students generally and underserved students in particular.

NEXT FRONTIERS FOR REDESIGNING COMMUNITY COLLEGES

The experiences of colleges that have adopted guided pathways practices and research by CCRC and others point to five next frontiers of community college reform.

Ensuring that programs lead to good jobs and further education

Community colleges that adopted guided pathways early have generally made great strides mapping out clearer programs of study and aligning advising systems that support students to graduation. They have paid less attention, however, to redesigning existing programs and developing new ones to better prepare students for jobs that pay a living wage and offer opportunities for learning and advancement or for transfer to a bachelor's degree program without excess credits. In other words, community colleges have clarified existing program pathways, but they have not done enough to interrogate where those pathways lead.

As we have noted, most jobs paying enough to support an individual let alone a family require at least a bachelor's degree. Two-thirds of community college associate degrees are intended to prepare students to transfer. Yet only about 16 percent of students who start at a community college transfer and earn a bachelor's degree in six years. The most common transfer degree offered by community colleges—the associate of arts in liberal arts or general studies—is not well designed to enable students to apply many of their credits toward a bachelor's degree in their specific field of interest. Having to take credits that do not apply toward their intended bachelor's major discourages many students from completing a bachelor's degree and adds to the time and cost for those who do persevere. Given the diversity of community college students, transfer has the potential to diversify bachelor's degree attainment. However, in reality, transfer is often more of a barrier to earning a bachelor's degree for students, particularly those from underrepresented groups, than a pathway to expand opportunities.

A growing number of community colleges offer bachelor's degrees. Most of these are in fields associated with jobs paying above a living wage. However, the number of graduates from these programs is small relative to the demand. Community colleges also award a substantial number of associate degrees in career-technical fields such as allied health and nursing, most of which are also associated with jobs paying at least a living wage.

The proliferation of automation and advanced technologies across industries and public and private investments in infrastructure, low-carbon technology, and advanced manufacturing have increased demand for skilled workers to fill technician jobs that pay well above a living wage and provide opportunities for career advancement. To meet the projected demand for these workers, community colleges will have to greatly expand their career-technical associate degree and bachelor's programs, particularly in engineering and science technology and industrial and construction technology. Community colleges will also need to continue to turn out at least as many graduates as they have in the past in fields such as allied health and nursing, computer and information technology, public safety, and business, which also offer living-wage jobs to individuals with community college workforce associate and bachelor's degrees.

In recruiting for jobs in these fields, employers want and need to create diverse workforces that reflect their customers and the communities in which they operate. However, women, students of color, and low-income students are underrepresented in most community college associate and bachelor's degree programs in high-demand fields. Colleges will not only need to expand but also diversify enrollments and completions in degree programs that enable students from underserved groups to enter and advance in careers in high-opportunity fields.

Because of the strong demand for workers to fill these jobs, colleges will have to recruit from the current workforce and collaborate with K–12 schools to build a supply of workers for the future. Community colleges often tout that their programs are designed to enable working students to "stack" credentials to advance to better jobs, but in practice, they too often fail to offer program sequences and guidance so that students can pursue the education and training needed to advance up career ladders while they are working. Instead, it is often left to students to figure out how to stack courses and credentials in a way that leads to better jobs and degrees. Short-term certificates theoretically can help underemployed workers enter career ladders in high-paying fields. In reality, low-income learners are overrepresented in certificate programs in low-wage fields and are underrepresented in short-term certificate programs in high-paying fields, which tend to enroll workers who are already in the industry and seeking to improve their skills. Too often, community college workforce programs are not designed or delivered so that working students can pursue the education and training needed to enter and advance in careers in high-demand, high-opportunity fields.

To ensure that their programs truly prepare students for success in employment and further education, it is not enough for colleges to map programs to completion and periodically review them in consultation with employers and universities. Instead, they need to develop much more dynamic partnerships in which they involve universities and employers in regularly reviewing and redesigning existing programs and developing new ones to make certain that their graduates can secure good jobs and pursue further education and training needed to achieve their education and career goals.

Teaching versatile learners in a fast-changing world

It is essential that community college program curricula align with the requirements for well-paying career path jobs or transfer in a major. But improving curricular alignment is not enough. The teaching and learning that take place throughout programs are vital. Classroom instruction and other learning activities must help students develop the skills they need to succeed in upper-division bachelor's coursework and in a fast-changing, highly technological workplace.

Research on the skills employers look for in potential new hires for well-paying career-path jobs indicates that effective communication, problem-solving, critical thinking, and the ability to learn as technology changes are as important as technical skills and content knowledge. Research on teaching and learning in college suggests that an essential strategy for helping students develop these skills is active learning, in which they are asked to engage in critical thinking, problem-solving, questioning, and analysis. Other research has shown the importance of contextualizing instruction—making it relevant to students' lives and goals—for enhancing engagement in learning. Students also benefit from opportunities to apply what they learn outside the classroom, particularly through work-based learning opportunities, such as clinicals, apprenticeships, co-ops, internships, and service learning. Students who participate in these opportunities are more attractive to employers, as it may demonstrate that they have developed skills they can apply to real-world problems and circumstances. Work-based learning also enables students to develop contacts and networks that broaden their career prospects and help them find jobs.

The fourth pillar of the guided pathways model—ensuring that students are learning across their programs—has received the least attention in guided pathways reforms to date, despite the importance of offering students rich learning opportunities inside and out of the classroom. This is not to say that innovation in teaching at community colleges is lacking. The problem is that it is too often fragmented.

Many community colleges have made a concerted effort to improve student success in introductory college-level math and English composition courses. Improving the academic support that students receive as part of such courses has led to increases in the rates at which students complete college math and composition in their first year. Those improvements, however, generally have not translated into greater student success in other program gateway courses that are critical for student progression and retention. Similarly, many community colleges have sought to strengthen online teaching in response to the rapid growth of online courses. They have also worked to make course content more relevant and culturally responsive to a diverse student body. But too often those efforts have been focused within groups of faculty or programs rather than across all faculty. Community colleges have long provided work-based learning opportunities to students in nursing and other career-technical programs and have also offered service learning, undergraduate research, and other cocurricular opportunities. Yet few colleges have sought to extend experiential learning opportunities to all students regardless of program.

Community colleges typically provide resources to support faculty professional development, and many have a teaching and learning center to organize training and other activities to help faculty become more effective teachers.

Participation is often voluntary, however, and the focus is typically on improving instruction in the courses faculty teach, not on improving learning across programs. The challenge for colleges is creating a culture and infrastructure to support instructional innovation that engages students across programs and prepares them to become versatile learners who can thrive as they pursue further education and navigate a fast-changing workplace.

Creating a more engaging recruitment and onboarding experience

Redesigning urged colleges to improve career and college assessment, information about programs of study, and advising to help students explore options and identify a path forward. Many colleges have done this. Yet recent research suggests that while improving information and advising for student decision-making is essential, it is equally important to talk with students about their interests and goals, connect them with people and programs in fields of interest, offer them challenging and inspiring coursework from the start, and work with them to develop an educational plan that shows a path to achieving their goals.

Based on our research on early adopters of guided pathways, CCRC developed the Ask-Connect-Inspire-Plan (ACIP) framework to guide colleges to create a more engaging and effective program onboarding experience that starts with efforts to recruit prospective students. We have introduced ACIP to scores of colleges through numerous online workshops and institutes since spring 2021, and we have seen encouraging progress among those that have implemented these ideas. It will require more work, however, to tailor ACIP practices for students from groups that often are not well served by conventional onboarding practices, such as older returning students, first-generation students, veterans, and those in adult basic skills programs. In addition, colleges generally take a very passive approach to recruiting students. ACIP can be applied to rethink how colleges encourage both prospective students and those who are enrolled but do not have a plan to enter their programs.

Helping students complete programs on schedule and affordably

The discussion on student services in chapter 2 of *Redesigning* emphasized the importance of holistic advising and other services that support success. Research since then has provided further evidence that such wraparound supports are especially important for first-generation students and others unfamiliar with how to navigate college. However, even colleges that have made significant progress implementing these supports often neglect to pay attention to how long it takes students to complete and how much it costs them to do so. Time and cost needed to complete a program are of paramount importance to students and are gaining more attention from policy makers. Yet surveys of community college students find that too many do not receive guidance and support to complete their programs in a timely matter.

The challenge for community colleges is providing high-quality advising and support for on-time completion to all students given their extremely limited budgets for such activities. Early adopters of guided pathways have offered cost-effective case-management advising at scale by embedding academic advisors in program areas (or in meta-majors) who work with faculty to support students. They use technology to monitor student progress and to facilitate communication between advisors and support staff, faculty, and students. Mandatory high-quality advising for all students can help keep them on the path and a timeline to completion.

Some guided pathways early adopter colleges have also begun taking a more intentional approach to scheduling courses. Doing so can benefit the many students who have substantial work and family obligations that can get in the way of course-taking. A growing number of colleges, for example, have found success offering courses in condensed seven- or eight-week terms. Scheduling also is critical for advancing equity, because students from underrepresented groups are the least likely to have the time and resources to squander when they cannot access the courses they need. Many colleges still schedule classes unsystematically, rolling over schedules from previous years without examining students' plans or time preferences. This makes it difficult for students to take the courses they need to progress when they need them, and it leads colleges to cancel course sections with low enrollment, which hurts students, faculty, and the college.

Community colleges also have begun to recognize that nonacademic needs—such as food and housing insecurity, monetary support beyond financial aid, and mental health issues—create barriers to on-time completion. Many colleges, including early adopters of guided pathways, rely on a variety of supports to address these needs. But the challenge is doing so on a substantial scale without diverting limited staff and resources from the core business of providing high-quality programs, instruction, academic support, and student advising.

Rethinking dual enrollment as an on-ramp to college and career opportunity

Dual enrollment, in which high school students take college-level courses that confer both high school and college credit, has grown rapidly in recent years. One-third of recent high school graduates have taken at least one dual enrollment course, and about 70 percent of all dual enrollment courses are offered through community colleges.[17] Indeed, dual enrollment is the only segment that has grown over the past decade.

As important as dual enrollment has become, many community colleges take a laissez-faire approach to it, neglecting to help students with career and college exploration and failing to offer courses that could give them a head start on a program in a field that interests them. Too many colleges also fail to support access to dual enrollment for first-generation college students, students of color, English learners, students with disabilities, and other underserved students. It is not surprising, then, that gaps in participation in dual enrollment programs, sometimes called "programs of privilege," persist by student race/ethnicity and income. Because there often is no alignment between courses offered and taken and the requirements of programs that students might be interested in, the resulting course-taking choices by students have sometimes been characterized as "random acts of dual enrollment."

Dual enrollment has traditionally been aimed at students who are already college bound. Colleges and high schools often do little to encourage the millions of high school students enrolled in career-technical education to use dual enrollment to start a career-technical associate, apprenticeship, or bachelor's degree while in high school. As a result, dual enrollment has yet to realize its full potential to expand college access by providing an immersive introduction to postsecondary education in fields that interest different kinds of students. Instead, it tends to provide whatever courses might happen to be available to students who are planning to attend college anyway. Even as dual enrollment has continued to grow at community colleges, enrollment at these institutions among recent high school graduates has declined. Community colleges are thus failing to capitalize on the opportunity to persuade dual enrollment students to enter their programs after high school.

Community colleges have an opportunity to broaden the benefits of dual enrollment by taking a more strategic approach. They can provide a head start on postsecondary education for more students; at the same time, they can build a stronger supply of post–high school enrollments. In CCRC's research on guided pathways and dual enrollment, we observed colleges that extended guided pathways practices to K–12 dual enrollment programming to expand college access and opportunities for underserved students. In this emerging approach, which we call dual enrollment equity pathways (DEEP), community colleges partner with middle and high schools to prepare underserved students to pursue postsecondary education and training after high school. CCRC has been researching the implementation of DEEP practices in different contexts since 2021 with the aim of guiding adoption by college–K–12 partnerships on a large scale.

GIVING STUDENTS COMPELLING REASONS TO ENROLL AND COMPLETE

Although there are complex causes for the community college enrollment declines we discussed earlier, one reason is that many students see insufficient value in community college and are, in a real sense, voting with their feet. In the current environment in which students and potential students have limited time and resources to pursue education, tight labor markets make the opportunity costs of attending community college high. Students have other postsecondary education options as well. Additionally, many prospective students or people they know have not had a positive experience with community colleges or public education more generally, particularly those in groups that have been poorly served by our education systems in the past.

Although it is not always well recognized, community college students bring extraordinary talent and drive to the college experience. The many students from underserved groups that these colleges serve often navigate more formidable challenges than those from privileged backgrounds—and typically do so with fewer resources and support. Outside of school, they exhibit skills and interests that are not measured by the narrowly focused standardized tests traditionally used to assess readiness for college. Many former students have profited from their education at a community college and enjoyed great success, whereas others have been stymied by prerequisite developmental courses they never finished or betrayed by credits that did not transfer to their four-year destination college. These are ways community colleges may fail to capitalize on students' motivation—and even quash it.

Early adopter guided pathways colleges have implemented large-scale changes that help students better navigate the journey to completion. However, to achieve better and more equitable outcomes—and to recruit and retain more students in a highly competitive market—community colleges must not only remove barriers to completion but also strengthen pathways to success in employment and further education after graduation, and thus give students good reasons to enroll and complete. The next frontiers of community college reform that we have outlined and that we examine in depth in this book are designed to do just that, by

- ensuring that all programs prepare students to secure jobs that pay a living wage or to transfer with no excess credits to bachelor's degree programs in their field of interest;
- teaching students in ways that enable them to develop the versatile skills needed to thrive in a rapidly changing workplace and society;
- strengthening recruitment and helping incoming students—especially those without strong outside guidance and networks—to choose, plan, and gain momentum in a program of study;
- providing case-managed advising, progress monitoring, and student-centered scheduling to enable students with many responsibilities and pressures outside of school to complete their programs in as little time and at as little cost as possible; and
- giving K–12 dual enrollment students a reason to enroll in community college after high school by building on-ramps to debt-free postsecondary programs that lead to well-paying career-path jobs.

PURPOSE AND ORGANIZATION OF THIS BOOK

In the coming pages, we draw on research from CCRC and others since *Redesigning* was published and on innovations in practice by community colleges nationally to show practitioners and state policy makers how they can build on prior guided pathways reforms to implement further innovations in the five frontiers. The goal is informing further transformation by community colleges to ensure that their programs lead to good jobs and further education and can be completed in a reasonable time and cost—and thus make students' investment of time, money, and effort to enroll and complete worth it.

If community colleges are to fulfill their mission to support upward mobility through education, maintaining a clear focus on equity is crucial. Community colleges have taken steps to increase employee diversity, promote inclusion, and respect individual differences. Creating a more diverse and caring campus is essential. But colleges also need to ensure that underserved students receive high-quality guidance and instruction that prepares them for career-path employment and further education at the bachelor's level and beyond. As we have learned, however, colleges cannot close equity gaps merely by improving programs and supports for all students. They also need to ensure that students from underserved groups benefit from improved practices by customizing efforts to match their needs. This dimension of equity and how colleges can achieve it are a major focus of this book.

In chapter 1, we summarize findings from two large CCRC evaluations of the progress colleges have made in adopting large-scale changes following the guided pathways model and the effects on student progression and equity. Chapters 2 through 6 provide lessons from research conducted by CCRC and others to further transform college practice in the five frontiers of reform previously highlighted: ensuring the postcompletion value of college programs for employment and baccalaureate transfer (chapter 2); strengthening teaching and learning to help students develop the versatile skills needed to thrive in a fast-changing workplace and society (chapter 3); improving recruitment and enriching students' experience in exploring, selecting, and planning a program (chapter 4); revamping advising, scheduling, and supports to help busy students complete programs affordably and on schedule (chapter 5); and building on-ramps from high school to postsecondary degree pathways for underrepresented students (chapter 6). Chapter 7 offers lessons for college leaders on rethinking college organization and finance to implement and sustain the next frontiers of reforms. Chapter 8 guides policy makers and system leaders in funding and supporting colleges to undertake and sustain these reforms over time.

Chapters 2 through 8 include examples and case studies that illustrate how colleges and state agencies have approached the reforms we describe. Each chapter concludes with recommended actions colleges can take to improve practice in the given reform area.

CCRC's research on how leaders and practitioners have managed the large-scale changes associated with guided pathways reforms reveals a broad insight: colleges that improved practice and the student experience most effectively devoted a great deal of energy to inviting stakeholders to think in new ways about how they help students succeed. Changing mindsets is critical to changing college culture. The two must occur in tandem for sustainable whole-college change to take hold and endure. Therefore, in our chapters on new frontiers, we also examine mindset changes necessary to enact and sustain further innovations that strengthen pathways to educational and career success for students.

CHAPTER 1

Lessons from Two Major Guided Pathways Evaluations

In *Redesigning America's Community Colleges: A Clearer Path to Student Success,* Thomas R. Bailey, Shanna Smith Jaggars, and coauthor of this book, Davis Jenkins, examined why community colleges failed to improve student retention and completion rates despite concerted reforms since the early 2000s.[1] One reason, they argued, was that most reforms either benefited a small number of students and were not scaled or they affected larger numbers but provided only low-intensity, light-touch support. In addition, most reforms targeted only one segment of the student experience, typically college orientation, developmental education, or the first year of courses. Instructional reforms typically involved strengthened tutoring and other supplemental academic supports rather than improvements to classroom teaching and tended to be provided in developmental education, college math, and English composition. As a result, most faculty were largely disconnected from these reforms.

The authors also cited a more fundamental reason for the lack of marked improvements in completion rates: the reforms changed the conventional community college education model incrementally instead of producing a more thorough reinvention. That model, which had prevailed since the 1960s when community colleges were integral to the country's historic effort to expand access to higher education, was laudably effective in expanding access to low-cost college coursework. It was not designed, however, to help students enter and complete affordable programs that prepared them for further education and employment. According to the *Redesigning* authors: "In particular, the emphasis on low-cost college enrollment has encouraged colleges to offer an array of often-disconnected courses, programs, and support services that students are expected to navigate mostly on their own. Students are confused by the plethora of poorly explained program, transfer, and career options; moreover, on closer scrutiny, many programs do not clearly lead to the further education and employment outcomes they are advertised to help students achieve."[2]

The authors urged colleges to move away from this conventional cafeteria style or self-service model: "Instead, [colleges] need to engage faculty and student services professionals in creating more clearly structured, educationally coherent program pathways that lead to students' end goals, and in rethinking instruction and student support services in ways that facilitate students' learning and success as they progress along these paths. In short, to maximize both access and success, a fundamental redesign is necessary."[3]

The first four chapters of *Redesigning* describe how the guided pathways approach contrasts with the cafeteria-college model in four essential functional areas: program structure and information, intake and support, instruction, and developmental education. The most salient contrasts are summarized in table 1.1.

TABLE 1.1 Cafeteria college and guided pathways models compared

Area	*Cafeteria college*	*Guided pathways*
Program structure and information	• Programs siloed by field and type • Program paths unclear; too many choices	• Programs organized by field or meta-major • Default full-program maps
Intake and support	• Optional career/college planning • General education for undecided students • Student progress not monitored	• Educational plans required • Exploratory majors for undecided students • Proactive progress tracking, feedback, and support
Instruction	• Course learning outcomes • Focus on covering content rather than learning skills • Fragmented classroom instructional improvement efforts • Online instruction used to improve access to learning	• Program learning outcomes • Learning-facilitation teaching focused on building student metacognition • Collaborative inquiry approach to improving instruction • Technology used to enhance learning
Developmental education	• Prerequisite remediation in math, writing, and reading	• Corequisite integrated academic support in college-level math and composition

Citing research on organizational effectiveness in education and other sectors, the authors advocated for aligning key practices within these functional areas to change the experience in- and outside the classroom for all students, not just groups targeted by specific interventions, across their college journeys. Specifically, the authors argued that reforms should focus on better helping students choose, enter, and complete programs to prepare them for employment and further education.

The authors made clear that though some evidence cited in *Redesigning* to support the guided pathways model relied on rigorous causal studies, other evidence was descriptive and suggestive. The two- and four-year colleges described in the book that were undertaking reforms along these lines had seen promising results, but most initiatives were still in the early stages. And except for Guttman Community College in the City University of New York, a small, new college designed on guided pathways principles, large universities like Arizona State University, Florida State University, and Georgia State University were further along in making these reforms at scale than community colleges. The authors acknowledged that many of the practices they described "reflect[ed] evidence-based hypotheses of how colleges can become more effective, rather than proven solutions."[4]

The authors also recognized that colleges operating under different conditions would inevitably implement the guided pathways model differently. Rather than prescribing a single approach, the authors invited colleges interested in undertaking whole-college reform to adapt the general principles of guided pathways practice and design specific approaches to their circumstances. They also expressed hope that *Redesigning* would lead to a growing community of practice: "As more and more colleges redesign their practices based on the model, we will accrue a growing body of evidence regarding specific implementation approaches, which will help future college leaders in their own efforts."[5]

In this chapter, we describe how the Community College Research Center (CCRC), along with college, state, and intermediary partners, codified and refined a framework and assessment tools to implement guided pathways and measure the scale at which colleges adopt practices aligned with the model. We then present lessons from CCRC's two multiyear evaluations examining how readily nearly a hundred colleges across the country were able to implement guided pathways reforms at scale and the effects on student outcomes. We conclude with areas of practice that these evaluations indicate are ripe for further reform and improvement.

TRANSLATING THEORY INTO PRACTICE

CCRC spent two years before *Redesigning*'s publication working with Complete College America (CCA) and state higher education agencies in Georgia, Indiana, and Tennessee to help two- and four-year public colleges adopt guided pathways reforms. Together with the National Center for Inquiry & Improvement, CCRC also partnered with student success centers in Arkansas and Michigan to provide their colleges workshops on implementing guided pathways reforms.

What was missing from these early efforts, however, was a clear, jargon-free framework and assessment tool to show faculty, staff, and others what guided pathways might look like in practice and to help them plan and evaluate guided pathways reforms. In fall 2015, CCRC and CCA worked with Tristan Denley, then–vice-chancellor for academic affairs at the Tennessee Board of Regents, to develop a prototype scale-of-adoption assessment tool for member institutions. The prototype called for grouping practices into three categories: clarifying paths to student end goals, helping students get on a path, and keeping students on path. The assessment also asked colleges to summarize their progress on practices in each area, and then to detail next steps and the assistance they needed from the Board of Regents.

CCRC added a fourth area of practice—that is, ensuring that students learn across their programs—and turned the prototype into an implementation framework and institutional assessment tool to help faculty and staff in colleges learn about the guided pathways model, plan reforms, and formatively evaluate their scale of adoption across students and programs. CCRC first administered the full guided pathways Scale of Adoption Assessment (SOAA) in spring 2016 with the thirty colleges involved in the American Association of Community Colleges (AACC) Pathways Project, which we describe in more detail later in the chapter.

Although the areas of practice outlined in the SOAA were not explicitly identified in *Redesigning*, what came to be known as the four pillars of guided pathways are fully consistent with the model outlined in the book. The SOAA practices address four general features of the cafeteria college model highlighted in *Redesigning* that, while helpful in expanding access to college coursework, tend to create barriers to student persistence and success in programs aligned with jobs and further education. First, the programmatic paths to career and further education are often unclear, with students frequently overwhelmed by the number of choices available. Second, entering students typically receive limited support for career and college exploration and planning, leaving them without the direction and motivation that accompanies a clear plan. Third, because colleges generally do not monitor students' progress, students often self-advise, and as a result, they often take courses that do not apply to a credential aligned with their goals. Fourth, standardized placement tests divert too many students into prerequisite remedial (or developmental) courses in math and English composition when what they need is help succeeding in college-level courses. Moreover, instructional innovation under the cafeteria model typically focuses on improving student performance in individual courses rather than ensuring that they build essential knowledge and skills across their programs.

Redesigning encouraged colleges to align guided pathways practices to produce complementary benefits for learning and progression into and through a program. Figure 1.1 shows how practices under the four pillars theoretically should interact to shape students' experiences, which in turn should encourage behaviors that improve their progression and success. For example, clear

FIGURE 1.1 Guided pathways theory of change

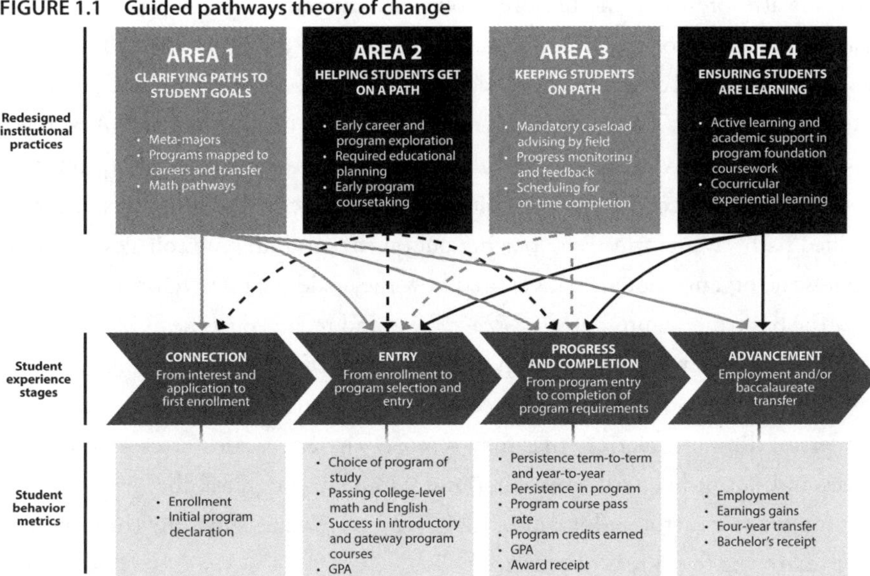

program maps (top panel, box 1) and career exploration (top panel, box 2) at the connection and entry stages will increase the likelihood that students will choose a program suited to their strengths and interests. Integrating academic support (top panel, box 2) and active learning (top panel, box 4) into program foundation or gateway courses will increase their confidence and motivation to progress to higher-level coursework. Improvements in educational planning (top panel, box 2) and monitoring (top panel, box 3) will help students progress through and complete a program that prepares them to secure a job or transfer to a bachelor's program.

Redesigning did not prescribe a sequence for colleges to follow to enact reforms across these four practice areas. But mapping programs to career and educational goals can guide new students in career and academic exploration and planning, enabling staff to schedule classes and monitor progress to ensure timely completion. Mapping also helps faculty sequence courses and set learning outcomes to help students master foundational knowledge and competencies and ensure that they are building skills as they progress. As it turns out, most early adopter colleges began their reforms with the mapping pillar.

REFINING OUR THINKING BY STUDYING PRACTICE

Since 2015, CCRC has conducted research on implementing guided pathways reforms at more than one hundred colleges nationally, including thirty AACC Pathways Project colleges in seventeen states; all seventy community and technical colleges in Ohio, Tennessee, and Washington; and twenty colleges in California's Guided Pathways Demonstration Project. We administered the SOAA to these colleges regularly, with follow-up calls to validate and gain insight into their responses. We also conducted site visits at forty-eight colleges to understand how guided pathways reforms were playing out on the ground, how colleges managed large-scale organizational changes, and how they paid for these reforms.

The basic model presented in *Redesigning* and reflected in the SOAA remains sound. Lessons from our research on early adopter colleges and other research on efforts to improve community college student success, however, refined our understanding of practices that may remove barriers to success created by colleges and better help students enter and complete programs that lead to well-paying jobs or further education. Table 1.2 summarizes how our thinking has evolved in the four areas of practice.[6]

TABLE 1.2 Evolution of CCRC's thinking about guided pathways

Area of practice	*Redesigning America's Community Colleges*	*CCRC's refined thinking*
1. Clarifying paths to student end goals	• Use meta-majors and maps to clarify and simplify students' choices	• Build academic and career communities in each meta-major field to help students build networks with faculty, students, and others • Work with employers and universities to develop and update program maps • Guide students to take a math sequence appropriate to their field of study
2. Helping students get on a path	• Ensure that all new students receive career and transfer information and advising	• Ensure that new students participate in guided exploration to choose a pathway • Help every student develop an individualized educational plan
3. Keeping students on path	• Provide holistic wraparound advising and other supports	• Provide case management advising by meta-major and use students' educational plans to monitor progress and schedule classes
4. Ensuring that students are learning across their programs	• Use multiple measures to place students into appropriate developmental or college-level courses and provide corequisite remediation when possible • Establish program learning outcomes and promote faculty development through collaborative inquiry	• Teach students to be effective learners in college-level program foundation courses (not just math and English composition) • Embed active and experiential learning in all programs

Based on what we learned, we revised the list of practices under the SOAA's four pillars. Table 1.3 details practices that research since *Redesigning* indicates are critical for helping students explore interests, choose a program, and gain early momentum.[7] CCRC considers a college to have fully implemented a foundational set of guided pathways when it uses these model practices at scale for all or nearly all entering students.

Note that these practices generally focus on student experiences during their first year. This is intentional. Nationally, nearly 40 percent of students who start

TABLE 1.3 Updated guided pathways model practices

Practice	*Measure*
Practice area 1: Clarifying paths to student end goals	
1a. Meta-majors	Programs organized by meta-major and students' meta-major tracked
1b. Career and technical education (CTE) program	CTE programs mapped to related jobs/careers
1c. Transfer program maps	Transfer programs mapped to related majors
1d. Math pathways	Program-specific math sequences mapped
Practice area 2: Helping students get on a path	
2a. Meta-major exposure	Either a mandatory orientation or a mandatory first-year experience course and either meta-major content or field-focused events
2b. Required career assessment and advising	All new students participate in career and program exploration and advising
2c. Early program-related course-taking	Students advised to take program-relevant course in term one
2d. Mandatory educational planning	All students helped to develop educational plan in term one and can see plan online
Practice area 3: Keeping students on path	
3a. Mandatory ongoing advising	Mandatory advising for returning students
3b. Caseload advising by field	Caseload advising by advisors assigned by meta-major
3c. Progress monitoring and feedback	Students' progress is monitored based on their plans, with alerts when students fall "off plan"
3d. Scheduling for on-time completion	Classes scheduled based on students' plans
Practice area 4: Ensuring that students are learning across their programs	
4a. Corequisite college math	Students placed in corequisite math and corequisite support aligned with math subject
4b. Program foundation course improvement	Instructional improvement in program foundation courses other than math by meta-major

at a community college do not return to any college for a second year, and attrition rates for students of color and low-income students are even higher.[8] Improving persistence through the first year and into the second is critical. We also found that focusing guided pathways reforms on first-year students is a good place for colleges to start work on implementing these complex reforms.

Since *Redesigning* was first published in 2015, CCRC has used this updated model in two major evaluations of how colleges have adopted guided pathways reforms and the effects of these reforms on student outcomes. We turn to these next.

EVALUATING WHOLE-COLLEGE REFORMS

Redesigning's authors acknowledged that it would not be easy to evaluate a whole-college reform model like guided pathways. To assess the impact of an educational innovation, researchers typically examine the outcomes for subjects (in this case, students) who experience the "treatment" compared with a control group of students who do not, ideally with students randomly assigned to a group. It is impossible to evaluate guided pathways reforms this way. For one, the "treatment" is multifaceted, changing many aspects of practice across the student's journey into and through programs. Although the model does include a list of crucial principles of practices, it does not prescribe precisely how and in what order to implement them, leaving each college to follow its own path and timeline. Implementing guided pathways also involves changing practices in ways that benefit all students, so it is not feasible to assign students to comparable treatment and control groups. It is not surprising, then, that there have been few efforts to evaluate the effects of whole-college reforms in community colleges or higher education in general.[9]

CCRC documented colleges reporting substantially improved completion rates and other measures of success at scale, something they attribute at least in part to guided pathways reforms.[10] However, colleges that improve student success typically make many changes, some of which have only a tangential relationship to guided pathways. Of course, external factors outside of colleges' control also can affect enrollment and completion—from personal crises and local plant closings to a pandemic.

Unprecedented opportunities to evaluate whole-college reforms

Is it feasible for colleges to implement guided pathways at scale? Do guided pathways improve student outcomes? If so, do some groups benefit more or less than others? Two major evaluations of efforts to support guided pathways reforms across large groups of community colleges helped CCRC answer these questions. The first was an evaluation of the AACC Pathways Project. Launched in late 2015, the project supported a cohort of community colleges to implement guided pathways reforms.[11] AACC adopted CCRC's four-pillar guided pathways model as the framework.[12]

To participate in the project, AACC selected thirty colleges—representing seventeen states and varying widely by size, governance, and mix of programs and students—whose leaders embraced the challenge of redesigning the community college experience for students at scale using the guided pathways model. In 2016 and 2017, administrators, faculty, and staff from these colleges took part in six three-day institutes, during which they learned about the model from national experts, analyzed institutional data, examined the student experience at their institutions, and redesigned college policies and practices following the guided pathways framework.

CCRC served as the lead research organization and used the colleges as sites for research on the specific practices implemented, how they managed the large-scale changes, and how much the reforms cost and how colleges paid for them.[13] CCRC's evaluation of the project assessed the connection between the scale of practices implemented and data on student progression at each college.

The second study was based on research CCRC launched in fall 2019, with funding from the National Science Foundation (NSF). The goal was to examine more rigorously the implementation and scale of adoption of guided pathways reforms, as well as how these reforms affected student participation and success in science, technology, engineering, and math (STEM) programs and in general. CCRC partnered with state agencies in Ohio, Tennessee, and Washington with a combined seventy public two-year colleges. These states had launched initiatives to help community colleges (and, in the case of Tennessee, public regional universities) adopt guided pathways practices. All three states shared information about the guided pathways model and held institutes with national experts, coaching, and other supports to help colleges implement reforms at scale.

In the next two sections, we describe how we measured the scale at which colleges in these two studies adopted guided pathways practices and the effects of adoption on student progress. In the sections that follow, we present key findings on whether colleges implemented guided pathways reforms at scale and the effects of these reforms on student outcomes.

Measuring the scale of adoption of guided pathways reforms

Both studies used versions of our SOAA to measure the scale at which colleges implemented the guided pathways model practices shown in table 1.3. We used the SOAA for the AACC Pathways Project to help colleges educate faculty and staff about the model and to plan and monitor its implementation. We administered the SOAA to all thirty AACC Pathways colleges in spring 2016 at the start of the project; in the falls of 2016, 2017, 2018, and 2020; and in spring 2022. Each time, teams of administrators, faculty, and staff completed the SOAA. Our researchers verified the information and gleaned details about how they were managing the changes. For the final summative evaluation, we used data from the spring 2022 SOAA and made follow-up calls to identify where the thirty colleges stood in adopting the practices.

For the NSF study, we developed a survey based on the updated guided pathways model discussed in the last section.[14] We designed questions to capture what percent of programs or first-time-in-college students were affected by the practices and when colleges implemented them at scale, which we defined as affecting at least 80 percent of programs or first-time-in-college students. We piloted the SOAA survey with one college in each of the three states, and then we administered it to all community and technical colleges across the three states. An average of four people per college—administrators and faculty familiar with their institution's guided pathways—completed the surveys, and we received a response rate of 91 percent.

Measuring the effects of adoption on student outcomes

One challenge of evaluating whole-college reforms is that it takes several years for their effects on completion rates and other outcomes to play out. For this reason, CCRC used early momentum metrics (EMMs) to measure the progress of first-year students with no previous college experience or credits, including dual enrollment courses taken in high school.

Research by CCRC and others has found that EMMs correlate with success in community college completion and baccalaureate transfer for students generally, with especially strong benefits for students of color and low-income students.[15] Thus, year-over-year improvements in such metrics indicate that more students likely will complete or transfer successfully. EMMs are distinct from metrics such as the Integrated Postsecondary Education Data System's 150 percent graduation rate, which (for associate degree-granting institutions) takes three years to measure and includes only first-time full-time students, not the part-time students who account for most community college enrollments. Because EMMs are based on one-year outcomes for all entering students in credit programs (including full- and part-time students), boosting those metrics requires improving the experience of large numbers of entering students, not just those who might benefit from targeted interventions.

Given the guided pathways theory of change—that colleges need to align complementary practices across the student experience to improve outcomes—we hypothesized that those colleges implementing at scale a fully integrated set of guided pathways model practices would see greater increases in EMMs after scaling than colleges that were still scaling. Table 1.4 shows the EMMs used in the AACC Pathways Project and NSF studies. For the former, the thirty colleges reported aggregate EMM data on first-time students from fall 2012 to fall

TABLE 1.4 Early momentum metrics

Credit momentum	*College course completion*	*Gateway math and English completion*	*Persistence*
• Earned six or more college credits in term one • Earned twelve or more college credits in term one • Earned fifteen or more college credits in year one • Earned twenty-four or more college credits in year one • Earned thirty or more college credits in year one	• College-level course completion rate in students' first academic year • Average college credits attempted in year one • Average college credits completed in year one	• Completed college math in year one • Completed college English in year one • Completed both college math and college English in year one	• Persisted from term one to term two • Persisted from year one to year two

2020—for all students and for subgroups by race and ethnicity. As a result, it was possible to examine year-over-year trends for each college before and after the first AACC Pathways Project institute in early 2016. We might expect that more recent large-scale reforms would have improved these annual metrics compared with the pre-institute period.

In contrast, the NSF study relied on CCRC researchers calculating and analyzing EMMs using transcript-level administrative data on more than eight hundred thousand first-time-in-college students.[16] The three partner states shared these data with CCRC on cohorts of students who started at a two-year public college in the given state between 2010 and 2020. CCRC used the data to trace their progress through the 2020–2021 academic year.

Can colleges feasibly implement guided pathways at scale?

Both evaluations identified some colleges that implemented most of the guided pathways model practices shown in table 1.3 *at scale*—that is, for at least 80 percent of programs or entering students. Eleven of the thirty AACC Pathways colleges had implemented most of the model at scale by fall 2021.[17] Another twelve were still scaling these practices, with most on track to do so by fall 2022. Six other colleges had taken steps to map programs and redesign the program onboarding experience but had not yet scaled corequisite support in math or carried out other reforms.[18]

In the three states involved in the NSF study, a smaller proportion had implemented a substantial number of the model practices at scale.[19] Table 1.5 shows the number of colleges in each state that had implemented nine to fourteen

TABLE 1.5 Guided pathways adoption among colleges in the National Science Foundation study states in 2022

	High adopters (nine or more practices implemented at scale)	*Medium adopters (five to eight practices implemented at scale)*	*Low adopters (four or fewer practices implemented at scale)*
Ohio	7	9	3
Tennessee	6	7	0
Washington	5	13	12
Total number of colleges	19	29	15

(high adopters), five to eight (medium adopters), or four or fewer (low adopters) practices at scale.

Across these three states, colleges tended to implement and scale guided pathways practices from practice areas 1 and 2 first (clarifying paths to student end goals and helping students get on a path). These practices generally are required before implementing areas 3 and 4 (keeping students on path and ensuring that students are learning across programs).[20] Adopting corequisite math (4a) bucked this trend, as colleges could implement it on a more independent timeline.[21] Regardless of the level of adoption, colleges in all three states were most likely to scale practices in practice area 1, including mapping pathways in career-technical education (1b) and transfer programs (1c) and identifying key math pathways within those maps (1d). Most colleges also encouraged early program gateway course-taking (2c). In general, low-adopter colleges were less likely than others to scale program advising (2b and 3a), planning (2d), and progress-monitoring practices (3c). Scheduling for on-time completion (3d), a critical structure and form of support for promoting student programs, was the least likely to have been implemented at scale among all colleges.

Both studies show that while some colleges successfully adopted guided pathways model practices, it took several years for them to implement them at scale, and most were still trying to scale these practices by the end of each study period. The remaining colleges either had made little progress scaling or had made some progress but still were using prerequisite remediation in math. Many colleges in both studies were on track to implement guided pathways at scale by fall 2020 or 2021 but had to put their efforts on hold when COVID-19 hit. Yet nearly all of them have resumed, indicating in interviews their belief that guided pathways practices were even more important to attracting and retaining students in the postpandemic environment.

CCRC's research since *Redesigning* was published points to reasons why it takes so long to implement guided pathways reforms at scale. To begin with, it is a heavy lift to fundamentally change an educational model followed for decades. It requires strong, sustained leadership, active involvement from stakeholders across the college, and skilled implementation over several years—in most cases at least five.[22] Instituting whole-college reforms has been particularly challenging in a period of declining enrollments, increased competition, uncertain state funding, and generational leadership turnover. Notably, many colleges in both studies spent a great deal of time early on engaging faculty in mapping programs, redesigning websites, and pursuing other efforts to improve the quality of program information. While important, these efforts do not substantially change the experience for most students and are unlikely by themselves to improve student outcomes.

The NSF study also provides evidence that state policies can influence the trajectory with which colleges adopt guided pathways practices. The Washington State Board for Community and Technical Colleges, with funding from College Spark Washington, developed a program to pilot guided pathways reforms at ten colleges in two cohort stages, one from 2016 and another from 2018. These colleges received grants to support their work. Following the pilot's rollout, the state legislature in 2019 approved funding for guided pathways at all state technical and community colleges.[23] The influence of these policy actions is evident in figure 1.2, which shows when colleges in Washington implemented practices in the four practice areas at scale.

Is there evidence that guided pathways improves student outcomes?

Both studies found links between adopting guided pathways practices and improvements in leading indicators of student success in the longer term, although the findings from the NSF study, which relied on more rigorous quantitative analysis, were mixed.

Findings from the AACC Pathways Project. Using descriptive data on EMM trends, we found that most of the thirty colleges saw improvements in the majority of EMMs over the five years after the initiative started compared with several

FIGURE 1.2 At-scale adoption of practice areas 1–4 over time among Washington colleges

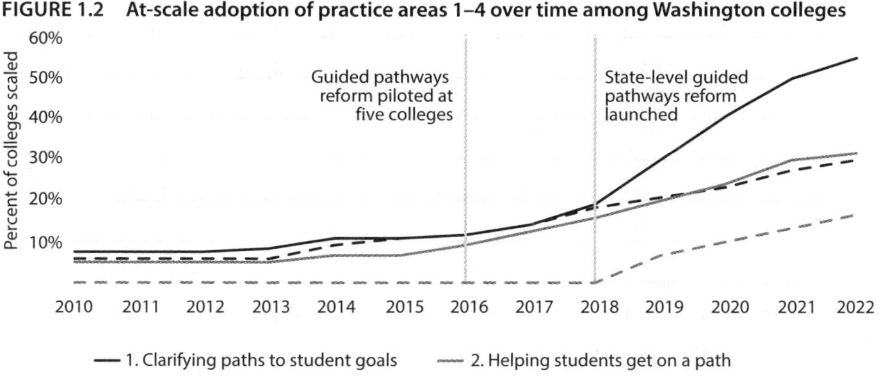

FIGURE 1.3 Trends in meeting college credit thresholds by AACC Pathways college group

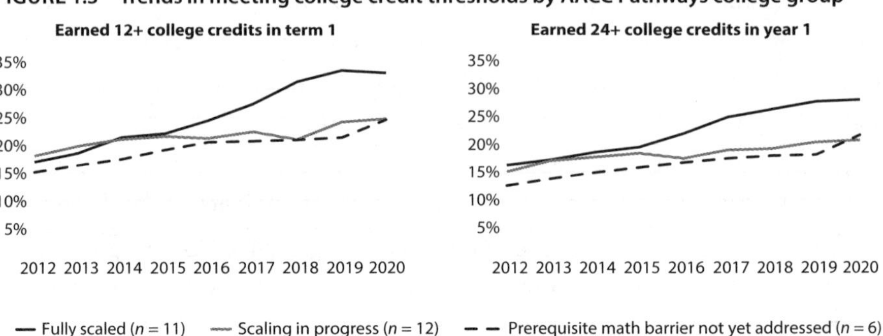

years before.[24] Notably, however, colleges that adopted a fully scaled set of model practices saw markedly higher increases in EMMs. For example, as shown in figure 1.3, the trend lines for both EMMs—on students earning at least twelve credits in the first term and earning at least fifteen in the first year—for the eleven fully scaled colleges diverge from those for the other two groups starting in 2016 and increase at a higher rate. This is what we hypothesized for colleges further along in redesigning practices that affect the student experience, such as program planning and progress monitoring.

We also saw larger increases in the rates at which first-year students successfully completed college math and English courses after the AACC Pathways Project began at colleges that adopted a fully scaled set of practices than for those that did not. These EMMs are important because college-level math and English composition are required for virtually all degree programs. Moreover, research has shown that failing math impedes momentum for many college students, particularly those from underserved groups.[25]

The AACC Pathways Project did not see positive differences for fully scaled colleges for two EMMs: the college-level course completion rate and the rate of persistence from term one to term two. The persistence finding is particularly concerning, because research shows the importance of continuous enrollment without stopping out.[26] We discuss the implications of both findings for further reform in the final section of this chapter.

When we disaggregated EMM trends for the three groups of AACC Pathways colleges by student race/ethnicity, we found that, after 2016, average rates for all racial/ethnic groups in the fully scaled group increased more rapidly than in the other groups, which was consistent with the overall trends. Similar gaps

FIGURE 1.4 Trends in "earned twelve or more college credits in term one by race/ethnicity": Two AACC Pathways college groups compared

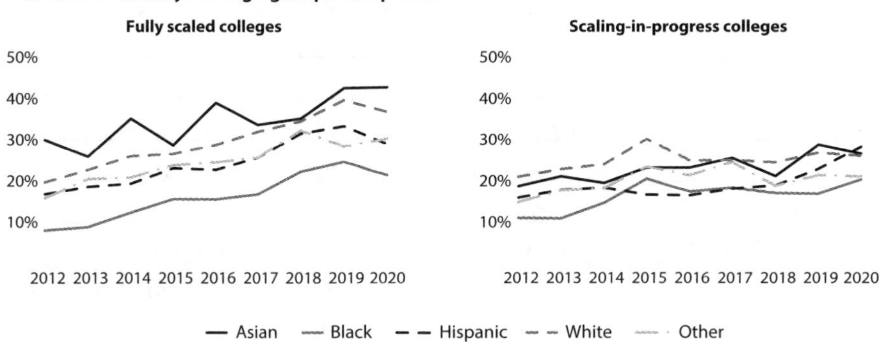

between racial/ethnic groups, however, remained for the fully scaled colleges. In other words, even though we observed a greater rate of improvement in EMMs across all student groups among colleges that fully scaled the model, those colleges did not close equity gaps. This pattern is evident in figure 1.4, which compares trends by student race/ethnicity between the fully scaled colleges and scaling-in-progress colleges for the "earned twelve or more college credits in term one by race/ethnicity" EMM.

Findings from the NSF study. We conducted three multivariate analyses using the colleges' institutional assessment responses and student administrative data to examine whether an association existed between adopting guided pathways practices and early student momentum.[27] Although the findings were mixed, the study provided insight into the effects of component practices of the model.

The first analysis examined whether launching statewide guided pathways reforms led to improvements in early momentum. We did not find consistently positive trends among colleges in Ohio and Washington, but we observed notable improvements in Tennessee, specifically in college-level credits earned in the first year and in fall-to-fall persistence. The methodology did not allow us to know whether the changes observed were due solely to guided pathways reforms or to others adopted at the same time. In 2014, the state launched the Tennessee Promise free college program, making it impossible to disentangle the effects of guided pathways on student success—for example, more students may have succeeded because they received tuition support from the Promise program. In this case, improvements in student momentum observed may have been the result of multiple reforms.

In the second analysis, we used responses from the SOAA survey to examine trends in student momentum before and after colleges scaled at least five practices. We found that increasing the intensity of adoption to at least five practices was not strongly associated with improvements in early student outcomes. Drawing conclusions for Washington may have been premature, however, given that we could examine only two years of data following the launch of its statewide initiative in 2018.

In the third analysis, we used regression analysis and data-mining techniques to isolate the effects on early student momentum of specific guided pathways model practices and combinations of practices. Interestingly, we found that on their own, some specific practices may benefit early student outcomes while others may hinder them. For example, corequisite college math was positively associated with college-level credits earned in the first year in Tennessee and Washington, whereas math pathways were associated with substantial increases in college-level math credits earned in the first year in all three states. In contrast, mapping career-technical programs and mandatory educational planning, by themselves, were negatively correlated with persistence (although the negative effects were small).

When examining the effects of guided pathways practices in combination, we found that adopting practices across practice areas was associated with larger improvements in early academic success than adopting any one individually. In Tennessee, adopting practices in areas 1 (clarifying paths to student end goals) and 3 (keeping students on path) resulted in a nearly twofold increase in college-level credits earned, compared with adopting any single practice or with the moderate- or high-intensity adoption of practices. The combination of adopting practices in areas 1, 2 (helping students get on a path), and 3 was associated with improvements in math and STEM credits earned in Tennessee and Washington and with student persistence in Washington. Ohio colleges achieved more significant gains in the number of college-level credits earned by adopting multiple practices within area 3 as opposed to adopting practices together across different areas.[28]

DRAWING CONCLUSIONS FOR PRACTICE AND FURTHER REFORM

According to the AACC Pathways Project evaluation, compared with colleges still scaling guided pathways reforms, colleges that adopted a more fully integrated set of practices at scale saw markedly higher rates of improvement in college credit accumulation and in passing college math in the first year (although not in student persistence). In contrast, the NSF study did not find any evidence that adopting at least five guided pathways practices was associated with improvements in early momentum across colleges in Ohio, Tennessee, and Washington. The NSF study did find, however, that the complementary adoption of practices within and across the practice areas correlated with larger improvements in early academic success than adopting any individual practice.

Thus, the findings of both studies are broadly consistent with the central premise of guided pathways: improving student success requires colleges to implement at scale a set of complementary practices that change the experience for all students, not just particular groups, in entering and progressing in a program. The two studies also point to specific areas for further reform if community colleges are to change students' experiences in ways that substantially improve outcomes for all while closing equity gaps. We discuss these in more detail in subsequent chapters.

Remove prerequisite remediation, particularly in math

The two evaluations provide evidence about the importance of corequisite remediation and math pathways. These practices are intended to ensure that entering students take college-level math courses as opposed to prerequisite remediation and that these courses are aligned to their programs. The AACC Pathways colleges that made substantial reforms to student onboarding and advising but kept in place prerequisite math did not see any marked improvements in early student momentum. In the NSF study, Tennessee's community colleges—in which we observed improved early student outcomes—began using corequisite math remediation and math pathways in 2015 and 2016. In contrast, corequisite math was much less common in Ohio and especially less so in Washington. This could be one reason why the NSF study did not find evidence of improved trends after the two states launched guided pathways reforms.

Strengthen program gateway courses outside of math and composition

Research indicates that corequisite and other reforms to developmental education, although necessary, are insufficient for improving student success beyond math and English composition course completion.[29] The fact that neither the

AACC Pathways nor the NSF study found evidence of improved success rates in college-level courses in other subjects is consistent with our prior research, which revealed that even colleges further along in scaling guided pathways reforms generally did not do much to strengthen pedagogy outside of math and English. Strengthening active and contextualized learning across program foundation courses and throughout programs is a critically needed next frontier for the guided pathways reform movement. How colleges can do this is the focus of chapter 3.

Offer ongoing advising and predictable schedules to help students complete plans

Both studies found that average persistence rates did not increase, suggesting that although it is important to help students onboard and gain credit momentum in a program, students also need help staying in college and completing on time. In fact, the NSF study revealed that combinations of practices that included those in practice area 3 (keeping students on path) had the strongest associations with early student success. Mapping out programs, organizing them more coherently, and improving information about them for students—as many colleges in the NSF study did—is insufficient to change student experiences and outcomes. Similarly, helping incoming students explore career and college interests and develop an educational plan is unlikely to help them progress unless they also receive ongoing advising (ideally by advisors who are knowledgeable about their field) and unless students and advisors use the plans to monitor progress and schedule classes. Improving scheduling for on-time completion—a critical guided pathways practice that was the least likely to be adopted by colleges in both studies—is much needed by community college students, who typically juggle myriad responsibilities and have little time and resources for school. How to provide better support to students for on-time completion is the focus of chapter 5.

Tailor guided pathways practices for students from underserved groups

In the AACC Pathways study, we saw improvements in key leading indicators for all racial/ethnic groups of students, but equity gaps nevertheless persisted. This finding supports the idea that adopting guided pathways reforms is not sufficient to close equity gaps. We saw the need in associated research to personalize practices according to the needs of student groups. Put differently, even with guided pathways, colleges must be proactive in personalizing support for students, particularly those from groups that have not been well served by our education system. Indeed, early adopter AACC Pathways colleges that saw improvements for students overall are now scrutinizing their reforms through an equity lens to ensure that these practices do not unwittingly reinforce tracking by race/ethnicity, income, gender, and other factors. We discuss how to tailor guided pathways practices to students from underserved groups in subsequent chapters, especially chapters 4 and 5.

Build on-ramps to career-path postsecondary programs for underserved K–12 students

The roots of equity gaps between student groups by race/ethnicity and family income are complex and include inequitable access to well-resourced primary and secondary schools. This realization spurred some colleges to extend guided pathways practices to underserved K–12 students by rethinking high school dual enrollment as a more equitable and effective on-ramp to career-path postsecondary programs after high school. In chapter 6, we describe in more detail how colleges can create such dual enrollment equity pathways.

CCRC's evaluations of guided pathways focused on efforts by colleges to redesign how they help students enter and complete programs successfully because colleges focused on these goals in their early reforms. These early reforms and evaluations paid less attention to designing and teaching programs in ways that ensured they would have postcompletion value for students in terms of employment and transfer. That is the topic of the next chapter.

CHAPTER 2

Ensuring Programs Lead to Good Jobs and Further Education

Community colleges that were early adopters of guided pathways made great strides in mapping clearer paths of study and aligning advising systems to support students through to graduation. They have made much less effort, however, to review and redesign existing programs and develop new ones to ensure that graduates succeed in the labor market and further education at the bachelor's level and beyond.

A 2023 Strada Education Foundation survey of students who had recently attended a community college (including some graduates and some who stopped out) found that career motivations were the most common reason for enrolling.[1] The survey also found that students primarily motivated by their careers were less likely to believe their community college education helped them achieve their desired outcomes than those motivated by personal or community-oriented reasons. Respondents earning less than a median income of $48,000 annually were markedly less likely to say their education was worth the cost or that it helped them achieve their goals. Students who completed an associate degree or transferred to a four-year institution valued their education more than those who did not.

The Strada findings are concerning when examined with data on program outcomes at community colleges. As noted in the introduction, only slightly more than 40 percent of students who start a program at a community college complete a degree or certificate at any institution within six years—meaning most come away with no credential. Of the more than 1.45 million credentials that community colleges award each year, more than 90 percent are designed to lead to direct employment or transfer to a bachelor's program rather than for personal edification (see text box and figure 2.1 for an overview). Students who enroll in these programs should expect them to lead to living-wage jobs and career advancement or enable them to earn a bachelor's degree affordably. Unfortunately, many if not most community college programs do not help students achieve those goals.

To recruit and retain students in today's extremely competitive higher education marketplace, community colleges must ensure their programs are worth the time and resources to complete. Moreover, colleges cannot meet their goals for upward mobility and equity solely by increasing completion rates by low-income students, students of color, and other underserved populations for just any credential. To achieve more equitable outcomes, community colleges must enable students from underserved groups to earn credentials that transfer efficiently or lead directly to well-paying career-path jobs.

In this chapter, we examine why too many community college transfer and workforce programs fail to achieve these goals. We then describe colleges' efforts to work with employers and four-year colleges to map programs to post-completion success so students can transfer to a bachelor's program with no excess credits or enter living-wage career-path jobs in high-demand fields. In the final section, we outline actions colleges can take to ensure that their programs expand economic and educational opportunity for students.

Overview of Community College Credit Program Awards

Of the more than 1.45 million credit program credentials community colleges awarded in 2021–2022, nearly 60 percent were associate degrees (figure 2.1). Most of the rest were certificates, and only 1 percent were bachelor's degrees.

Two-thirds of associate degrees were designed to prepare students to transfer to bachelor's programs. The remaining third and most certificates were workforce or career-technical credentials intended to prepare students to enter directly into or advance in jobs. The remaining certificates (including 44 percent of those from programs lasting at least a year) were in liberal arts and sciences. Because these credentials generally are not recognized by employers or universities, they are presumably designed for students seeking to advance their knowledge for personal interest rather than career reasons.

FIGURE 2.1 Community college awards by program outcome: Academic year 2021–2022

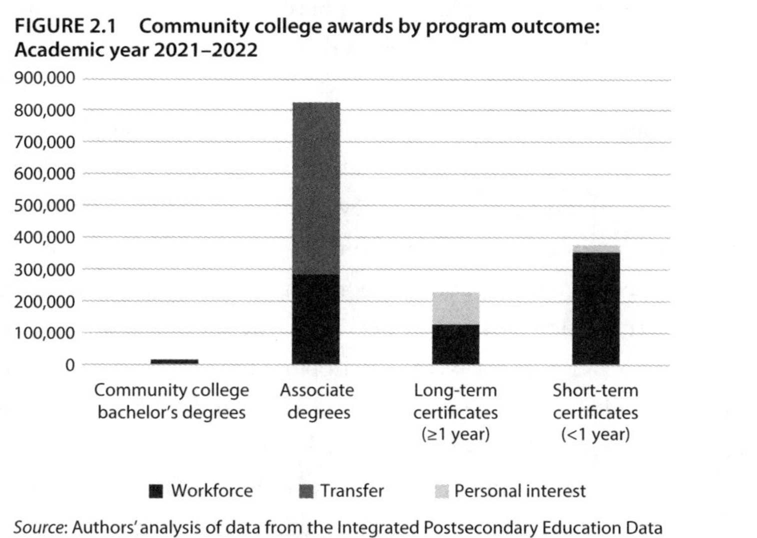

Source: Authors' analysis of data from the Integrated Postsecondary Education Data System (IPEDS) on more than 1.45 million credentials awarded by 916 community colleges in academic year 2021–2022.

Not shown in this figure are credentials obtained through noncredit workforce training programs, which in some cases award occupational certificates that prepare students to take industry certification tests. These certifications are ineligible for Title IV federal financial aid. There are no good national data available on the number of noncredit certificates or certifications awarded by community colleges each year.

DELIVERING AN AFFORDABLE PATH TO A BACHELOR'S DEGREE

Most jobs that pay a living wage for one person, much less that can support a family, are held by workers with at least a bachelor's degree.[2] That share has increased steadily since the 1980s and is expected to continue to increase over the next decade. It makes sense that most students who start college at a community college say in surveys that they aspire to earn a bachelor's degree.[3]

Yet only about one-third who start at a community college transfer to a four-year institution, and of those, fewer than half (48 percent) earn a bachelor's degree within six years of starting.[4] As a result, only 16 percent of community college starters earn a bachelor's degree within six years. Transfer outcomes are even worse among students of color and those from low-income families. For example, of the 29 percent of Black students who transfer, only 32 percent earn a bachelor's degree within six years, which means transferring to a four-year institution is a valuable path to a bachelor's degree for fewer than one in ten Black community college starters.

Many students planning to transfer earn a substantial number of credits, or in some cases an associate degree, but they never transfer.[5] Among those who do, too many earn far more credits than they need, requiring more time and money.[6] Transfer students of color and those from low-income families are more likely to earn excess credits.[7] That means the poorest students often have to pay more and spend more time completing their degrees. Other evidence suggests that many students who earn lots of excess credits drop out in frustration before completing a degree.[8] Credits lost at the point of transfer tend to reduce the labor market returns to transfer students who do earn a bachelor's degree.[9]

Unless students continue on to earn a bachelor's degree, having a transfer associate degree alone generally does not enable students to obtain well-paying jobs, a fact many community college educators fail to recognize. For example, an associate of arts degree in liberal arts or general studies, by far the most common transfer degree, is associated with near-term earnings for graduates well below a living wage.[10] Associate of arts graduates who transfer must thus continue to rely on low-wage jobs even as they take additional credits to earn their bachelor's degree.

Scrapping the broken, inequitable 2+2 model

Responsibility for this problem lies both with community colleges and transfer universities. A key root of the problem is the conventional 2+2 model, subscribed to by community colleges and universities, in which advisors recommend students delay selecting a major and instead take "general education" liberal arts and sciences courses in their first two years, leaving major courses for junior and senior years. Students who earn associate degrees under this model typically accumulate a grab bag of liberal arts and sciences credits that they have trouble transferring to specific majors. Advising transfer students to take general education courses before choosing a major is a big reason they end up with excess credits, because they need to take the right lower-division credits for their intended major while they are still in community college to ensure those credits will be accepted toward a bachelor's in their field of interest.[11] This situation can prevent transfer students from entering high-remuneration fields, such as science, technology, engineering, and math (STEM), nursing, and business, which have strict lower-division requirements. For example, students pursuing STEM majors may need to take advanced introductory chemistry, not general introductory chemistry.[12] Students who intend to transfer but are unaware of pre-major requirements may lock themselves out of these fields. Unfortunately, many students find out too late that they have taken courses that do not apply to their majors. This is likely one reason why a smaller proportion of community college transfer students who complete a bachelor's do so in STEM fields compared with those who start at a four-year institution.[13] Given that the 2+2 model does not provide a clear path to transfer in a major, it is not surprising that fewer than 10 percent of students who transfer follow this pattern.[14]

Most four-year institutions do not follow the equivalent of the 2+2 model with students who enter as freshmen. Some large universities require students to apply to specific colleges, which means committing to a field of study even before enrolling. Broad-access institutions like Florida International University that have improved outcomes and narrowed equity gaps require students to choose at least a preliminary major or major field of study in the first term or two.[15] Even at liberal arts colleges, first-year students typically take courses in major fields early and tend to follow curriculum tracks depending on whether they plan to major in English, arts and humanities, social and behavioral sciences, or STEM.

This misalignment of community college transfer degrees with bachelor's majors is evident in table 2.1, which compares the field of study of the approximately 541,000 transfer associate degrees awarded by community colleges in the 2021–2022 academic year to those of the nearly 1.39 million bachelor's degrees awarded by public four-year institutions during the same period. Note that 60 percent of community college transfer associate degrees were in liberal arts or general studies, compared with only 4 percent of public four-year bachelor's degrees. Of the transfer associate degrees aligned with four-year major fields, most were in business (12 percent); social and behavioral sciences (9 percent); or art, humanities, and English (6 percent). Only 10 percent of transfer associate degrees were in STEM fields, compared with 23 percent of bachelor's degree awards from public four-year institutions. This misalignment is one reason why only 40 percent of community college students earn an associate degree before transferring.[16] In theory, given the diversity of community college students,

TABLE 2.1 Community college transfer associate degrees and public four-year bachelor's degrees by program area: Academic year 2021–2022

	Community college transfer associate degrees		*Public four-year bachelor's degrees*	
Program area	*Awards*	*Share of all awards*	*Awards*	*Share of all awards*
Liberal arts or general studies	324,380	60%	49,034	4%
Arts, humanities, and English	32,519	6%	86,113	6%
Communication and design*	5,242	1%	78,092	6%
Social and behavioral sciences	46,713	9%	218,754	16%
Business	64,983	12%	63,109	5%
Education and child care	9,501	2%	36,515	3%
Human services and public administration*	1,771	0%	49,165	4%
Law, public safety, and corrections*	424	0%	253,832	18%
Allied health and nursing*	2,349	0%	177,064	13%
STEM				
Biosciences	33,834	6%	102,728	7%
Physical sciences	9,679	2%	43,987	3%
Computer and information sciences	4,836	1%	81,651	6%
Engineering	5,566	1%	100,460	7%
Industrial and applied technology*	0	0%	12,508	1%
Agriculture and natural resources*	86	0%	34,639	2%
Total	541,883	100%	1,387,651	100%

* Most community college associate degrees in these fields are designed to prepare students for direct entry into the workforce rather than to transfer.

Source: Authors' analysis of IPEDS awards data from academic year 2021–2022.

transfer is a potential mechanism for diversifying bachelor's degree attainment, particularly in STEM and other high-opportunity fields. In reality, however, the transfer option is often more of a barrier to bachelor's attainment for underrepresented students than a pathway to expand opportunities.

The conventional 2+2 model, which front-loads general education courses, is well meaning; in practice, however, it often does not work for students. Although the 2+2 transfer path may sound like an affordable route to earn a bachelor's degree, students who take it likely will have to earn more credits—and spend more time and money—unless they understand what their intended major requires. Without clear, structured major-specific transfer pathways mapped by community colleges and their four-year partners, transfer too often replicates and reinforces existing inequities.

Mapping pre-major transfer pathways

Even in states with regulations ensuring the transferability of general education core courses, students who do not know which community college courses will apply toward their major often end up taking additional courses to satisfy specific major requirements.[17] Therefore, community colleges need to work with universities to backward-map transfer programs starting with bachelor's degrees in specific majors. The mapping must be done with each transfer institution because requirements can vary across universities even for the same major. Processes also need to be in place to update maps as program requirements change.

Many if not most community colleges have established articulation agreements with transfer destinations, but these agreements are hard for students to decipher and are often out of date. Relatively few community colleges work with four-year partners to map structured transfer pathways to degrees in specific majors and keep them current. A small but growing number of community college four-year partnerships, however, are seeking to expand access to bachelor's degrees for large numbers of students, especially those from underserved groups, through so-called dual- or concurrent-admissions programs. Two well-known examples are the University of Central Florida's (UCF) Direct Connect to UCF partnership with Valencia College and other Orlando-area community colleges, and the ADVANCE Program established by George Mason University and Northern Virginia Community College.[18] Both partnerships guarantee admission to a bachelor's degree program in a specific major at the university. Students receive joint advising and help creating and following plans based on curriculum maps developed for each major.

Most community college students have numerous transfer destination options, particularly in areas with many nearby four-year institutions. It is challenging to map transfer pathways in specific majors to more than a few four-year transfer destinations. Institutions like the Alamo Colleges District in Texas show not only that it is possible to map transfer paths to multiple universities but also that the process can improve outcomes for students, diversify four-year college student bodies, and benefit the community college by retaining more students through to their associate degree before they transfer.

Case Study: Strengthening Success Through Transfer Advising Guides at the Alamo Colleges[19]

In the past, too few students who started college at one of the five Alamo Colleges in Texas successfully transferred and completed a bachelor's degree. Additionally, many who intended to transfer earned substantially more community college credits than required. For example, the average student who completed an associate degree earned more than ninety credits before transferring, even though transfer associate degrees generally require around sixty credits. In many cases, however, students had to take additional courses for a major (or switch to another one), adding to the time and cost of earning a bachelor's degree and increasing the chances of falling short.

As part of the American Association of Community Colleges (AACC) Pathways Project, the Alamo College District organized its programs into six meta-major fields called the Alamo Institutes. Administrators reassigned deans to oversee the institutes, which included academic transfer and career-technical, credit, and noncredit programs. The district created advisory boards of employers and university personnel to guide students in each institute.

Alamo leveraged a regional transfer compact to develop transfer advising guides (TAGs) for hundreds of majors to more than twenty public and private universities in Central Texas. The TAGs show the courses that students should take depending on their major and whether they plan to attend a public or private four-year institution. Figure 2.2 is based on the Alamo TAGs and shows the courses that three groups of students intending to transfer to a public or private university partner can take without

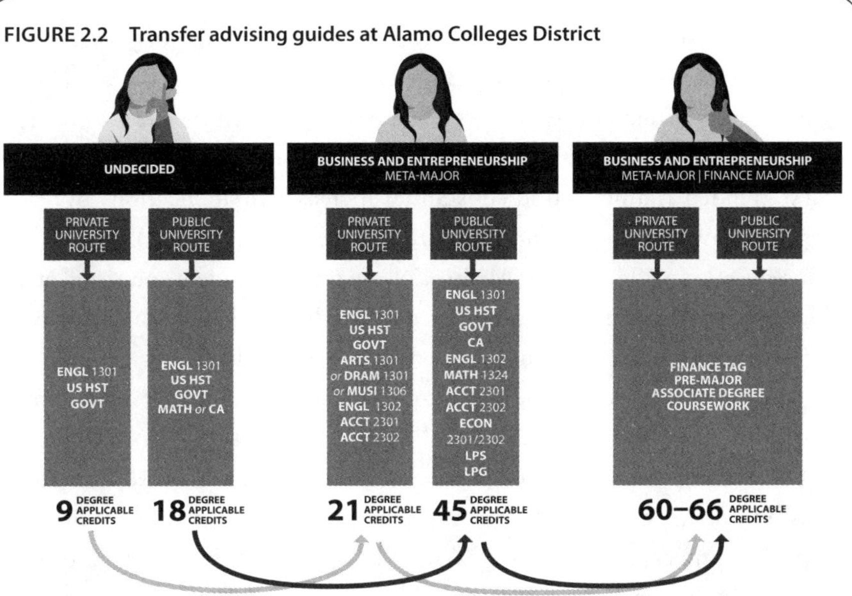

FIGURE 2.2 Transfer advising guides at Alamo Colleges District

Source: Adapted with permission from a presentation slide from the Alamo Colleges District.

losing credits: (1) those who are undecided on a major, (2) those who are interested in business but have not decided on a specific major, and (3) those who want to major in finance.

Through the parallel AlamoADVISE initiative, the colleges reassigned existing advisors and hired new ones to advise students in each institute. They also reorganized intake and advising for new students to help them navigate enrollment, explore interests, and secure an advisor. Advisors help all transfer students develop an individualized educational plan based on the TAG for their field. Students seeking to enter the labor market directly receive help developing a workforce program plan. Students are required to connect with their advisor before registering for classes at fifteen-, thirty-, and forty-five-credit checkpoints to ensure that they are on track to complete their plans. Six curriculum analysts at the Alamo District work with four-year partners to update TAGs as requirements change and universities offer new programs.

Through these efforts, the Alamo Colleges have decreased the average number of credit hours to an associate degree for transfer students from ninety-two in the 2014–2015 academic year to seventy-seven for 2022–2023.[20] The average has dropped to sixty-five for transfer students who started at one of the colleges. Research conducted in 2021 with the University of Texas at San Antonio (UTSA), where half of undergraduates attended Alamo, found substantial increases in applications by Alamo students (up 46 percent from 2016) and enrollments (up 32 percent). Moreover, UTSA found that Alamo College transfer students persisted at a higher rate (88 percent versus 83 percent) and had higher graduation rates (69 percent versus 63 percent) than native UTSA students.

Alamo estimates that the average student who follows a plan based on one of its seamless TAGs with a public university in the South & Central Texas Transfer Compact would save more than $40,000 in tuition and fees by starting at Alamo and transferring, and students transferring to a private university could save $65,000. They could save even more by starting on a transfer path through Alamos Colleges' large and growing high school dual credit programs or by participating in the Alamo Promise tuition-free program for recent high school graduates.

We understand that community colleges may be reluctant to focus on mapping major-specific pathways to bachelor's programs, particularly given that they often compete with universities for lower-division students; that universities are reluctant to allow community colleges to teach major-specific courses; and, in many states, that universities resist community colleges' efforts to offer their own bachelor's degrees. Yet demand for an affordable path to a bachelor's degree is unlikely to decrease given the strong economic returns. We contend that community colleges can recruit and retain more students by marketing themselves as low-cost, high-quality pathways to bachelor's degrees in high-opportunity fields. Helping transfer students earn associate degrees through so-called reverse transfer or "credit where it is due" initiatives, although well intentioned, may benefit colleges and state systems by increasing completion rates. They fail to address, however, the problem of students not taking courses that will count toward a bachelor's in their desired major.[21] Rather than awarding credit for a degree after the fact, community and four-year partners need to map pathways to bachelor's degrees in specific majors and help all students develop individualized major transfer plans *prospectively* so students can apply their community college credits toward a bachelor's degree *and* earn an associate degree along the way.

EXPANDING AND DIVERSIFYING THE TECHNICIAN WORKFORCE

The proliferation of automation and advanced technologies across fields has increased demand for skilled workers to fill technician jobs that pay well above a living wage and provide opportunities for career advancement. The technician workforce is aging and is predominantly male and white, especially in computer and information technology, engineering technology, and industrial and construction technology and trades. To replace them and fill the new jobs being created, employers need a diverse workforce that reflects their customers and the communities in which they operate. Most of the projected new jobs in these fields will require a bachelor's degree or higher, but demand is expected to remain strong for workers with less than a bachelor's degree, particularly those with associate degrees in allied health, nursing, and industrial and construction technology and trades.[22] These developments combine to create opportunities for community colleges to expand and diversify workforce programs that will increase upward mobility for students and communities and help build talent for their local economies.

Growing and diversifying community college bachelor's degrees

Transferring to a four-year college to pursue a bachelor's is not feasible for many students, particularly those who cannot move and who need to work. So the dismal transfer outcomes for older working students who start at a community college are not surprising.[23]

A growing number of community colleges nationally offer bachelor's degree programs for students who cannot move to pursue one. Students in bachelor's programs at community colleges tend to be more diverse in age, race, and income than those in four-year institutions.[24] Evidence also suggests these programs generally lead to good job opportunities for older students, who are more likely to be place-bound. Although such programs are growing, the number of bachelor's degrees awarded by community colleges is still small: 16,548 in 2021 to 2022 compared with the 1.39 million awarded by public universities. Most were in fields in which graduates can secure well-paying jobs with good career prospects. The largest numbers were in business (6,531 degrees awarded). Bachelor's degrees in nursing and allied health were second (4,156 degrees awarded).

Community colleges awarded fewer bachelor's degrees in other high-demand fields, including 1,689 in computer and information technology, 635 in education, and 494 in engineering and science technology. These numbers are tiny relative to the projected demand for workers with bachelor's degrees in teaching, information technology, computer and engineering technology, and industrial and construction technology fields, among others.[25] Women and students of color were underrepresented among community college bachelor's graduates in some of these high-demand fields, as shown in the shaded cells in table 2.2.[26]

TABLE 2.2 Community college bachelor's degrees by program area: Academic year 2021–2022

		Share of awards earned by subgroup			
Program area	*Awards*	*Female*	*Black*	*Hispanic*	*White*
Business	6,531	67%	14%	27%	47%
Allied health and nursing	4,156	85%	14%	23%	50%
Computer and information technology	1,689	23%	11%	27%	43%
Communication and design	1,181	77%	7%	24%	40%
Education	635	87%	7%	23%	54%
Public safety and corrections	586	55%	22%	29%	42%
Child care	410	95%	10%	28%	49%
Industrial technology and trades	362	28%	7%	17%	56%
Human services and public administration	310	84%	28%	16%	47%
Science and science technology	269	66%	9%	26%	36%
Engineering and engineering technology	191	12%	7%	24%	51%
Agriculture and natural resources	129	65%	5%	14%	69%
Liberal arts and general studies	59	42%	2%	2%	86%
Social and behavioral sciences	32	75%	9%	9%	25%
Personal services	8	63%	0%	13%	63%
Total	16,548	67%	13%	25%	47%

Note: In rows of high-demand program areas, shaded cells indicate that women or students of color were underrepresented among bachelor's degree earners relative to their representation among all community college bachelor's degree earners.

Source: Authors' analysis of IPEDS awards data from 916 community colleges from academic year 2021–2022.

Community colleges need to greatly expand and diversify their bachelor's programs in these fields to help meet the strong projected demand for workers with bachelor's degrees.

Expanding and diversifying high-return workforce associate degrees

Community colleges offer a substantial number of associate degrees in career-technical fields (often called workforce or applied associate degrees) that can lead to jobs paying well above a living wage and provide opportunities for career advancement. As shown in table 2.3, nearly half (48 percent) of the more than 286,000 career-technical associate degrees awarded by community colleges from

TABLE 2.3 Community college workforce associate degrees by program area and estimated earnings: Academic year 2021–2022

		Median earnings (in 2019 dollars)	*Share of awards earned by subgroup*			
Program area	*Awards*		*Female*	*Black*	*Hispanic*	*White*
Well above a living wage						
Nursing	58,529	$57,989	86%	11%	16%	59%
Allied health technology	35,547	$44,483	79%	8%	17%	61%
Industrial technology and trades	33,642	$41,004	14%	7%	19%	62%
Engineering technology	6,139	$47,862	13%	7%	14%	65%
Science technology	2,641	$46,636	62%	16%	20%	45%
Subtotal	136,498		63%	9%	17%	60%
Share of awards	48%					
Near a living wage						
Public safety and corrections	33,049	$31,824	52%	11%	35%	44%
Computer and information technology	26,277	$35,351	24%	12%	17%	50%
Business	19,063	$29,057	68%	13%	21%	49%
Allied health (other)	15,491	$33,193	73%	10%	36%	34%
Agriculture and natural resources	8,613	$31,957	58%	2%	15%	73%

continued

TABLE 2.3 ***continued***

Program area	*Awards*	*Median earnings (in 2019 dollars)*	*Share of awards earned by subgroup*			
			Female	*Black*	*Hispanic*	*White*
Funeral and mortuary science	699	$36,021	73%	18%	14%	61%
Subtotal	103,192		52%	11%	26%	47%
Share of awards	36%					
Well below a living wage						
Education and child care	14,711	$20,738	96%	14%	38%	36%
Communication and design	13,471	$25,231	60%	8%	27%	47%
Health administrative services	6,067	$29,624	94%	19%	14%	54%
Culinary services	3,976	$25,624	63%	18%	21%	44%
Human services and public administration	3,819	$26,269	85%	20%	27%	43%
Mental and public health	3,645	$28,269	80%	23%	17%	47%
Cosmetology	1,077	$18,838	97%	14%	29%	44%
Subtotal	46,766		80%	14%	28%	44%
Share of awards	16%					
Total	286,456		62%	11%	22%	53%

Note: Light shaded cells indicate program areas associated with earnings well above a living wage in which women or students of color were underrepresented among graduates. Dark shaded cells indicate program areas associated with earnings well below a living wage in which women or students of color were overrepresented among graduates.

Source: Authors' analysis of IPEDS awards data from 916 community colleges from academic year 2021–2022 matched to College Scorecard earnings data, which are median annual earnings in calendar years 2017 and 2018 for federal financial aid recipients who completed a community college workforce award in the given field in academic years 2014–2015 and 2015–2016 and were not enrolled in an institution of higher education during the measurement years (inflation-adjusted to 2019 dollars). According to the Massachusetts Institute of Technology Living Wage Calculator, in 2019, the living wage for an individual with no children nationally was about $35,000.

2021 to 2022 were associated with median earnings well above a living wage two years after award completion.[27] More than one-third (36 percent) of the awards were associated with median earnings near a living wage, and only 16 percent were associated with jobs paying well below a living wage.

Over the next several years, many parts of the country are projected to face shortages of skilled workers for well-paying jobs that require postsecondary technical education but not a bachelor's degree.[28] In most regions, community colleges and other providers are producing far fewer graduates with associate degrees or apprenticeships in industrial and construction technology and trades. In some regions, demand is projected to outstrip the supply of workers with postsecondary education and training in health technology, public safety, and engineering and science technology.

Table 2.3 also shows the lack of diversity among community college workforce associate degree graduates in many of the higher earning fields. Women are unsurprisingly overrepresented in allied health and nursing, but they are underrepresented in industrial technology and trades, computer and information technology, and engineering technology. Black students are underrepresented in industrial technology and trades and engineering technology, and Hispanic graduates are underrepresented in nearly all the fields associated with median earnings well above a living wage. In contrast, women and Black and Hispanic students are overrepresented in fields paying well below a living wage. As with bachelor's programs, to meet projected demand and provide opportunities for upward mobility for their communities, community colleges need to expand and diversify associate degree programs in high-demand, well-paying career-technical fields.

Building career ladders in high-demand fields for working students

Associate degree programs in nursing and allied health tend to be highly selective because of limitations on the number of clinical spots. Some colleges have tried to diversify these programs by deemphasizing standardized tests and prerequisite courses, which too often weed out students who otherwise might thrive. Even career-technical associate degree programs that are not formally selective tend to be rigorous and take time to complete. In most fields, it helps to work in the industry while pursuing a degree, because such experience increases the value of applicants with degrees, and as mentioned, it is hard for students to support themselves and their families on low-wage service jobs while in school. Community colleges offer certificate programs in nursing, allied health, and other well-paying, high-demand fields, such as industrial technology and advanced manufacturing, that provide stepping stones to jobs that may pay near a living wage and thus enable students to support themselves while they pursue applied associate degrees. Examples include advanced certificate programs in licensed practical nursing, phlebotomy, and machining technology. Although certificates lasting a year or more in these fields appear to improve employment rates and stability, workers with certificates generally need to pursue degrees to advance to jobs that pay above living wages and have strong career advancement opportunities.[29]

Colleges often use the term "stacking credentials" to refer to earning certificates or industry-skill certifications that lead to jobs offering progressively higher wages and allow students to gain experience while pursuing degrees. Although certificates may stack on paper, in practice, too many colleges fail to offer program sequences and advising to help students advance to better jobs while also taking courses toward a degree. Moreover, career-technical courses are often not well integrated with liberal arts and sciences courses, which are required components of all degree programs. Instead, students must figure out themselves how to stack courses and credentials in a way that leads to better jobs and degrees.

Short-term certificates can theoretically provide an on-ramp for underemployed workers to career ladders in high-paying fields. But in reality, low-income learners are overrepresented in certificate programs in low-wage fields (e.g., child care and nursing assistance) and are underrepresented in short-term certificates programs in high-paying fields (e.g., engineering technology, manufacturing, and information technology), which tend to enroll workers already in the industry seeking to enhance their skills.[30] Low-income students account for a large percentage of students earning noncredit certificates, which rarely lead to credit-bearing credentials.[31] Very short training programs (less than ten weeks) often lead low-income students to jobs paying poverty-level wages and, in some cases, high debt.[32] Despite their promise as an on-ramp to career ladders, short-term certificates tend to lead to low-paying dead-end jobs. Moreover, they often do not help students take the next step toward better paying jobs and degrees.

From stacking credentials to learning-and-earning career ladders. As we have emphasized, many if not most community college students need to work to support themselves and their families. Employers in fields with expanding demand need workers immediately. Colleges therefore need to create program sequences that enable students to quickly get a foothold in a high-demand field and pursue the education and training needed to advance up job ladders while they are working. A growing number of colleges are developing such learning-and-earning ladder programs in well-paying, high-demand fields in their communities. Key features of these programs are highlighted in the following text box.[33]

Key Features of Learning-and-Earning Career Ladders

Learning-and-earning ladder maps. Colleges work with employers, industry groups, and universities to map programs that enable students to earn the credentials needed to advance to progressively higher-paying jobs while earning credit toward associate and bachelor's degrees. The maps show how much time students need to complete each rung, along with examples of the jobs and related wages they can expect to get at each stage.

Fast-start foothold training. These short-term training programs enable working adults to secure entry-level technical jobs in high-demand fields. Fast-start training emphasizes foundational workplace and applied technology skills through hands-on instruction that prepares students to earn industry certifications they can use to land jobs paying above minimum wage. Completers will have the means and motivation to pursue further training to move up the ladder, but colleges will need to encourage and support students at each rung to progress to the next.

Curriculum maps. These maps are developed with industry and four-year college content experts to integrate instruction in applied technical fundamentals with teaching communication, problem-solving, and other essential workplace competencies. Coursework in liberal arts and sciences should emphasize these skills and integrate with technical courses to fulfill degree requirements.

Work-based learning. Curriculum maps can include embedded work-based learning that may give students academic credit for on-the-job learning and employer-sponsored training. Apprenticeships are a well-tested model for industry-led on-the-job learning that complements learning in classrooms and labs. Colleges are now offering apprenticeship programs in fields outside of the trades, including healthcare, education, and computing and information technology.

Scheduled and delivered for working adults. Programs are offered on schedules, including evenings, weekends, and summers, and through online and hybrid modalities that make learning accessible to working adults. Rather than leaving it to students to figure out how to complete their programs, colleges provide clear schedules with beginning and end dates (e.g., three-week fast-track training or fifteen-month associate degree programs with embedded certificates).

On-ramps from high school. Colleges embed college-level courses from degree programs in high-opportunity fields into career-technical courses, career academies, and other high school programs. This lets students earn college credits and, in some cases, industry-skill certifications or college certificates, a first step on a learning-and-earning ladder to degrees and career-path jobs. Students can then get entry-level jobs immediately after high school that pay more than low-skill service jobs, supporting themselves and gaining valuable work experience while they pursue an associate degree, an apprenticeship, or a bachelor's degree.

Over the past decade, Lorain County Community College (LCCC) in Ohio has developed learning-and-earning career ladder programs with local employers and economic development groups to meet expanding demand for microelectromechanical technicians across a wide range of industries in Northeast Ohio. Its work demonstrates the key features of these types of programs.

Case Study: Building Learning-and-Earning Career Ladders at Lorain County Community College

In 2013, LCCC found that a growing number of regional manufacturers and other employers were embedding smart chips to make their products more competitive. To accomplish this, employers needed technicians with different skills than the then-current technical workforce or graduates of the college's existing manufacturing and engineering technology programs. Because employers did not have a clear idea about what they wanted, they hired applicants with engineering degrees, which was expensive and led to high turnover. Local employers critically needed workers with the right skills to upgrade existing products and launch new ones to stay competitive.

Learning together to build a supply of new talent. LCCC staff and faculty worked closely with employers to analyze these jobs. Faculty studied skills listed in job postings, which often included outdated job titles, and visited workplaces to talk with employees and supervisors about their jobs and see the work firsthand. Staff and faculty then mapped a sequence of programs that would enable workers to enter and advance to higher-level microelectromechanical technician jobs while pursuing associate and bachelor's degrees in the field.

At each rung of LCCC's microelectromechanical systems (MEMS) learning-and-earning career ladder (see figure 2.3), students receive hands-on instruction in applied technical fundamentals. After completing each

FIGURE 2.3 MEMS career ladder map at LCCC

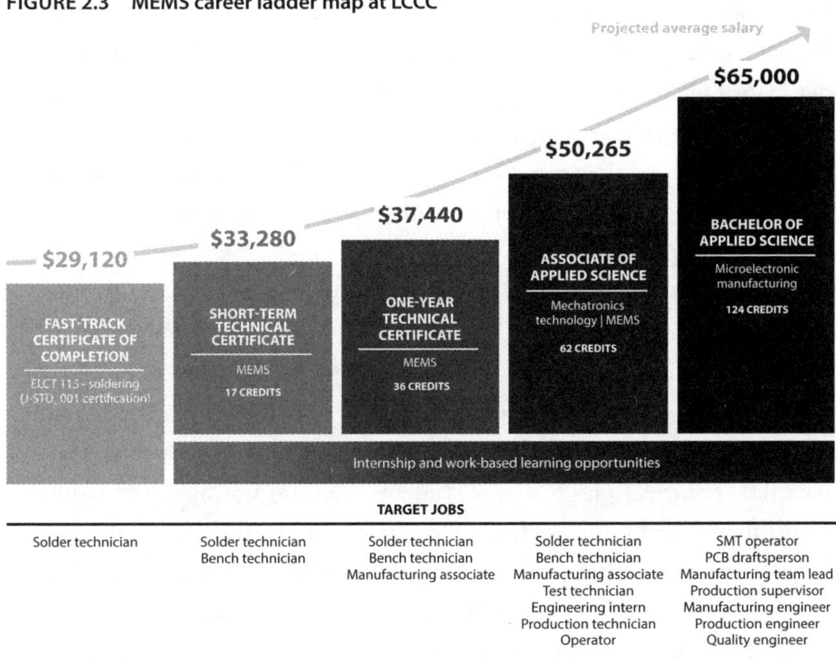

Source: Adapted with permission from a presentation slide from LCCC.

rung, students earn credentials qualifying them for better jobs, and their credits apply to new associate and bachelor of applied science programs in MEMS.

Ladders out of poverty that supply diverse talent to local industries. LCCC created a short-term fast-track training program that leads to a nationally recognized certificate in soldering to help inexperienced workers get a foothold onto a career ladder in industries that need workers with MEMS skills. Students who complete the fast-track program can secure entry-level technician jobs, which provides them with industry experience and allows them to earn money while continuing their part-time training. The college is working with local community organizations to recruit more women and people of color, who are underrepresented in MEMS jobs in the region, into the program.

Active recruitment and support to help students progress to higher rungs. Because the learning ladder has multiple on and off points, the risk exists that students will not seek to advance to higher rungs once they find a job. Faculty and advisors, however, emphasize that the more classes students take, the more they can advance in their careers while using ladder maps to help them develop an educational plan. LCCC also schedules classes at times that are convenient to working students. Staff say retention is high, something they attribute to talented faculty who provide hands-on learning from the start and opportunities to network with faculty, other students, and potential employers.

On-ramps to career-path degree programs after high school. Nearly half of local high school students take college courses through LCCC's College Credit Plus dual enrollment program. A big obstacle for the remaining half is not having the grades or test scores to qualify. Starting in 2022, LCCC participated in a waiver program that lets it offer career-technical courses to high school students who did not meet the requirements for academic courses like college math and English. The college also began offering certification training in MEMS as well as in healthcare and other fields. LCCC not only gives high school students a head start on a learning-and-earning career ladder program but also brings them to campus to meet with faculty, students, and employers so they can build networks in the field. In 2023, the Ohio legislature expanded funding for high school dual enrollment career-technical education. The college will focus on low-income first-generation students who do not have plans to continue education and training after high school.

Using learning-and-earning ladder maps to update program offerings, build employer ownership, and recruit more employers. The MEMS ladder maps and curricula are not static. LCCC shares them with workforce partners to help design and update curriculum and instruction at each level. This practice has created a sense of ownership and has encouraged employers to urge (and in some cases financially support) workers to participate. The college has also used ladder maps to show employers what other companies are paying for similar roles, which has led to wage increases to attract and retain workers.

Additionally, LCCC uses the maps with new employers in a wide range of industries. The MEMS ladder, which was originally used with five employers, now has more than eighty. In 2022, Intel announced plans to build a new fabrication facility near Columbus, Ohio. Although the site is more than two hours away from LCCC, the college has worked with nearby employers to add semiconductor-related training to the MEMS curriculum so that the facility can become part of the labor force supply chain for microelectronics manufacturers, electric vehicle makers, and other firms in the region.

Leading a regional effort to build capacity. LCCC is leading work with eight other Ohio colleges and high school partners to build capacity for educating workers in semiconductors and related advanced technology fields. This includes collaboratively developing curriculum for colleges and high schools and creating opportunities for them to use LCCC's specialized equipment and trained faculty. The college is focused on helping students develop foundational skills in applied technology, as well as in communication, problem-solving, and teamwork—skills that will enable them to find employment in a wide range of industries and adapt as technology changes.

LCCC and other colleges working with employers to map career ladder programs and curricula can build strong partnerships benefiting students, employers, and colleges. New technologies are changing jobs in many industries in ways not reflected in federal and state labor market data or even in more up-to-date commercial job information sources. Keeping programs current can be done only through ongoing dialogue with employers and workers, particularly in fields in which the core skills are changing and creating new job opportunities. Thus, working with employers to develop and update job ladder and curriculum maps can help employers update job descriptions and pay-and-promotion ladders. This gives employers a sense of ownership and makes them more likely to hire graduates and recommend the programs to current and prospective employees.

Focus on teaching fundamentals, not training for specific jobs. Although community colleges should be responsive to employer needs, they should also be wary of building programs around specific technologies or jobs. Narrowly focused programs are not sustainable because local labor markets quickly become saturated, leaving students stranded and programs obsolete. Instead, colleges should focus on teaching applied technology fundamentals and add modules that equip students with cutting-edge skills.

For example, Southwest Wisconsin Technical College (SWTC) found that a relatively small number of jobs were being created by solar farms in the rural part of Wisconsin the college serves. However, the college identified a much larger demand across a wide array of industries for technicians who can install and manage energy systems to cut energy costs and move to noncarbon sources. These jobs include construction and building inspector, energy program coordinator, energy auditor, energy control system specialist, energy conservation representative, environmental field technician, and weatherization inspector. The college is working with employers across industries and with faculty from the University of Wisconsin–Platteville's Sustainable and Renewable Energy Systems program to develop a sequence of programs that will enable students to enter and advance in these jobs while pursuing associate and bachelor's degree programs. SWTC has identified a common set of competencies employers want from potential employees. In addition to basic technical skills, including solar photovoltaic technology fundamentals, calculating investment payment, and energy systems installation and maintenance, employers are looking for applicants with demonstrated competence in oral and written communication, problem-solving, project management, and team leadership. SWTC has integrated teaching and learning of both types of skills in the living-learning lab it created using its own energy management system as well as on the job through apprenticeships and internships.

TAKING ACTION TO ENSURE PROGRAMS LEAD TO GOOD JOBS OR TRANSFER

Accreditation agencies require colleges to have procedures to regularly review specific programs to ensure quality. But colleges generally do not perform global assessments to ensure that all programs lead to good jobs and further education. Doing so requires college leaders to raise awareness about the impact that ensuring the college's programs are worth completing can have on recruiting and retaining students. This also requires reorienting program reviews to focus as much on post-program student jobs and further education as on success in completing programs.

Assess the postcompletion value of all programs

Having faculty and staff assess the postcompletion value of their programs is an effective strategy for demonstrating the importance of programs that enable students to achieve their employment and transfer goals. The Community College Research Center (CCRC) and the Aspen Institute's College Excellence Program developed a taxonomy for this purpose (see table 2.4).[34] We recommend using this taxonomy to analyze all awards from a college in the most recent year by academic division, credential type, and program. Data on the gender, race/ethnicity, and age of program graduates can help assess whether certain groups are underrepresented among graduates of higher-value programs or overrepresented among lower-value program graduates.

The academic divisions that award credentials should lead these analyses because they have the authority and know-how to change them. The analysis should also include awards given by noncredit workforce or adult basic education divisions. Faculty, chairs, and deans should examine the postcompletion value of all awards along with the characteristics of students who earn them with the following questions in mind:

- What awards are our students earning? In what fields or majors? At what levels?
- Which awards enable students to secure or advance in jobs directly? Which prepare students for bachelor's degrees in specific major fields?

TABLE 2.4 Taxonomy to assess postcompletion value of community college programs

Program value category	*Program credential allows completers to . . .*
Transfer high value	Transfer all or most of their credits toward a bachelor's degree in their major field of interest. *Examples*: AS-engineering, AA-English, statewide premajor transfer associate degrees, such as California's CCC-associate degree for transfer.
Transfer low value	Transfer many of their credits only as electives rather than major-applicable credits. *Examples*: AA-liberal arts or general studies, AA-general business.
Workforce high value	Secure jobs paying well above living wages and offering strong career advancement opportunities. *Examples*: AD-nursing, AAS-industrial maintenance technology, one-year or more certificate-line worker, community college bachelor's degrees in career fields.
Workforce medium value	Secure jobs paying more than the prevailing wage for low-skill work and that serve, with further training, as stepping stones leading to living-wage jobs. *Examples*: one-year or more certificate-licensed practical nurse, one-year or more certificate-welding technology, one-year or more certificate-emergency medical technician.
Workforce low value	Secure jobs paying at or less than prevailing wages for low-skill work that do not provide opportunities for advancement without extensive education or training. *Examples*: certified nursing assistant, AAS-certificate-culinary, AAS-certificate-cosmetology, AAS-veterinary tech.
Workforce upskilling	Develop and document skills of value in the labor market that may not by themselves enable students to secure or advance to better-paying jobs. *Examples*: less than one-year certificate-environmental management, "skills badges."
Competitive admissions preselection (for program enrollment analysis only)	Enables students to satisfy prerequisite requirements and compete for admission in selective, limited-access programs, such as nursing, respiratory therapy, and engineering technology. Most students in these tracks will not be admitted into their program of choice.
Not in a program (for program enrollment analysis only)	Tracks that absent an educational plan do not prepare students to advance to better jobs, build workforce or academic skills, or transfer in a major. *Examples*: undecided degree-seeking students, adult basic education students, high school dual enrollment students.

- Are graduates from each of our programs able to secure or advance in jobs paying above a living wage or to transfer to a bachelor's program in their major with no excess credits?
- How feasible is it for our workforce certificate graduates to pursue further education at the associate and bachelor's levels that will help them advance to better jobs?
- Is award attainment equitable across programs and student groups? Are some groups underrepresented among graduates of programs with higher postcompletion value? Are some overrepresented among graduates of programs with low or unclear value for employment or transfer?
- How can the college and divisions redesign lower-value programs to increase their value for employment or transfer?

This way of assessing programs may raise fears of program elimination and faculty and staff losing their jobs. Leaders need to communicate to faculty and other stakeholders that students are more likely to enroll and persist in programs that enable them to advance to better jobs or transfer efficiently in a major (and less likely to enroll and persist in programs that do not have clear postcompletion value). Our experience with colleges completing such an assessment is that it is more effective (and in most cases more accurate) to discuss the need to strengthen programs rather than eliminate them. College leaders must provide adequate support to division administrators and faculty to revamp programs identified as having lower or unclear value for careers or transfer.

Institutionalize career and transfer program mapping

Transfer pathways maps, learning-and-earning ladders, and curriculum guides should become integral to college processes for reviewing programs and developing new ones. Employer and university partners must be actively involved in developing these maps and guides. As with efforts to assess the postcompletion value of programs, pathways and program mapping should be the responsibility of the academic divisions overseeing them. It is essential, however, that the process include advisors and other student support services staff as well as employer and four-year college personnel. Key features of each type of map are discussed in the next text box.

Essential Features of Pathways and Program Maps

Learning-and-Earning Career Ladder Maps

- Show credentials awarded at each ladder rung.
- Show time needed to complete each rung.
- List sample local jobs with entry-level salaries that completers can secure on completing each rung.

Transfer Advising Guides

- List courses students need to take at the community college to transfer with no excess credits to specific majors at specific universities.
- List grade point averages and other program entrance requirements for each transfer major program.
- Ideally show the types of local jobs and career paths open to individuals with bachelor's degrees in the given field.

Program Curriculum Guides

- Show the sequence of courses and other learning experiences students must complete.
- Highlight the gateway courses in which students must perform well to succeed in a program or major.
- Include embedded work-based or other cocurricular experiential learning as integral parts of the curriculum.

Colleges need to adopt processes to display transfer and career ladder maps on program websites and to incorporate updated curriculum guides into college catalogs. They also need processes and staff to work with employers and universities to regularly update both kinds of maps as transfer and job requirements change.

Use maps to guide other reforms

Regularly reviewing and updating pathway and program maps seems like a great deal of work, and it is. But it can be valuable in multiple ways. As mentioned, working with employers to map career ladders and program curricula will not only help ensure that graduates can get jobs but also build a sense of program ownership among employers and cultivate new employer partners. Collaboratively mapping transfer pathways and curriculum maps with universities can have similar effects. Perhaps most important, colleges can no longer leave it to students to figure out how to negotiate transfer pathways or career ladders on their own.

Maps can also help guide other reforms necessary for ensuring that students are learning and for guiding them into and through programs, which we discuss in the chapters that follow. For example, curriculum maps developed in collaboration with industry and four-year college content experts can guide efforts by faculty to strengthen pedagogy within programs to ensure that students develop the skills they need to succeed in bachelor's programs and career-path employment. Transfer pathway and career ladder maps can help students explore options and develop career and college goals. Once students have chosen a program direction, these curriculum maps are essential for helping students develop individualized educational plans. Colleges can also use these plans to monitor students' progress and schedule classes so they can complete transfer pathway or career ladder programs as quickly and affordably as possible.

Developing well-mapped programs will not ensure that underserved students are well represented in programs with high value for careers or transfer. Colleges must also rethink onboarding and recruitment to help underserved students enter high-value workforce or transfer programs. Transfer and career ladder maps can help tailor marketing, recruitment, onboarding, and advising to busy working students concerned about taking the shortest path to better jobs or a bachelor's degree. Additionally, maps can help colleges work with employers and community groups to recruit underemployed workers onto the first step of learning-and-earning ladders. They also can be used with K–12 partners to recruit high school career-technical education students and others into workforce associate and bachelor's degree programs in high-demand fields right after high school.

Providing the dedicated staffing and infrastructure to support regular assessment and mapping across programs (along with the other reforms needed) will require colleges to organize and budget in new ways. We discuss how colleges can do this in chapter 7.

CHAPTER 3

Teaching Versatile Learners for a Fast-Changing World

It is not enough to align program curricula with transfer requirements for a major or with career-path employment, as discussed in chapter 2. Teaching also must enable students to develop the skills to thrive in upper-division bachelor's degree programs and in a fast-changing workplace and society.

In an analysis of the competencies employers want, Georgetown University's Center on Education and the Workforce found that communication was not only the most in-demand skill across occupations, it also was the most valuable, because jobs involving complex communication tend to pay more.[1] Other valuable skills include problem-solving, complex thinking, and teaching and learning, suggesting that communicating effectively, thinking critically, and learning from and teaching others are as important as technical skills.

The report cites research showing that economic shifts, particularly increasing levels of automation, have increased the demand for and value of cognitive skills compared with physical and manual skills since the 1970s. This trend has also been a key driver of the increasing returns to bachelor's degrees, which employers see as a signal for strong communication, problem-solving, and learning skills.[2] Thinking in ways computers cannot and learning and adapting as technology and work processes change over time are critical to thriving in today's workforce.

Community colleges must ensure that students seeking to transfer and enter career-path jobs develop communication, problem-solving, and learning skills from the start, along with technical knowledge and skills. Research suggests two strategies effective in teaching these skills are contextualizing content across subjects to make it relevant to students' goals and integrating opportunities for active learning, in which students are engaged in critical thinking, problem-solving, questioning, and analysis. Research on community college students in particular finds that contextualized instruction and active learning help them not only develop the skills essential for further education and careers but also build intrinsic motivation to persist in challenging programs.

As we previously noted, research by the Community College Research Center (CCRC) and others studying early efforts to implement guided pathways reforms has found that the fourth pillar—ensuring that students are learning across their programs—is by far the least developed practice area.[3] One reason is that it is often easier for a college to change advising and other student supports outside of the classroom than it is to change teaching across all courses. Community college instructional reforms have centered on math and English composition, but even in these areas, they have tended to focus on course placement policies and structure rather than on improving curriculum or pedagogy. Many community colleges have sought to strengthen online teaching and make content relevant and culturally responsive to a diverse student body, but that work is often isolated to groups of faculty or programs and is largely separate from guided pathways reforms.

In fairness, teaching through contextualization and active learning is difficult and represents a significant departure from traditional approaches delivered mainly through lectures. Many students are not used to teaching that requires them to write purposefully, speak publicly, think critically, solve hard problems, and demonstrate mastery of learning. Although they may benefit from these strategies, some students may resist it. Teaching through active learning is particularly difficult online. Typical community college structures for faculty development, such as teaching centers, focus on improving curriculum and teaching in individual classes rather than across programs, with participation often voluntary.

Of course, contextualized and active learning need not be confined to the classroom. Students benefit from opportunities to apply what they have learned outside the classroom through cocurricular and work-based learning activities. Job seekers increasingly need relevant experience in addition to degrees to secure well-paying jobs with good prospects for advancement. Community colleges have long provided work-based learning opportunities to students in nursing and other career-technical programs, as well as through service learning, undergraduate research, and other cocurricular opportunities. It is challenging, however, for colleges to extend these opportunities to all students regardless of program.

In this chapter, we examine how early adopters of guided pathways reforms are contextualizing subject matter and infusing active learning throughout their programs, especially in the foundational courses critical for preparing and motivating students to complete their programs. We discuss the challenges to active teaching and learning in courses and programs taught fully online. We also describe how a small but growing number of colleges are taking a more systematic approach to supporting faculty to adopt contextualized and active learning and other effective teaching techniques. We outline the changes in organization, practice, and mindset needed to institutionalize ongoing review and improvement to teaching. Finally, we present steps colleges can take to develop a culture of instructional innovation that enables students to become versatile learners who can thrive as they pursue further education and navigate a fast-changing workplace.

ENGAGING LEARNERS TO DEVELOP THINKING SKILLS

Beyond passing college math and English

Recent instructional reforms at community colleges have focused on helping students who arrive without strong math or writing skills pass college math and composition. The assumption is that if they can pass these courses, they will be prepared to succeed in others.

Redesigning America's Community Colleges devoted an entire chapter to showing the promise of using high school grades and measures other than standardized test scores alone to avoid placing students in prerequisite remedial courses that do not benefit them and instead mainstreaming most into college-level math and English courses with added corequisite academic support.

Research since *Redesigning* has provided further evidence that placing students into courses using an approach called "multiple measures assessment" (i.e., placement based on high school grades and other measures as opposed to a single standardized test score) and corequisite academic support can increase the rate at which students take and pass college-level math and English in their first year.[4] Other research has called into question the optimism among college practitioners and researchers that helping students avoid prerequisite developmental courses and pass college math and English would also increase their success beyond those subjects.[5]

In the first study of corequisite remediation at scale across all colleges in a state, CCRC researchers found that the Tennessee community college system's adoption of the corequisite model in 2015 and 2016 resulted in much higher pass rates in college-level math and English within one year compared with the traditional prerequisite developmental approach the colleges previously used.[6] In dissecting the effects of the corequisite model, however, the researchers found that it is not so much that corequisite support helps students but that placing them into prerequisite remediation hurts them. For math, the biggest benefit beyond allowing students immediate access to credit-bearing courses was guiding students into a math course sequence aligned with their programs—a practice often called math pathways.

Yet the researchers also found that while corequisite courses helped students pass introductory and subsequent courses in math and English, they had a limited impact on longer-term postsecondary outcomes. Other rigorous studies have also found limited benefits of corequisite remediation on success beyond introductory math and English courses.[7] So the corequisite model is not a silver bullet that guarantees students are prepared to succeed in other coursework.

Research on helping poorly prepared students master college math and composition finds that structural reforms like corequisite academic support benefit students more when accompanied by innovations in instruction. Specifically, instruction that engages students in real-world tasks and encourages them to contribute ideas, discuss concepts, and justify their thinking leads to strong outcomes when paired with changes to placement policies and course structure.[8]

Case Study: Enhancing Corequisite Support Through "Minds-On" Teaching at Cuyamaca College

Cuyamaca College, an early participant in the California Guided Pathways Project, which involved more than forty colleges in the state, was also among the first in California to completely transform math remediation.[9] In the past, three out of four entering students at Cuyamaca were referred to prerequisite remedial math courses—often multiple course sequences—based on standardized placement test scores. Not only did these courses not count for transfer credit toward a bachelor's degree, but most students dropped out before getting to the transfer-level math courses. Students of color fared even worse, as they were more likely than white students to be placed into remediation and even more likely to become discouraged and drop out before taking transfer-level math.

Recognizing that this approach was failing students and inspired by the developmental reform movement unfolding at institutions across the country, Cuyamaca in 2015 launched Math Pathways. This initiative transformed the college's approach to helping entering students master college-level math in three ways. First, it considered students' high school performance in determining how much extra support they needed. Second, it replaced one-size-fits-all remedial course sequences with bachelor's transfer-level courses that integrated tailored corequisite academic support for underprepared students. Third, it supported math faculty to adopt teaching practices that emphasized "minds-on" activities in collaborative, community-oriented spaces and called attention to the affective side of learning.

The effects on student success were striking. In the 2016–2017 academic year, nearly seven times as many underprepared students completed baccalaureate-level math in their first year than in the previous year—67 percent versus 10 percent. The rate at which Hispanic students completed transfer-level math in their first year increased more than four times, from 15 percent to 65 percent. First-time Black students enjoyed a ninefold increase in math success, from 6 percent to 55 percent.

One reason for such exceptional results is likely that unlike many colleges, Cuyamaca has combined multiple measures placement, math pathways, and corequisite reforms with complementing innovations in teaching. To create "minds-on" learning experiences for students, the math department adopted shared instructional design principles. Instead of the traditional paradigm of drilling students on decontextualized remedial skills, the principles called for engaging underprepared students in rigorous college-level work, with just-in-time remediation as needed, and for helping them reason their way through relevant, open-ended problems in a collaborative and supportive environment. Additionally, faculty encouraged students to become a community of learners willing to make mistakes and support each other's growth. Instead of treating struggle as a sign of failure, teachers wanted students to view it as a sign of learning. These design principles guided the development of common practices, such as activities that engage students in working on more basic math skills and concepts in the context of doing higher-level work and whole-class quizzes, in which groups of three to four students solve separate problems on whiteboards. Faculty also integrate activities that help students change their perspectives about education and their ability to succeed.

Despite growing adoption of corequisites, tens of thousands of students each year are still diverted from their college dreams by well-intended but ineffective placement tests and prerequisite remedial coursework in math and composition.[10] Although math and writing skills are important for success in college and careers, improving teaching and learning in these fields alone is not enough. Success in other introductory courses, such as Accounting 101 and 102, Advanced Introductory Chemistry, and Anatomy and Physiology predict program completion just as much as passing college math and English.[11] Colleges need to rethink academic support and instruction across such program gateway courses so students develop foundational skills they can apply across their programs.

Building skills and motivation in program gateway courses

Two strategies colleges are using to engage students and support learning are contextualization and active learning. In contextualization, the subject matter relates to real-world situations and issues of interest to students. This approach engages learners by showing the relevance of foundational content to their goals and their lives. Traditionally, first-year introductory courses are considered general education courses that cover the same content regardless of students' program pathways. Students in such courses may fail to grasp the relevance of foundational content and struggle to connect abstract concepts with material and activities in programmatic coursework. However, contextualizing curricula in introductory courses to programs and aligned careers may help students understand how course content relates to their interests and goals. Studies of contextualized instruction in community colleges find a positive relationship between it and student performance in program foundation and subsequent coursework.[12]

Early adopter guided pathways colleges use contextualization to ensure that students can apply the skills they learn in foundational courses across their programs. For example, faculty at Wallace State Community College in Alabama collaborated collegewide to incorporate meta-major-specific assignments into courses related to careers in students' fields, make course content relevant to the college's four meta-majors, and partner with advisors to support students' success in challenging gateway courses.[13]

Contextualizing instruction is important. But to ensure that students develop critical-thinking skills they can apply across learning in school and out, colleges also need to steer foundational courses away from instruction dominated by lectures to teaching that provides rich opportunities for active engagement.

A growing body of research finds that providing students with opportunities for active learning—defined as pedagogical approaches that "truly engage students intellectually and involve thinking, problem-solving, questioning, or analyzing information"[14]—is positively associated with mastery of course content, problem-solving skill development, academic performance, college persistence, and undergraduate degree completion.[15] Indeed, active learning is a central theme in guidance for college faculty based on research on effective methods for teaching undergraduates.[16]

Active learning may also help close equity gaps by race and gender. One meta-analysis showed that active learning approaches in science, technology, engineering, and mathematics (STEM) classrooms reduced equity gaps for underrepresented students by 33 percent on exam scores and 44 percent in course pass rates.[17] Students in classrooms that spent more time on active learning experienced the largest performance gains. Research on community college students finds active learning increases mastery and motivates students, particularly those from underrepresented groups, to persist in challenging programs, such as those in STEM.[18]

Instructors have many ways to encourage active learning in college classrooms: in-class polling; whole-class discussion; in-class, group-guided inquiry; tutorials or study guides to accompany lectures that students complete during a pause; problem-based learning, in which students consider real-world problems based on case studies; and "jigsaw" activities, in which students rotate among small groups to discuss topics.[19] Many of these strategies focus on group learning and peer engagement to solve problems. Theoretical frameworks that support active learning approaches show that learning is social and influenced and enhanced by groups working toward common goals.[20]

Case Study: Promoting Active Learning in A&P at Lorain County Community College

Anatomy and Physiology (A&P) is a key gateway course for students pursuing nursing and other health-related degrees. Because it is demanding and rigorous, it often is a barrier to degree progress for many students. In the past, success rates in A&P at Lorain County Community College (LCCC) in Ohio hovered between 30 and 40 percent—an unacceptably low rate for a college committed to student success. Even nursing students who passed struggled to apply what they had learned in the program's first course, Nursing 120, causing many to leave school. Pass rates on NCLEX, the National Council Licensure Examination in nursing, also were declining.

To address these challenges, some nursing faculty advocated for raising program entry requirements. Then-provost Jonathan Dryden resisted, arguing that the institution and the course caused the poor outcomes. Rather than using A&P to weed out students seeking degrees and careers in healthcare, he proposed a comprehensive course redesign to integrate lectures and labs, allow students to demonstrate mastery outside of testing, and provide abundant opportunities for hands-on learning.

Several other factors supported the redesign, including the expanding body of research on the benefits of active learning. Another was a Title III grant that enabled LCCC to increase its instructional design capacity. A third was a change in the Ohio statewide transfer policy requiring students to meet new learning outcomes in courses designated as general education in science, including the ability to "apply scientific knowledge." This created a sense of urgency: without a redesign, the course no longer would qualify as a general education transfer course, meaning that Ohio's four-year institutions would not accept the credits.

With these winds at their backs, the college convened faculty, instructional designers, tutors, and other student support staff—a group that dubbed itself the A&P Avengers. Members began by examining outcome data from A&P disaggregated by student characteristics. They saw that course pass rates were even lower among students of color and older students. They also observed passive instruction in A&P 1 and 2 that relied on high-stakes exams rewarding memorization rather than problem-solving and application of concepts. According to Aaron Weiss, dean of science and mathematics who supported the team's work and had been part of similar efforts to redesign developmental math, faculty wanted students to succeed but had not been trained to teach to students who never had rich learning experiences in school.

In 2021, the A&P Avengers began redesigning the course. Meghan Andrikanich, a biology instructor, was the lead faculty member and oversaw the comprehensive redesign of the course, with support from Jacob Bowman, an instructional designer. One of the biggest changes was integrating the lab and lecture components, which had been separate and led by different instructors. Robin Dahman, a biosciences instructor, said that in the earlier lecture-dominated model, there was often little connection between content and lab work. Since the redesign, she still gives frequent minilectures to introduce key topics. But students spend most of their class time—three hours, twice a week—on hands-on problem-solving that requires accessing, analyzing, and synthesizing information from outside the classroom. Dahman's students often work in teams. She creates flip cards with pictures that illustrate learning objectives; for example, the card for bodily systems used to remove waste features a garbage truck. Every station has whiteboards for students to write answers and teach concepts to one another. She creates four- to eight-minute videos on key topics for students to review at home on the college's learning platform.

Dahman said this method of teaching is challenging and time consuming. She and her colleagues regularly share ideas, but there is no cookie-cutter approach. Each instructor approaches topics in their own way and adapts their teaching based on the students. For example, Dahman teaches the younger students who typically attend morning sessions differently than the older working students who come for afternoon and evening classes. The hard work pays off, she says, in more engaged students: "Once students feel confident that you are truly invested in them and see how much you are doing to help them learn, they will work hard and put in the extra effort needed to succeed."[21]

The A&P Avengers implemented the redesigned course in 2022. By fall 2023, 66 percent of students passed the course with a C or higher, a thirty-point improvement over the old course and the highest success rate in A&P that Dryden observed during his tenure. Success rates for Black students jumped from 24 percent to 53 percent, a strong improvement despite equity gaps that the team continues to address. Additionally, success rates in Nursing 120 rose from 65 percent to nearly 90 percent, and scores on NCLEX among LCCC students are the second highest in the state after The Ohio State University, the state's flagship public university. The A&P Avengers mapped learning outcomes to the Ohio statewide transfer pathways, making LCCC's course the only one in the state that counts as an Ohio transfer lab course in STEM.

The college has created a general improvement process for courses that examines outcome data and includes support from professional instructional designers and faculty professional development to infuse active learning into gateway courses. For example, faculty saw substantial improvements in pass rates in Biology 1 and 2 and Microbiology—all critical foundations for healthcare and biosciences fields—by redesigning them to integrate lab and lecture and expanding opportunities for hands-on learning.

The challenge of active teaching and learning online

Active learning engages students and improves course outcomes. Online learning environments present significant challenges, however, to providing the active learning opportunities students need. *Redesigning* addressed the importance of technology for providing flexible learning options to busy students with complicated schedules. Enrollment in online courses and programs at community colleges has been growing for years—during the 2020–2021 academic year,

65 percent of public two-year students had taken online courses—and the pandemic has accelerated its growth dramatically.[22]

Online learning offers potentially positive benefits for community college students, including letting those with full-time jobs or children complete programs conveniently. Research shows that students who take all their courses online in community colleges are more likely to be older, women, married with children, enrolled part time, and working thirty or more hours per week.[23]

Yet research on the impacts of online learning in community colleges paints a complicated picture of its effects, which emphasizes the need to balance online and in-person learning and to provide adequate supports for online learners.[24] For example, Black, Hispanic, and low-income students have worse outcomes for community college degree completion if they primarily take courses online, but these groups may also benefit from the flexibility.[25]

This research also finds that community college students who take all their courses online are less likely to succeed than those who take just some courses online. This may be due at least in part to the fact that online-only students are less likely to experience active or collaborative learning and meaningful engagement and have fewer opportunities to interact with other students or faculty.[26] CCRC's research shows that faculty find it challenging to teach their students in online classes because these students are often less engaged and excited to learn as a result of the isolation.[27]

An important takeaway from the research on effective online teaching and learning is that the amount of student interaction depends on the instructor's approach. Faculty can create more interaction and positively affect students' classroom experiences by signaling availability and responsiveness and deliberately fostering classroom interactions by encouraging students to introduce themselves, exchange contact information, work together during class, and form study groups outside of class.[28]

A guide produced by the Institute of Education Sciences describes how faculty foster engagement and active learning in online courses through technologies like online simulations, forums, Slack, social media, Zoom, or Google Docs.[29] The guide emphasizes the importance of faculty articulating expectations about how these tools play a role in the course, advance course goals, and define how students should engage with the tools inside and outside of class.

Although online courses offer greater accessibility to postsecondary learning for some students, research suggests that hybrid learning environments, which blend in-person and online learning in ways that prioritize in-person time for hands-on learning and one-on-one support, have the potential to produce the best learning and success.[30] Hybrid course models may improve outcomes for community college students by creating more flexibility and accessibility while maintaining meaningful in-person learning opportunities. Research shows that students in hybrid courses perform at least as well as those taking in-person courses at community colleges.[31] One effective hybrid approach is to flip the classroom by delivering lecture material and other course content online, while dedicating in-person class time for hands-on and experiential activities, problem-solving, group work, and individual instruction.[32]

When integrating technology into courses, it is important to keep in mind that online learning, whether hybrid or completely online, demands a higher level of academic autonomy, self-direction, help-seeking, and time management for students to be successful. Colleges should assess students' experiences with online learning and preferences; staff should explain what is necessary in terms of hours of study for online courses and help students develop a plan to complete course assignments on time.[33] Students also need to have appropriate technology resources. Colleges can address this by providing laptops and internet access, extending open computer lab hours, and building more robust student technology support infrastructure.

In the post–COVID-19 era, community colleges may feel additional pressure to offer courses online to compete with local four-year and for-profit colleges. It is important, however, to strike the right balance. As mentioned, introductory program gateway courses are pivotal for retention and engagement in programs because they offer important venues for active learning. Community colleges should be cautious about offering these courses in fully online formats (including to high school dual enrollment students). Given the loss of community and negative learning impacts associated with asynchronous online courses, colleges should be judicious in offering foundational courses in fully asynchronous formats. Finally, it is important to provide professional development to faculty who are teaching online courses so they can adopt approaches that build community and actively engage students in learning.

Opportunities for applied learning beyond the classroom

Students benefit when they apply what they have learned outside the classroom. Such opportunities are particularly impactful when integrated into relevant occupational experiences, as is the case with work-based learning in college, including clinicals, apprenticeships, co-ops in career-technical programs, and service learning. Research shows the benefits of work-based learning while in college for graduates, specifically through paid internships or other work-based learning opportunities.[34] The number of community college students who take advantage of these opportunities, however, is quite small. A national survey found that only 13 percent had participated in an internship during the prior twelve months, compared with 41 percent of seniors and 22 percent of juniors at four-year institutions.[35] Work-based learning makes a clear connection between knowledge and skills developed through courses and jobs, which gives students a jump on developing relevant professional experiences.

Surveys of US employers suggest that relevant work experience is the most important factor in assessing job applications from recent college graduates, even more than relevant coursework.[36] Indeed, students with internships in college are more likely to receive offers for interviews.[37] Students who complete paid internships also are more likely to receive job offers and higher introductory salaries.[38] More broadly, students who complete degrees while working are more likely to transition to managerial positions. The type of work-based learning opportunity, however, matters for later outcomes. For example, unpaid internships do not appear to contribute to a greater likelihood of obtaining employment or earning higher salaries.[39] And although it is common for students to work during college, they are less likely to hold jobs related to their programs or long-term career goals.[40]

Some research reveals patterns of class and racial/ethnic inequity in participation in internships: Black and Hispanic students have lower participation rates than white students at predominantly white institutions. Additionally, working during college may have detrimental impacts on academic performance, and these may be greater for low-income students and students of color, particularly at community colleges with weak support structures. When integrated with coursework, working during college is more connected to and compatible with learning and enables students to gain valuable professional experience.[41]

The lack of opportunities for program-relevant experiential learning will remain a barrier to gainful employment and upward mobility for most students unless community colleges can expand experiential learning not only through work-based learning activities but also in the classroom.[42] Few community colleges offer internships and work-based learning opportunities to large numbers of students beyond nursing and programs where work-based experiences are integral. The Alamo Colleges are a notable exception.

Case Study: Extending Experiential Learning to All Students in the Alamo Colleges

In 2019, the Alamo Colleges in Texas launched a major new initiative: providing the more than seventy thousand students enrolled across the five colleges in the district with practical, meaningful, field-relevant and career-connected experiences. The AlamoEXPERIENCE experiential learning model has two main objectives: (1) addressing the common complaint from employers that many students they hire cannot translate what they learned in the classroom to practice in the workplace, and (2) expanding opportunities for students to network with professionals in fields of interest to solidify their academic and career goals and expand job prospects.

Alamo offers four types of work-based learning:

- Cocurricular, which includes academic experiences such as project-based learning, research projects, reflective essays, or a course portfolio. Faculty also provide opportunities for students to interact with professionals in fields relevant to the course or program. In an education program, for example, this could be a teacher coming into a class and answering questions from students.
- Extracurricular, in which students participate in career-oriented activities outside of class, such as attending a job fair or a presentation from a local employer or nonprofit.
- Service learning, in which students volunteer to serve the community, often at a local organization relevant to their field of study.
- Field experience, in which a student participates in a formal paid internship, clinical, or other hands-on workplace engagement relevant

to their program. For students unable to participate in an internship full time because of other commitments, Alamo also offers shorter, part-time paid micro-internships—some of which allow students to participate online, whereas others require students to be at a work site.

Alamo has developed experiential learning transcripts that track and describe the learning outcomes of each experiential learning experience in which a student participates. This is noted automatically on their transcript in some cases, such as when they complete a class with an experiential learning component or when they attend an experiential learning event and record attendance through a scannable code. Other times, dedicated experiential learning staff members input this information manually. Students can download and draw from their experiential transcript to develop resumes and job application materials or share it with an employer directly.

Faculty have incorporated cocurricular learning opportunities into every program. The Alamo Colleges District is also working to catalog and publicize the specific types of experiential learning opportunities available to students in each program. More than two-thirds of students have cocurricular learning experiences on their transcripts. But only about half that number have participated in a field engagement activity, the most valuable and highest-intensity option offered. Alamo's goal is to provide every student with a field experience in their program by graduation.

MAKING CONTINUOUS INSTRUCTIONAL INNOVATION PART OF THE CULTURE

Embedding active, contextualized, applied, and work-based learning opportunities into programs has the potential to strengthen the learning experiences of community college students at scale. These changes, however, represent a significant departure from business as usual for colleges that approach introductory courses as general education requirements with little connection to programmatic learning objectives, and for faculty who rely too greatly on passive approaches to learning like lecture and memorization. Thus, changing curriculum and teaching and learning requires transforming professional development for full-time and part-time faculty. Specifically, colleges need to create structures and a culture that support ongoing cross-disciplinary, faculty-led professional development focused on contextualized, active, and applied learning in the classroom.

South Puget Sound Community College (SPSCC) in Washington provides an excellent case study of how a college, as a central part of its work on guided pathways reform, can build organizational infrastructure, processes, and culture to support faculty-led innovation and teaching across programs. In our work with community colleges nationally, we have frequently heard that faculty unions can be barriers to reform and innovation. SPSCC shows that it is possible to build processes and culture for faculty-led innovation in teaching in a college with strong unions.

Case Study: Encouraging Faculty Innovation at South Puget Sound Community College

South Puget Sound Community College (SPSCC) in Washington takes seriously the idea of guided pathways as a whole-college reform. Since embarking on these reforms in 2017, SPSCC has used the model as a framework for rethinking how it does everything—from reorganizing programs, redesigning advising for program onboarding, and monitoring progress continually to changing the physical classroom structure, reallocating budgets, and improving the student experience. The college has since designed its strategic plans to measure progress in these efforts.

Faculty-led innovation in curriculum and instruction. From the start, SPSCC's guided pathways work was led by faculty. Top administrators put to a faculty vote whether to apply for a grant from College Spark Washington to implement guided pathways reforms. Faculty leadership is undoubtedly why SPSCC has made more changes than many other guided pathways early adopter colleges on the fourth pillar, ensuring that students are learning across their programs.

Guided pathways reforms began in the Transition Studies (adult basic education and English for Speakers of Other Languages) program, for which faculty contextualized the curriculum to help students choose a career and associated program pathway. Additionally, the Transition Studies Department expanded Integrated Basic Education and Skills Training

(I-BEST) into all pathways, including transfer and professional technical degree programs, by framing I-BEST as an equity strategy. Faculty-led efforts in Transition Studies ignited guided pathways collegewide. Faculty replaced prerequisite remediation in math and composition with increased support in college courses early in the work, but then expanded the effort by reviewing all prerequisite requirements and eliminating unnecessary ones. In the past, students were required to take college composition as a prerequisite for almost every humanities and social science course. The college removed this prerequisite for most courses after a review in which departments had to provide evidence showing the necessity to student success.

Such moves helped bring about a change in mindset in which faculty were responsible not only for teaching the content of their disciplines but also for teaching skills that were transferable across students' programs. College learning and assessment staff have worked with faculty to strengthen the rubrics and methods faculty use to assess mastery of "collegewide abilities" identified as essential across programs: analytical reasoning, effective communication, information literacy, multicultural awareness, and social responsibility. SPSCC regularly provides training to faculty to ensure consistency in assessment results across programs.

Faculty also adopted contextualized teaching practices across programs after research showed that students are more likely to develop the sorts of foundational competencies reflected in the collegewide abilities requirement if they learn concrete applications in a relevant, interesting, and specific context. SPSCC has incorporated a question into course evaluations: "How are you able to connect the content of this course to your career and/or personal goals?" This accountability for ensuring that students can apply what they are learning in individual courses more broadly has led to formal professional development activities and informal dialogue among faculty on using contextualization effectively in teaching.

Making innovation in teaching a central part of what faculty do. As part of its guided pathways reforms, SPSCC also sought to systematize innovation in teaching across faculty and disciplines, particularly by helping faculty use data to improve teaching and student success. To this end, the college developed student success data dashboards at the program, course, and section levels, disaggregated by key demographics. Leaders said most faculty did not know how to use data to improve their practice, so the college has devoted a great deal of effort to teaching them. The academic deans developed a guide that leads faculty through a guided inquiry process of collecting data on student success, describing patterns in the data, interpreting the findings and devising strategies to improve results, and outlining actions for testing improvements. Faculty must include a summary of their analysis-and-action plan as part of their annual professional development review with their dean.

Rethinking program review to focus on instructional improvements. More recently, the college revamped its program review process. In the past, faculty and administrators reviewed student data and planned improvements to curricula and instruction annually. According to administrators, many faculty viewed the process as perfunctory rather than something that improved programs systematically.

The new model is a three-year process. The first year involves data analysis, which culminates in an action plan; in years two and three, faculty implement their action plan. Additionally in year three, program faculty submit to the student learning assessment committee a report on what they have learned and the outcomes they achieved. The process provides the time and structure to consider their student success data more deeply. Teaching and learning staff say it is important to provide faculty with the right mix of structured guidance and flexibility in using data for improvement because they are best positioned to decide what will work with their students and programs.

Accordingly, different departments have focused on different problems or challenges, such as improving instruction in foundational program courses using the collegewide abilities. Others have compared success rates between online, hybrid, and in-person modalities and explored ways that faculty can enhance their teaching.

Making teaching excellence a central criterion for faculty hiring, promotion, tenure, and annual review. In 2024, a faculty working group, with support from the college's Center for Teaching & Online

Learning, published a teaching excellence guide that succinctly outlines course standards representing core teaching beliefs across programs. The college requires faculty to use the data inquiry-and-action process as part of their pretenure and post-tenure reviews. Faculty also must use their program or department's action plan to inform their individual professional development plans, which they update annually. Thus, the work of faculty to improve their teaching contributes to larger shared goals and strategies for improving instruction at the discipline and program levels. Finally, SPSCC provides stipends for faculty who apply to improve instruction in key areas, such as open education resources or culturally responsive pedagogy.

Changing organization and staffing to sustain a focus on excellent teaching. SPSCC has made organizational changes and invested resources so faculty can sustain these practices. Academic deans act as instructional leaders, working with faculty to carry out program reviews, observe classroom teaching, and help create individual professional development plans. The college also invested in a center for teaching and learning with dedicated staff expert in assessment of learning, online teaching, and other key areas. Staff also have convened communities of practice on their own and organized a day each quarter for minisymposia on issues they are confronting, including alternative assessment strategies and reformed approaches to grading students' work.

Combined, these strategies have created a faculty-led process collegewide as well as a culture of continuous improvement in instruction across programs. Whereas many faculty previously viewed learning assessment and program reviews as perfunctory, they now approach them much more enthusiastically. They recognize that working with colleagues to improve their craft not only helps students succeed but also serves as a powerful professional development experience.

Since SPSCC has implemented these and other reforms, it has seen marked improvements in student progression and outcomes.[43] For example, the percentage of first-time, full-time students earning college-level math and English credits increased, with the largest gains among historically underrepresented students. The rate at which such students earned college math credits in their first term increased from 24.6 percent in 2017 to 40.1 percent in 2022. Fall-to-fall persistence rates also increased during that period for all groups, particularly underrepresented students. For example, the college saw increases in the fall-to-fall retention rates for African American students from 48 percent in 2017 to 60 percent in 2022. Thanks to these and other improvements, the college was a finalist for the Aspen Institute Prize for Community College Excellence in 2023 and 2025.

TAKING ACTION TO INSTITUTIONALIZE INNOVATION IN TEACHING AND LEARNING

Time in the classroom often represents the vast majority of the college experience for community college students. Thus, improving teaching and learning, particularly in foundation program courses, is a key strategy for enriching the student experience in ways that tap their motivation to learn and pursue a program. Because innovations in teaching typically are led by faculty members, the extent to which students experience contextualized and active learning may vary widely between courses. To scale contextualized and active teaching and learning across programs, we suggest that college leaders cultivate the mindset that pedagogical and curricular reforms are central to student success, use an inquiry-and-action team-based approach for faculty to lead improvements to teaching, and ensure continuous improvement by creating structures that institutionalize innovations in teaching and learning.

Mindset: Reimagine innovation in teaching and learning as a key success strategy

Because teaching is deeply entrenched in institutional culture, a commitment to instructional improvement must become part of college culture to be sustained. Mindset shifts, therefore, are critical. Colleges need to make innovation in teaching and learning a central focus to improve student success. Mindset shifts among faculty are an important precursor to these reforms. Faculty may see it as their job to teach content and support student success in their courses and departments. It is important, however, that they reconceptualize their roles as teaching core knowledge, skills, and competencies beyond their fields that are transferrable across programs, such as analytical reasoning, effective communication, information literacy, multicultural awareness, and social responsibility. One way to cultivate this mindset is to ensure that instructional reform is an ongoing, collaborative process involving faculty within and across disciplines and divisions.

Planning: Form faculty teams to recommend improvements in program foundational courses

To encourage faculty involvement in improving teaching, some early adopter guided pathways colleges have found success using inquiry-and-action teams to implement improvements in critical program foundational courses by meta-major.[44] These teams provide practical strategies for grassroots leadership on instructional improvement by faculty and staff (supported by upper-level administrators), uniting faculty from different disciplines within the same meta-major. Including advisors and student services staff fosters collaboration between areas that typically operate independently, leaving participants more informed about their students and the roles of their teammates and thus better equipped to support students. Institutional research staff help teams gather and analyze data to inform their work. These teams should represent a coalition of the willing—volunteers who value the work and want to improve their craft and the student experience—although it is important that faculty, especially part-time instructors, receive appropriate compensation.

The teams should meet regularly and follow a systemic process that includes using data to identify student needs, selecting improvement strategies and creating purpose statements, creating detailed implementation plans with measurable objectives, and implementing and assessing effectiveness. Colleges need to ensure that faculty have the skills to design, implement, and evaluate pedagogical innovations. For example, faculty may need training to interpret data to ensure that instructional improvements are based on evidence. Faculty also need assistance keeping abreast of research on effective teaching methods. Colleges can help by engaging faculty in developing research-based standards or expectations for effective teaching practice across programs.

Inquiry-and-action teams provide a grassroots method for working with colleagues to improve student outcomes. When properly organized, they are much more action oriented than typical college committees, which too often get bogged down in deliberation.

Implementation: Institutionalize ongoing improvements to teaching and learning

To sustain a focus on continuous improvement in teaching and learning, colleges must alter organizational structures and processes, including hiring and promotion, faculty and staff roles, program review, and professional development.

Hiring can be lengthy and time consuming for colleges. Changes to the process can help colleges communicate a commitment to teaching and learning and attract faculty and staff who share these values. Colleges can require job candidates to provide examples of experience with contextualized and active learning that demonstrate a commitment to teaching, mentoring, and supporting students from underserved groups. To create accountability mechanisms, colleges can consider changing the adjunct promotion, faculty tenure, and post-tenure evaluation processes to include evaluations of classroom teaching and providing incentives for faculty to experiment with new approaches.

Institutionalizing continuous improvement in teaching may require organizational changes in which deans and chairs act as pedagogic leaders and support instructional improvement with faculty. This part of administrative jobs is as important as leading departments and programs. It also requires making instructional assessment a focus of program review.

Administrators should form a working group to assess whether their college's program review process includes a strong focus on improving instruction that leads to real improvements in teaching and learning. The group should recommend how to redesign the process to be more than a perfunctory exercise and to guide faculty to more effective teaching.

Finally, embedding contextualized active- and applied-learning opportunities into introductory courses has the potential to transform the learning experiences of community college students at scale, as all students participate in introductory coursework. To achieve this, colleges must dedicate time to ongoing professional development by incentivizing full-time and adjunct faculty to participate. These activities should be developed and led by faculty and instructional leaders and focus on incorporating contextualized active- and applied-learning opportunities into all introductory coursework. Disciplinary faculty can focus on contextualizing curricula to the program and relevant careers and embedding active learning. Cross-disciplinary faculty can focus on developing strategies to support collegewide abilities and skills, such as communicating effectively, thinking critically, and teaching others, which are essential to becoming versatile leaners in a fast-changing world.

CHAPTER 4

Creating a More Engaging Recruitment and Onboarding Experience

Think about the typical onboarding experience in most community colleges. What does it entail? Onboarding usually starts after a student fills out an application and is accepted. The student receives information on policies and procedures and often must take placement tests to determine whether they are eligible to take college-level courses. Onboarding traditionally concludes when students register for their first-term classes. At many colleges, onboarding activities such as orientation or advising are optional or online, meaning that many students never meet with someone from the college to discuss interests, goals, or concerns and potential challenges before classes start. Although this process may help students get enrolled for the first day of class, it is not designed to help them learn about different programs, decide on a direction, or develop a plan to meet their goals. It also does not help college staff and faculty learn about students' lives, their strengths, or the barriers they may face.

In 2021, the Community College Research Center (CCRC) developed a framework for a more immersive kind of onboarding, called Ask-Connect-Inspire-Plan (ACIP), as part of our work on guided pathways to help community colleges create a more engaging and effective recruitment and onboarding experience. Unlike the typical experience, ACIP begins before students even apply and extends through the first year. Furthermore, ACIP focuses on helping students learn about different programs, develop an educational plan, and gain momentum and confidence about that plan. We refer to this as program onboarding rather than simply onboarding to the college. It can help community colleges be more successful in helping students to enroll in and complete a program aligned with their interests and goals. Like other guided pathways reform practices, ACIP also requires colleges to consider how to adapt and personalize ACIP practices for different students, including those who often are not well served by conventional onboarding practices, such as first-generation students, students returning to colleges after a long hiatus, veterans, and adults enrolled in basic skills programs.

Yet students need to be motivated to even apply before colleges can help them onboard into a program. Community college marketing and recruitment often focuses too narrowly on the accessibility and relative affordability of courses and the wide array of programs available to students. In an era of stagnating enrollment, community colleges need to make the case to students and their families that their career or bachelor's pathway can start at a community college. And they need to recruit students not just to the college but to programs that will help them achieve their goals.

In this chapter, we review why rethinking students' early experiences before matriculation and throughout their first year could lead to improvements in their longer-term outcomes. We examine the components of the ACIP framework and explain how research on student engagement and retention informs each component. We then explore the importance of personalizing ACIP practices to different student groups. Next, we discuss how ACIP provides a way to rethink marketing and recruitment more strategically as processes to help students find a path to a career. Finally, we provide guidance for reimagining program recruitment and onboarding to help students get on a clear path to success from the start.

RECOGNIZING THE CRITICAL ROLE OF ONBOARDING FOR COMPLETION AND POSTGRADUATION SUCCESS

Early guided pathways work by community colleges revealed many of the long-standing barriers preventing students from entering and completing programs of study. Although an open-door mission may sound welcoming, in practice, community colleges often leave it up to students to apply, choose a program aligned with their interests and goals, figure out what courses to take, and find people who can help them navigate the institution.

Additionally, many community colleges still require students to take placement tests to assess their readiness for college-level math and English composition. These high-stakes assessments prevent many students from taking college-level classes in their first term or first year, including those in topics of interest to them. Instead, the results of those tests—which CCRC and others have shown to have low predictive value—often place students into one or more remedial courses, often in algebra and writing, before they can take most college-level courses. A recent survey found that 86 percent of community colleges offer prerequisite developmental education courses in math and 82 percent offer them in English, which delays entry to college-level coursework and may discourage students just as they are beginning.[1]

Forty-five percent of students who start at a community college do not return to their starting institution in the second year.[2] Year-one attrition rates from community colleges are high because students often are left to onboard themselves, are diverted away from college-level courses, and are not helped to enter a path aligned with their goals. Colleges lose students at multiple points in their first year, starting before the first day of classes. Many students who apply to higher education institutions, including community colleges, never matriculate. And low-income community college students are more likely than similar high-income students to experience summer melt—a particular worry given the number of low-income students at community colleges.[3] Findings from an informal survey found that even when students enroll, colleges lose between 20 and 30 percent of new students before census day, which typically occurs the second or third week of classes in a term.[4]

Guided pathways colleges have identified and addressed many structural barriers to enrollment and persistence, but they have focused less on whether the typical recruitment and onboarding experience helps students pursue an educational pathway aligned with their interests and goals. In the following section, we describe the ACIP framework for reimagining program recruitment and onboarding, focusing on the motivational aspects of these processes: How can colleges tap into students' excitement about going to college, help them explore their career and academic interests and goals, teach them about different programs, introduce them to faculty and peers in their fields of interest, and help them develop an individualized educational plan that will show them the path to meeting their educational and career goals?

RETHINKING ONBOARDING USING ACIP

The goal of ACIP program onboarding is to support all incoming students—regardless of their educational experiences, background, or goals—as they learn about different programs and careers, make connections in their desired field, take college-level classes that will light their fire for learning, and develop full-program educational plans.

A few key features of ACIP differentiate it from the typical onboarding experience. First, onboarding under ACIP begins before the application process and extends throughout the first year. The onboarding is not a one-time intervention or a single meeting between advisor and student. Rather, ACIP provides a framework for frequent interactions and relationship-building to discuss students' goals, interests, and plans as well as how they may evolve over time.

Second, colleges can use ACIP to rethink how recruitment can be part of onboarding. Although community colleges typically send recruiters to high schools and college fairs, most potential students are not actively recruited to a college, much less into a program. Often, colleges do not have a system for connecting incoming students with faculty, peers, or advisors in a field of interest.

Changing mindsets about onboarding

The overarching mindset shift that runs through ACIP is moving from a process focused on onboarding students into the college and developing a first-term schedule to a process focused on onboarding students into programs and helping them (1) explore interests and options, (2) choose a program direction, and (3) develop a customized educational plan to meet their goals. Research suggests that this type of developmental process ought to play out over time, which is why CCRC presents ACIP to inform a new student onboarding experience that extends through the first year. Students often change their minds about their goals, and as they learn more about different programs of study and careers, they may want to switch to different programs. Because ACIP facilitates exploration and learning, the goal is not for students to pick a program right away and stick with it; instead, we encourage colleges to develop strategies for helping students make an initial choice and then continue to learn and explore throughout their first year.

Next, we provide an overview of each component of the ACIP framework, and the mindset shifts necessary to move to this type of program onboarding.[5]

ASK: Colleges engage every student in ongoing conversations about their interests, strengths, aspirations, and life circumstances to help them explore programs and career paths aligned with their goals.

Ask promotes conversations with new students about important topics, including program and career interests and work and family responsibilities. Students talk with multiple people at a college to clarify their interests and goals. Faculty, advisors, and staff learn about students' goals, interests, and lives to provide the ongoing support they need to be successful in their program and as a college student.

Ongoing conversations about programs and career goals form the foundation of *Ask* because many community college students are still undecided about their program of study by the end of their first year. Delaying or never deciding on a program is problematic given the research showing that students who choose a program aligned with their goals are more likely to complete it.[6] Student surveys conducted by the Center for Community College Student Engagement found that fewer than half of new students reported meeting with someone at their college about the jobs to which their program might lead. In fact, students were as likely to seek advice from family, friends, and other students as they were to receive advising from college faculty and staff.[7] At the same time, students who did talk with an advisor felt more engaged and scored higher on a variety of measures of engagement. When asked what would help them choose a program or area of study, entering community college students told CCRC researchers that they wanted to talk to a faculty member or an advisor who knows the field.[8]

Many students also said college staff members never asked about their commitments outside of school, including work and family, to help determine their courseload. College personnel often need to initiate these conversations, because some students are uncomfortable asking questions or do not even know what questions to ask in the first place.

To effectively adopt *Ask* practices, colleges need to consider how to scale these practices to all incoming students, including those in dual enrollment programs, those coming from high school, adult learners, and those returning with some college experience. College personnel should discuss interests and goals with students so they can learn about different programs and careers. These conversations should happen with every student, not just those who identify as "undecided" or are coming directly from high school. College faculty, staff, and advisors should talk with students about their outside responsibilities and explain how those responsibilities might affect their college experience. They should also inform students about potentially useful supports, including tutoring, counseling, and basic needs or other campus resources. Most important, these *Ask* practices need to continue beyond an initial advising meeting.

Genesee Community College in New York developed an innovative way to learn information about new students, the Hi 5 Questions, which asks them the following questions:

- What excites you about your major and going to college?
- What are your educational and career goals?
- What do you like to learn about and how do you like to learn (modality)?
- What are your obligations outside of school?
- Have you seen the accepted student checklist? Where are you in the process?

Continuing students receive a different set of questions:

- How are your current classes going? How did your last semester go?
- Are you happy with your current major?
- What is one highlight, event, or person who affected your semester positively?
- How do you feel about where you are today and your progress?
- Have you reviewed your degree audit lately? Do you have any holds? Do you know which classes you need to graduate?

Genesee reorganized intake and onboarding and developed a new process for student success coaches to ensure that every new and continuing student is asked these questions. It created the Student Success Center, which includes advising, records and registration, financial aid, student accounts, and coaches, who receive cross-training in all areas and are assigned to students based on program area.

Other colleges have developed surveys for students to complete before their first meeting with an advisor. Institutional researchers and student services leaders at Lorain County Community College (LCCC) in Ohio developed a new student survey to help advisors collect information about new students' goals and their lives outside of college. Advisors know before the first mandatory meeting a student's level of certainty about their major, their level of family and community support for completing a credential, their work situation, and whether they are caring for dependents or other family members.

CONNECT: Colleges and academic departments organize opportunities for every student to meet with faculty, students, alumni, and employers in fields of interest and to access college and community resources that can support their needs.

Connect is informed by research on student engagement and how connections within an institution can help students develop meaningful relationships and feel like they belong, which in turn can facilitate persistence. *Connect* practices help students find and build a community within the college and develop relationships with peers, faculty, advisors, and others who can support them as they progress through their program.

Such connections benefit students in many ways. For instance, those who feel a strong sense of belonging at their institution report higher grade point averages.[9] Students who develop connections with faculty and other students are more likely to complete their programs.[10] Students intending to transfer who have ongoing relationships with an advisor receive better information about requirements, which leads to higher confidence and results in a greater likelihood of successfully transferring and graduating from a four-year institution.[11]

Adopting *Connect* practices is important for community colleges. Most community college students commute to campus and do not spend extended time before or after classes on campus meeting with faculty or peers. Even if students desire relationships on campus, they may not seek them out. Many work and juggle family responsibilities, making it difficult to set aside time to form connections. Moreover, some students may experience imposter syndrome—believing they are not talented or prepared enough to be in college. This problem has been noted especially among first-generation students and students of color.[12] *Connect* practices lead to meaningful connections if they are proactive, sustained, and informed by what college faculty and staff learn about students through *Ask*.[13]

Lessons learned from guided pathways colleges highlight the importance of involving faculty and academic departments in new student activities focused on networking and careers. For example, St. Petersburg College in Florida hosts a week of virtual and in-person events for each career and academic community, its term for meta-major. Students can learn about different fields of study and associated careers by networking with professionals in those fields and can hear from faculty about projects they are working on or papers they are writing.[14]

Like *Ask*, *Connect* practices depend on college staff and faculty being proactive about initiating relationships. One of the goals of *Connect* is ensuring that if students have a problem, they know and trust someone on campus to help them solve it. A recent study found that nearly 40 percent of students who reported needing support for mental or emotional health challenges did not know where to find it at their college.[15] Another survey found that fewer than two-thirds of community college students were aware of academic advising at their institution.[16] Those who knew about it were more likely to report feeling that they belonged, that they were on track to graduate, and that they were confident about passing their courses.

Central Carolina Community College (CCCC) in North Carolina created seven career communities (or meta-majors) that include all credit and noncredit transfer and workforce programs, including continuing education. CCCC created a brand, color scheme, and merchandise for each career community to build group identity and foster a sense of belonging. Students start interacting with career communities at orientation, where they meet the education navigator assigned to the community they are interested in. Throughout the year, each career community regularly hosts social and educational events where students can meet faculty, learn about programs, and confirm or change their programs. These opportunities to connect extend to college recruitment events, with CCCC faculty hosting career community tours and panels for high school students and for the broader community so that adults can also learn about the college's various programs.

INSPIRE: Every student takes at least one well-taught college-level course on a topic that interests them during their first term.

First-year students typically receive limited advice about what courses to take, and they are often told to take math or English or to "get gen eds out of the way." *Inspire*, however, is interested in courses beyond math and English; it is about helping students take courses that will engage them with what they are learning. Inspiring courses can prompt students to explore their academic and career interests, build the confidence to tackle future coursework, and build a community with other learners and faculty.

The typical first-year experience at community colleges highlights some of the barriers to *Inspire*. Many colleges place students into developmental math, English, or reading courses—or all three—which limits what else they can take during their first year. *Inspire* is concerned not just with what courses students take but also with the teaching of these courses to ensure that students engage with the course content and each other. In chapter 3, we emphasized the importance of supporting instructors to ensure student learning and success by embedding opportunities for contextualized and active learning, particularly in foundational program gateway courses.

Inspire is intended to boost motivation during the first term and first year. This can happen by taking a course in a topic of interest or in the students' chosen program. In some cases, an inspiring class may fulfill both goals. The primary goal is tapping students' motivation. Imagine a new student in an associate degree program in biology who cannot take any biology courses during their first term because of prerequisite requirements or lack of information. In her research with community college students in science, technology, engineering, and mathematics (STEM) programs, University of Wisconsin faculty member Xueli Wang found that transfer-intending students were more likely to persist in STEM if they took a STEM course in their first term, and then took the required math courses in a subsequent term.[17] Colleges are laying the groundwork for *Inspire* by creating program maps that include taking program-relevant courses during the first term. This helps advisors ensure that students take a strong introductory course in a field to determine whether they want to continue.

However, an inspiring course does not have to be in the students' field. It can be any college-level course in a topic of interest, including humanities, fine arts, or social sciences. As our CCRC colleagues found in a study about taking humanities courses in Michigan community colleges, faculty in these disciplines can *Inspire* by building "connections across disciplines and across time periods, places, and peoples."[18]

PLAN: Every student receives help developing a full-program educational plan that shows them a path to their goals.

Making an educational plan is a critical part of program onboarding. Such a plan, tailored to each student, provides a term-by-term look at the courses in their program so they can see time to completion. Because many students will change their minds about their program and need to change their course schedules, it is helpful to think about educational planning as a process that starts with creating an initial plan, and then updating it as needed over time.

An educational plan is like a contract between a student and the college. The student should know what courses they need to complete their program and how long it should take them to do so. Likewise, full-program educational plans give colleges information about the courses students need and when they need them to complete on schedule. We will go into more depth in chapter 5 about how to use educational plans for advising and scheduling.

Unfortunately, most community college students do not know what classes they need to take next or how long it will be until they graduate. Surveys show that many students never talk to anyone about time to completion or the cost of their programs.[19] One survey found that fewer than half of community college students discussed what courses to take and when with an advisor.[20] A separate survey of students who left community college found that one-quarter did not know how many semesters they had left to complete their program.[21]

Although critical to students' long-term success, educational planning can be challenging to scale to all students during their first term. Caseloads are still too large at many colleges for an advisor to meet one on one with every student to develop an educational plan. To address this obstacle, many early adopter colleges are embedding educational planning into a required first-year experience course. For example, Jackson College in Michigan helps every student make a full-program educational plan as part of the required first-year experience course called Seminar in Life Pathways. But first, the college assigns student success navigators (i.e., advisors) based on program. Students meet with their navigator before enrolling to complete a survey about their interests and needs, confirm their initial program choice, and begin developing their educational plan. Program maps are a starting point, but the navigators tailor plans based on students' needs, often encouraging summer classes. The college connects these plans to registration: when students register for the following semester, navigators review their plans and meet with students to adjust them as needed.

Case Study: Building Student Success Plans at Southwest Wisconsin Technical College

In May 2023, Southwest Wisconsin Technical College's (SWTC) leadership team set a new goal: help all incoming students develop a tailored success plan detailing a path to achieve their career goals, including career, educational, and financial components. Meetings between students and staff from career services, advising, and financial aid inform these plans, as does a new survey administered during student orientation. It asks about educational and career interests, work schedules, family responsibilities, and basic needs like food, housing, transportation, and child care.

The plans take shape in three steps. First, students meet with a career development facilitator to complete a career assessment and learn about SWTC programs aligned with their strengths, interests, and goals. Then students work with an academic advisor to develop a semester-by-semester course schedule. These customized academic plans include electives, work-based learning, and any support services needed to aid success. For example, the plan may specify that a student should meet with an academic success coach to review note-taking strategies or should enroll in a summer English language learner bridge course to work on English skills before classes begin.

Next, students and a financial aid representative use a tool that SWTC created to develop a budget and financial plan. Students enter expenses like tuition and fees, rent, utilities, and child care, as well as income from financial aid and jobs. Students can see their complete financial picture, including potential gaps in their ability to pay tuition and expenses. In those instances, financial aid staff connect students with scholarships and other possible sources of income.

Ahead of the 2023–2024 academic year, SWTC set goals for how many students would make a success plan. They focused on a variety of students, including those in workforce education programs, transfer students, adult learners, and those in English language and dual enrollment programs. In fall 2023, about 40 percent of students worked with college staff to develop a plan. To further scale this practice, leaders realized that making a success plan needs to feel inevitable for all incoming students; they did this by building the process into onboarding. New student orientation became mandatory in fall 2024, with developing a success plan embedded into that experience. For incoming students to register for fall 2024 classes, they had to (1) complete a career assessment and student welcome survey, (2) develop an academic plan with supports and services, and (3) create a budget. Each student met with a recruiter or academic advisor to make the academic plan and with a financial aid staff member to make the budget and financial plan.

In spring 2024, SWTC started to administer career assessments to students in local high schools. SWTC's goal is for all high school sophomores to take the career assessment as they consider taking dual enrollment courses starting in eleventh grade. College staff touch base with students during their senior year to see if they are still interested in the same program and careers. If not, a recruiter or advisor helps them complete a new career assessment. By starting with high school sophomores, the college will be able to help students develop a success plan before they begin college classes.

SWTC is implementing a new customer relationship management system in which students, advisors, financial aid staff, and others can update plans. The college will tie registration for subsequent semesters to completing an advising check-in with a member of the student success team. Although the financial plans now cover one year, the financial aid staff is considering making follow-up appointments mandatory so students can update those plans as well.

Personalizing onboarding for different students

As discussed in chapter 1, according to the findings from the American Association of Community Colleges (AACC) Pathways Project evaluation, when improvements occurred in early momentum metrics for all students, the differences in outcomes between groups remained roughly constant. For example, the percentage point gap between Black and white students remained virtually the same throughout the project, even as outcomes for each group improved among colleges that made progress in scaling guided pathways practices.

A key takeaway from this research is that adopting practices that are not designed with student needs in mind is insufficient to close equity gaps in early momentum among underserved students. Colleges need to personalize guided pathways and ACIP practices based on students' distinct needs. This may require providing differentiated supports for specific groups of students, like older returning students, veterans, students of color, incarcerated students, English language learners, first-generation students, and others. In other cases, colleges will need to provide more personalized support based on a given student's needs. As our research with the AACC Pathways colleges revealed, these gaps continue to exist, in part, because of a lack of personalization of the practices. More work is needed in this area, however, to learn what different students need and to develop strategies for designing tailored student supports with these needs in mind.

In this section, we highlight how some colleges are moving toward personalized ACIP practices.

Personalizing* Ask *and* Connect *for adult students. In a study of community colleges in Tennessee, CCRC explored ways to personalize guided pathways reforms to adult students.[22] These colleges were designing new supports in large part because of anticipated enrollment increases of adult students following the adoption of Tennessee Reconnect, a scholarship program that offers free community college to older residents in the state who have not completed a credential. While considering what supports may benefit adult students, staff realized that adults were often exempted from mandatory participation in activities like orientation or a first-year experience course, which were often required of traditional-age students. Although well intentioned—primarily to reduce the barriers to enrollment—these exemptions can cause adult students to miss important connections and learning opportunities. We interviewed faculty, staff, and students about what support adult students need and want.

Motlow State Community College learned that adult students value one-on-one time with someone from the college during informational sessions. As a result, the college changed the format from a one-hour presentation to a twenty-minute presentation followed by one-on-one meetings. Staff noted that, like other students, some adults are more certain about their goals, whereas others are less certain about what credential and what field would help them achieve those goals. The college's new informational sessions engage adult students in advising conversations from the start.

Pellissippi State Community College developed an onboarding and advising process called Purposeful Advising With Students. Before registering for first-term courses, students meet with an advisor to discuss the results of a mandatory career interest survey. This is a valuable discussion for adult students who may not be aware of all the career opportunities related to their interests. Additionally, this meeting gives advisors the opportunity to explore how adult students' prior education and employment experiences relate to their desired career path.

Adult students at the colleges in our Tennessee study also valued connections and relationships with faculty, staff, and other students. The colleges responded by designing opportunities for connections inside and outside the classroom. For example, Nashville State Community College launched Reconnect Cafés, staffed by an advisor who reached out to the adult students in his caseload at least once a quarter, assisted with enrollment and registration, and provided a comfortable space in the cafés for students to gather between classes. In the classroom, faculty talked about the importance of helping adult students build confidence by encouraging them to share their experiences in class and to be a resource for younger students.

Although these examples of tailoring *Ask* and *Connect* to adult students are instructive, colleges can develop strategies for personalizing these practices to any student based on their needs, previous college experiences, and educational goals. LCCC's onboarding process consists of three steps: (1) an online orientation that gives students a general introduction to college before they meet with an advisor, (2) a mandatory intake meeting to help them explore and choose their major, and (3) a mandatory first-year experience course. Eight out of ten students taking their first class at LCCC, however, enter the college through diverse pipelines and partnerships, including high school dual enrollment, following completion of a general education development (GED) diploma, through an employer-sponsored program, or after military experience. The college responded by shaping these three steps to account for students' background. For example, LCCC's first-year experience course includes assignments and content that can be adapted for students who are new, returning, associated with an employer program, or transitioning after GED completion. Additionally, LCCC's caseload advising model has evolved over time to not only organize students by academic and career pathway but also assign advisors to specific populations, such as guest students from other colleges and universities, high school dual enrollment students, employer-based program enrollees, and those seeking fast-track (short-term certificate) programs.

The onboarding process at LCCC, while consistent in its aims, may be accelerated for some students, experienced in differently ordered steps by others, or boosted with more one-on-one advising when necessary. The college, however, ensures that all students, regardless of their prior experience, receive advising and are assigned a pathways advisor dedicated to helping them navigate the college and their academic program.

Tailoring* Inspire *practices. Students are inspired when they are excited about and engaged in what they are learning, which can help them develop the confidence to thrive in future coursework. Personalizing *Inspire* practices to each student is critical, because the class that inspires one student will not be the same for all. Therefore, advisors and others need to learn more about students as they are entering college to find the right classes for their first terms. The *Ask* practices previously described—learning about students' goals, interests, and aspirations—can help advisors identify classes that will engage students from the start, connect them to students and faculty with similar interests, and ensure that they are excited about college.

Tailoring* Plan *practices. Educational planning requires personalizing the process and the plan to each student. Most colleges start by developing clear program maps that lay out a program's courses in a recommended term-by-term sequence. These maps, however, are generic and static. Educational plans need to be tailored and dynamic, drawing on the courses in the program map and customized to a student's timeline for completion (i.e., how many courses they plan to take each term), goals (e.g., where they intend to transfer), and interests (e.g., what electives they want to take). The plans need regular updates to account for changing timelines or course sequences. Advisors and students can track progress through the student information system and note when students are off plan.

Sometimes, however, students need to make bigger changes to their plans and their goals by developing a plan B, particularly those in pre-nursing or other selective health programs that require students to apply for admission. Students interested in these programs typically take prerequisite courses for several years before applying. Unfortunately, community college nursing programs provide limited spots despite a national shortage of nurses, and many students who apply with high grades are not accepted. As a result, these high-achieving students leave without completing any credential despite their strong academic records, or they continue to take classes and reapply, putting them in a costly holding pattern with no guarantee of ever being accepted. It would benefit these students to have an alternative plan—one that takes into account their goals and provides them with another path to complete a credential and get a good job.

Case Study: Building Alternative Healthcare Pathways at Tulsa Community College

For years, many students at Tulsa Community College (TCC) in Oklahoma tried to get into selective-admission allied health science programs, including students with very good grades. The healthcare faculty and leadership recognized that many of these students were passionate about working in the field and wanted to help them learn about different programs as well as provide a new path for students in healthcare administration. First, the college created a noncredit seminar called Smart Start Orientation that is required for all students interested in allied health and nursing programs. Students can choose between an in-person or online version of the orientation, which is offered every fall and spring semester for new students. The college places a hold on students' accounts until they complete Smart Start, so students who begin in the fall, for example, cannot register for the spring until they complete the seminar. Health science faculty collaborate on presentations about the difficult nature of courses like biology and anatomy and physiology and the application process, and students meet with academic and career advisors. Students pick two programs they are interested in and attend breakout sessions to learn more about them and meet with program directors.

TCC also developed a new associate of science in healthcare administration program that is an alternative path to a good job in the health field. Health science faculty met with clinical partners in Tulsa to learn about job opportunities in hospitals and doctors' offices as well as the educational requirements of these positions. Students with an associate of science in healthcare administration would be eligible for jobs like case manager assistants, physician office coordinators, quality and improvement outcomes analysts, and medical records specialists, all of which pay living wages and include benefits. To be eligible for many of these jobs, employers look for candidates who have work experience (typically one year in a healthcare field). With this degree, however, employers may waive the work experience requirement.

The associate of science in healthcare administration is designed so students from twelve different TCC health science programs—including dental hygiene, nursing, occupational therapy, physical therapy, radiography technology, and others—can apply their credits to this degree program. Starting in fall 2025, students interested in any healthcare programs will be placed into the healthcare administration program alongside their specific program of interest.[23] A student pursuing radiography technology, for example, will be listed in both programs in the college's student information system so their advisor can guide the student on the correct program and general education courses for radiography, which will also apply to the associate of science in healthcare administration. Should this student not be one of the thirty accepted into the radiography technology program every year, they could complete the healthcare management program and reapply in the future.

A final benefit of this program is that it will transfer to two of TCC's university partners, Oklahoma State University and Northeastern State University, where students can pursue a bachelor's in healthcare administration. With a bachelor's degree, students could also apply for jobs in human resources or recruitment.

RETHINKING RECRUITMENT WITH STUDENTS' EDUCATIONAL AND CAREER GOALS IN MIND

Prospective students need a reason to apply to a community college, especially if they are uncertain about the value of higher education. Community colleges often send recruiters to high schools or community events, but more often colleges wait for students to come to them. Marketing and recruitment efforts typically emphasize their accessibility, relative affordability, and the wide array of choices available to students; they often fail to make a clear link between enrolling in college programs and achieving educational and career goals.

Given the increased costs of a community college education, the fierce competition from other education providers, and the high opportunity costs of attending college for many students, community colleges need to be much more purposeful in recruiting students. Students are more likely to enroll if they see a clear, affordable path to a college degree and career. Marketing and recruitment should highlight fields and jobs available to students who complete career-technical programs and promote the bachelor's degrees that transfer programs prepare students to enter efficiently and affordably.

Of course, many prospective students do not have a clear idea of the career or academic program they would like to enter, and even those with clearer goals generally do not have a plan for completion. Colleges should highlight their supports for students to explore interests, choose a program, and develop a plan. This means seeing marketing and recruitment as integral to program onboarding. It also means using the ACIP framework to redesign marketing and recruitment. Colleges should market and recruit for programs not just to prospective students but also to current ones, especially those in general studies tracks, those in noncredit workforce and adult basic education tracks, and those who do not have a program plan but do have a career goal.

Chapter 6 describes how colleges can rethink high school dual enrollment as an on-ramp to a college program after high school using practices that reflect the ACIP framework. Colleges are also using ACIP practices to recruit students who do not participate in dual enrollment. For example, Wallace State Community College in Alabama developed an annual fall showcase event in which tenth graders from local high schools visit and learn about the four meta-majors; visit program-specific booths grouped by meta-major; meet program faculty, staff, and current students; learn about careers related to different programs of study; and engage in program-relevant activities.[24]

It is much more difficult to recruit adults who are not in school. Working adults generally want a program that provides a clear path to a good job that can be completed efficiently and on days and times that accommodate work schedules. It is particularly challenging to recruit adults working low-wage jobs with no opportunities for advancement. They need programs that can be completed quickly and that lead to jobs paying enough to move them beyond month-to-month subsistence. Because they often work multiple low-wage jobs, they typically do not have the time for school, much less the money. That makes it challenging for colleges to develop and fund programs that provide economic mobility to underemployed adults. Valencia College in Florida has shown how this can be done on a large scale through its Accelerated Skills Training (AST) programs.

Case Study: Recruiting Adult Students into High-Demand Programs at Valencia College

About a decade ago, Valencia College in Florida launched the AST programs to meet the needs of employers looking for workers to fill well-paying, high-demand jobs and to support upward mobility for the underemployed. These noncredit programs are designed to enable graduates to secure a living-wage job in a short amount of time. Valencia works closely with employers to design these programs, the shortest of which (Commercial Truck Driving) is four weeks and the longest of which (Welding Technology) is twenty-eight weeks, to provide intensive hands-on learning based on employers' specific needs in such fields as advanced manufacturing, construction and maintenance, healthcare, and transportation and logistics. Across these programs, the college offers a total of fifty-three nationally recognized industry certifications.

The programs are not constrained by a semester-based schedule; the different programs start and end throughout Valencia College semesters depending on the length of the program. For example, the Robotics and Semiconductor Technician program is offered five times throughout the year and can serve up to one hundred students each year. There are no application fees and students receive tools and other equipment that they can take with them after graduation. Additionally, some programs do not require students to have a GED to enroll.

To help students complete their program and land good jobs, the AST program staff offer case management support, job placement assistance, and soft-skills training in topics like interviewing, communication, and financial literacy. In the 2022–2023 academic year, the AST programs served more than one thousand students, who earned nearly 3,500 credentials. More than 90 percent complete these programs and more than 80 percent land jobs related to their training.

Staff visit community events, barber shops, hair salons, apartment complexes, neighborhood centers, and health fairs to recruit students to these programs. They also conduct briefings at chambers of commerce and other business organizations and attend events with city and county officials to discuss Valencia's programs.

Despite the AST programs' high completion rates and strong track records enabling students to get good jobs in a short timeframe, prospective students still can have fears about returning to school. Valencia's recruiters are trained to help students address any perceived barriers to enrollment and success. To address their fears, Valencia hosts tours so prospective students can see the campus and start to feel comfortable. Many have concerns about basic needs like food, housing, and transportation, while others face child-care challenges. Program staff help students address each of these issues. For example, all students in AST programs are given an Orlando-area bus pass that is good for one year. Cost is another big concern. The programs are not eligible for Pell Grants, but Valencia draws from multiple sources (e.g., the federal Workforce Innovation and Opportunity Funds, grants from employers, and local municipalities) to help students cover tuition and other program costs like tools and equipment. As a result, 95 percent of participants have no out-of-pocket costs.

TAKING ACTION TO REIMAGINE PROGRAM RECRUITMENT AND ONBOARDING

Students' earliest experiences in community colleges are during recruitment and onboarding. This phase often is more focused on the steps of enrolling in college than on motivating students as they begin (or restart) their educational journeys. To help entering students get excited about their programs, colleges need to reimagine recruitment and onboarding not just as processes by which students apply and enroll at the college but as year-long developmental experiences focused on helping students explore, choose, and plan a program of study aligned with their interests and aspirations. With a new vision of recruitment and onboarding, college teams can begin to develop plans that involve faculty and staff throughout the college and that are informed by the ACIP framework. Finally, colleges can scale and personalize new practices in ways that make the recruitment and onboarding experience much more engaging for students and thus motivate them to enroll and persist in college programs.

Reimagine recruitment and onboarding to guide program selection and entry

Redesigning student recruitment and onboarding begins with cultivating a shared understanding that (1) typical onboarding focuses on college enrollment rather than program recruitment and entry, and (2) many students who start at a community college leave higher education in their first year because no one helps them build connections or develop an educational plan to achieve their goals.

One powerful way to help build this awareness is to engage faculty and staff in examining the outcomes of current onboarding practices, such as by assessing data on which students are enrolled in programs that clearly lead to strong baccalaureate transfer or job outcomes and which do not. Together with the Aspen Institute's College Excellence Program, CCRC developed a tool for conducting such an analysis; it uses the taxonomy described in chapter 2 to assess the post-completion value of a college's programs.[25]

This tool is designed to facilitate discussion and reflection on the following questions:

- How many students are enrolled in higher-value programs in that they either prepare students to transfer with no excess credits in a specific major field or secure a job paying a living wage and offering career advancement opportunities?
- How many students are enrolled in transfer programs that do not clearly prepare students to transfer in a specific major or secure a good job?
- Are certain groups of students by gender, race/ethnicity, age, geography, or other factors underrepresented in higher-value transfer or workforce programs or overrepresented in lower-value program paths, or in program tracks that do not have clear transfer or workforce outcomes?

Having helped scores of colleges conduct this analysis through in-person and online workshops, we find that, although the particulars vary, most colleges learn that large segments of their students are enrolled in program tracks that have weak labor market or baccalaureate transfer outcomes. This includes, for example, students in liberal arts or general studies or general business tracks, which do not prepare students to transfer with limited excess credits in a major and have limited labor market value, as well as students in culinary, early child care, and other workforce programs that lead to low-wage jobs. Women (outside of healthcare), students of color, and low-income students tend to be underrepresented in programs with stronger transfer and employment outcomes. Many students are in program tracks that are not clearly connected to degrees or jobs. This includes students who are undecided about a major, students who do not get into selective admission programs in healthcare, high school students taking dual enrollment courses, and adult basic education students.

For colleges that conduct this analysis, these findings invariably raise the question: If so many of our students are enrolled in low-return transfer or workforce programs, or are enrolled in tracks without clear degree or employment outcomes, what incentive do they have to persist and complete at our college? Ideally, this line of questioning in turn leads to the realization that, to improve retention, completion, and equity, we need to rethink the recruitment and program onboarding experience to help all entering students explore, plan, and gain momentum in a program of study aligned with their educational and career goals.

Use the ACIP framework to redesign program recruitment and onboarding

To begin the redesign process, colleges should examine the experience of entering the college and how college practices do and do not help students explore and plan a program of study aligned with their goals. How do we learn about their goals for a career and further education? How do we help them make connections with students, faculty, staff, employers, and others? Do we help them develop a full-program educational plan? If so, how do we update it?

To answer these questions, cross-sectional teams from academic and student services departments should map the typical student program onboarding experience for each part of the ACIP framework. Colleges should consider the typical experience of particular student populations, including returning adults, dual enrollment students, first-generation students, and any other groups that may be underserved.

These teams should then begin to map out the core principles for redesigning the recruitment and onboarding experience using the ACIP framework. What experience should the college provide to all students? How could the college personalize the experiences to groups that are not well served? How will ACIP recruitment and onboarding practices differ for different fields and programs?

Adopt ACIP at scale, personalized for different students

The ACIP framework is adaptable to any institution and will look different depending on the college's characteristics. As cross-functional teams implement plans for ACIP practices, they should ask the following important questions to maintain focus during recruitment and entry into a program (not just into the college generally) and throughout students' first year. Much of this plan can be tailored to the needs of individual students and different populations of students.

- Are we learning about students' interests, goals, and reasons for coming to our college?
- Are we connecting incoming students with students, faculty, advisors, and employers to help them build a network of people with similar interests?
- Are we lighting students' fire for learning with engaging first-term and first-year courses?
- Are we helping every student develop a customized educational plan that shows the courses they need to take and the timeline to complete a program of study that will enable them to advance their educational and career goals?

CHAPTER 5

Helping Students Complete Programs on Schedule and Affordably

Many things can get in the way of students completing programs—from college policies and classroom experiences to pressures at home or work. In response, colleges have their pick of well-intended reforms aimed at increasing the likelihood of student success. What is missing from many of these initiatives, however, is an emphasis not just on completion, but on completion that is on schedule and affordable. More than half (57 percent) of students who obtained an associate degree in the 2014–2015 academic year had been enrolled for four or more years; only 7 percent completed within two years.[1] Although the per-term cost of attendance at community colleges is relatively low in most states, the negative financial impacts of prolonging attendance accumulate. The longer it takes students to complete a credential, the more the cost increases in terms of fees for registering each term, reduced financial aid, forgone earnings, and increased debt.[2] Time and cost to completion are of paramount importance to students, and this reality is increasingly gaining the attention of policy makers. Failing to consider time and cost creates barriers for all students, but it is especially detrimental for underserved students with limited time and resources.

Despite the importance of time to credential for community college students, survey data suggest vast numbers are not receiving individualized guidance on the length of time it will take them to complete their programs. On average, nearly two out of five (39 percent) students who participated in the 2018 Survey of Entering Student Engagement replied "no" when asked if anyone had talked to them about time to credential.[3] This information is crucial. Without a clear plan and timeline for completion, students may be more likely to leave higher education. A nationally representative survey of community college students' enrollment decisions during the pandemic found that a much higher percentage of those who left (23 percent) were uncertain how long it would take to complete their program than those who enrolled (4 percent).[4]

This chapter builds on the *Plan* component of the Ask-Connect-Inspire-Plan (ACIP) onboarding framework presented in chapter 4 by discussing how advisors and schedulers can use educational plans as part of a comprehensive shift to prioritize on-time completion. Full-program plans developed during onboarding provide the foundation for case management advising and ongoing progress monitoring that involves regularly reviewing and updating plans to ensure that students remain on schedule to completion. In addition, full-program plans allow colleges to forecast which classes to schedule and when to schedule them. Building course schedules based on students' plans ensures that they can take the classes they need when they need them to stay on track. It also prevents students from falling off their plans and needlessly extending the time to completion simply because classes are not offered when they can take them.

Taking the perspective that the amount of time it takes to complete a credential is a critical affordability issue, this chapter proposes three core strategies for keeping students on the path to on-time completion, each of which involves questioning implicit assumptions and making fundamental shifts in mindset to see conventional practices differently. These strategies are described in table 5.1.

TABLE 5.1 Core strategies for promoting on-time completion

Strategy	*Status quo*	*Changed practice*
1. Mandatory case management advising by field	Relying on generalist success coaches for ongoing advising and offering wraparound supports to students who seek help	Embedding advisors in program areas (meta-majors) who work with faculty and staff to advise and monitor progress of an assigned caseload of students
2. Ongoing progress-monitoring	Using technology tools to identify whether students are on plan or off plan in terms of course sequencing and performance	Using technology to provide proactive progress monitoring, feedback, and support to determine not only whether students are on plan or off plan but also whether they are on or off schedule to credential completion
3. Student-centered scheduling	Basing class schedules on a typical 9 a.m. to 5 p.m. workday	Viewing scheduling as an equity issue and building schedules to help students balance college with other obligations

To be effective, community colleges must implement these strategies together at scale, which is a tall order. Thus, a key focus of this chapter is exploring how to scale strategies to promote on-time completion. Advising reforms undertaken by guided pathways colleges, for example, show that using meta-majors as an organizing structure for case management advising can foster collaboration across faculty, advisors, and other student services staff, making it more feasible to scale mandatory case management and ongoing progress monitoring. Course scheduling inherently affects all students, making it easier to design scaled approaches.

Even with efforts to scale these three strategies in place, however, it likely will require additional supports to significantly increase on-time completion rates and reduce equity gaps. Addressing students' basic needs (e.g., food, housing, transportation, child care, healthcare, mental health) was not part of the original guided pathways model, but it plays a vital role in students' ability to complete on schedule. Without support of their basic needs, students may have to take fewer classes per term or temporarily stop taking classes, thereby extending the time required to complete a credential. In recent years, identifying scalable strategies that prevent unmet basic needs from derailing students' studies has become an increasingly important part of guided pathways work to keep students on path.

The remainder of this chapter reviews what we have learned about (1) mandatory case management advising by field, (2) ongoing progress monitoring, and (3) student-centered scheduling. This chapter also features case studies of several colleges that are engaged in this work. We then present emerging ideas to address support for basic needs to ensure that students can complete on time and, in so doing, complete more affordably. Finally, we conclude with practical tips and suggestions for colleges interested in taking action to improve practice in these areas.

INSTITUTING MANDATORY CASE MANAGEMENT ADVISING BY FIELD

A common thread throughout many student success initiatives is the importance of personalized advising or coaching.[5] The challenge for community colleges with limited resources is providing these services for all students. For example, discussions of how to scale support are notably absent from the What Works Clearinghouse guide on effective college advising practices.[6] The guide concludes that advising is more impactful when it is part of a larger system of holistic support. It recommends adopting four holistic advising practices: (1) integrated academic and nonacademic supports; (2) sustained, personalized relationships with students; (3) mentoring and coaching; and (4) incentives to encourage student engagement with advising. It does not, however, offer practical guidance to ensure that these supports reach all students.

Indeed, most intensive advising reforms shown to improve persistence and completion, such as the Accelerated Study in Associate Programs (ASAP) model, are limited to select populations and thus do not offer useful examples for scaling.[7] The Wilson Sheehan Lab for Economic Opportunities reviewed the program design and outcomes for eight comprehensive student success initiatives (including ASAP), defined as "multi-year individualized support that is designed to address multiple barriers to student success," at two- and four-year institutions.[8] A central component for most of these initiatives was high-touch case management by either advisors, counselors, navigators, or peer mentors for small caseloads of targeted groups. Other common program features included financial support for tuition assistance or expenses (e.g., textbooks, supplies, transportation) and academic support through educational planning and tutoring. Research suggests that these types of programs can increase student success, but it also highlights the difficulty of scaling these supports. Rigorous randomized controlled trials of each of the eight programs found several significant impacts on student persistence, completion, and earnings, but these results also linked positive outcomes to the intensity of service offerings, which raises questions about the cost of extending programs to more students.

Community colleges with limited resources face another challenge: advisors tend to be generalists who work with students in a wide range of programs. Although generalist advisors are an important resource, it is not feasible for them to know the requirements of every program a college offers. Without that level of in-depth knowledge, administrators cannot reasonably expect these advisors to provide meaningful case management.

Colleges implementing guided pathways reforms have sought to address the problem of limited resources for case management advising by embedding advisors into meta-majors and assigning them to students within specific programs. This approach has several advantages. First, it enables advisors to become specialists in a program's requirements as well as those for baccalaureate transfer programs and jobs that graduates from those programs are likely to pursue. Second, embedded advisors can work more closely with faculty and academic administrators to recruit students into programs. In some cases, colleges assign responsibility for recruiting and retaining students for meta-majors to completion teams of embedded academic advisors, a lead faculty member, career advisors, and others. Third, embedding advisors in meta-majors and building support systems and communities within them has the potential to increase student engagement and therefore increase the likelihood that students will complete their programs. It also creates networks through which students can learn about internships, jobs, and other opportunities for educational and career advancement, and gain support from faculty and peers.

The Community College Research Center (CCRC) reviewed the guided pathways practices adopted by the thirty community colleges participating in the American Association of Community Colleges (AACC) Pathways Project, a national six-year initiative to support implementing and scaling guided pathways (see chapter 1). The review found that the vast majority (twenty-four out of thirty) had either implemented case management advising at scale or were in the process of doing so. Many redesigned their advising systems by assigning advisors to work with students in specific meta-majors. A small number developed student support networks organized by meta-majors in which faculty and student services staff from departments such as tutoring and financial aid support professional advisors.[9]

LEVERAGING TECHNOLOGY FOR ONGOING PROGRESS MONITORING

Guided pathways colleges also are scaling personalized support by using technology tools that help advisors and faculty monitor students' progress. Technology plays a vital role in case management advising by equipping advisors and faculty with tools to monitor progress more effectively through shared platforms for communication and documentation. Although organizing advising by meta-major or field creates a structure for case management, technology can provide the necessary tools for actively following students' progress over time, identifying when to intervene, and connecting students with faculty, advisors, and support staff. To increase completion rates and close equity gaps, it is important that advising reforms provide consistent ongoing support throughout students' time in college to ensure that they stay on schedule.

One way colleges are accomplishing this is by requiring advising checkpoints to review and update educational plans, such as at the end of the first term before registering for the next. Another involves increasing faculty involvement through early alert systems, which let them proactively inform advisors about students who need additional support. Early alert systems also give advisors a convenient platform for sharing case notes and messaging to improve communication with faculty, students, and other staff.

The real value of technology tools to improve the student experience depends on how much they are used in everyday practice. These tools in and of themselves will not keep students on track for on-time completion.[10] For example, even when students have educational plans, advisors may not be actively using them to monitor progress. On average, most students from each institution responding to the 2019 Community College Survey of Student Engagement indicated that they had an educational plan and that they reviewed it each time they met with an advisor in person. An additional 19 percent of students, however, reported that even though they had an educational plan, they did not review their progress with their advisor each time they met.[11]

As with educational planning tools, the utility of early alert systems depends on high levels of faculty and staff engagement—without buy-in, the tools go unused. Research on implementing early alert systems shows that faculty and staff buy-in requires not only showing them how the tools increase communication and student support but also developing clear processes for submitting and responding to alerts.[12]

Most of the thirteen AACC Pathways colleges that offer fully scaled case management advising require students to develop an educational plan and regularly review their progress with an advisor. The colleges placing the greatest emphasis on mandatory advising require that students contact their advisor every term to register for classes. In addition, many of the AACC Pathways colleges are increasing faculty involvement in student support and fostering collaboration between faculty members and professional advisors through early alert systems.[13] Ten of the colleges had fully scaled early alerts, and at least another three were either in the process of scaling alerts or planning to do so as of spring 2022.[14]

Case Study: Monitoring Progress by Field at Northeast Wisconsin Technical College

When asked to describe Northeast Wisconsin Technical College's (NWTC) approach to keeping students on path for on-time completion, Kathryn Rogalski, vice president of academic affairs and workforce development, cited dedication to strong pathways and strong starts. She said the foundation for the guided pathways model and for all decision-making is keeping the student in mind. Faculty and staff evaluate any potential changes by asking, "What does this mean for students?" and "How do we make sure students don't have to be here longer?"

At the heart of NWTC's strategy is case management by field, which is provided not just by academic advisors but also by student support staff from enrollment services, financial aid, career services, and disability services—all of whom are assigned to a cluster of programs within a meta-major. Although case management advising had been in place for a long time in some programs, most clusters have adopted it only in the past several years. Three key features of the college's case management model are (1) fostering collaboration among academic affairs and student affairs, (2) emphasizing ongoing progress monitoring, and (3) using faculty mentors.

Fostering collaboration among academic affairs and student affairs. Academic advisors attend faculty meetings within the program to which they are assigned to stay informed about curriculum changes and other developments. They also participate in program advisory committees to hear directly from industry partners about the labor market for the fields in which they advise. Staff from other student support departments meet with faculty to learn about the programs to which they are assigned but do not attend faculty meetings. The assignment of student affairs teams to academic programs also builds and enhances relationships with faculty and academic leadership.

Emphasizing ongoing progress monitoring. To familiarize students with available support services from the start, and to give faculty and staff a holistic understanding of students' lives, all new students complete a welcome survey as part of the orientation and registration process. Based on their responses, staff from a range of departments, including academic advising, career services, financial aid, the library, and the resource center for basic needs, proactively reach out to offer support. Personalized educational plans then provide a foundation for ongoing progress monitoring. All students have access to sample program plans on the college's website. After orientation, they meet with their assigned academic advisor to create a personalized educational plan based on full-time or part-time enrollment, work schedules, family responsibilities, and preferred course modalities. October and March are academic planning months when faculty and staff encourage students to revisit their plans and discuss potential changes with their advisor. If students do not meet with their advisor in person or virtually, they can email a copy of their plan to their advisor before registering to confirm they are still on their pathway to completion. In addition to personalized educational plans, NWTC's early alert system helps faculty and staff monitor students' progress on their pathways. Faculty use early alerts and the "to do" feature in Starfish (a technology platform with early alert and case management functions) to raise flags about classroom concerns, share kudos to positively reinforce academic behaviors, assign students tasks, and refer them to advising and other supports.

Using faculty mentors. Because most advisors have relatively large caseloads—on average 600:1—faculty mentors also play a pivotal role in ongoing progress monitoring. In support of this effort, faculty have engaged in training on holistic coaching to build consistency in communicating with students and assessing student needs in and out of the classroom. Student participation in the faculty mentoring program declined during the pandemic, but between the 2018–2019 and 2020–2021 academic years, NWTC invited roughly 50 percent of new program students to participate, and about 70 percent of participants engaged with a mentor, representing approximately 35 percent of all new program students.[15]

NWTC's dedication to strong pathways and ensuring students complete on time has paid off. Since making the transition to case management advising by field, course withdrawals have decreased, while success rates and other measures of academic momentum have increased. Both the early alert system and the faculty mentoring program are associated with increased student success. Analyses of five years of data for more than nineteen thousand program students found that students with positively cleared flags (indicating a faculty or staff member reached out to the student and resolved the issue) completed more credentials and persisted to the next term and the next year at higher rates than students with uncleared flags (indicating the lack of an intervention).[16] In addition, quasi-experimental analyses have shown positive impacts of the faculty mentoring program on retention, and faculty mentoring is strongly correlated with a reduction in equity gaps among students from underserved groups. Using propensity score matching to control for gender, race/ethnicity, and age, these analyses indicated that students who interacted at least once with a faculty mentor had a ten-percentage-point higher retention rate from term one to term two, a nineteen-percentage-point higher retention rate from year one to year two, and a twenty-one-percentage-point higher completion rate than students who were invited to participate but did not interact with a mentor.[17]

SCHEDULING WITH ON-TIME COMPLETION IN MIND

Scheduling is a critical ingredient for on-time completion. Too often, colleges design schedules for dependent students enrolling directly after high school—some of whom have few scheduling constraints. Most community colleges, however, serve large numbers of students juggling jobs and family responsibilities with coursework and who have complex scheduling needs.[18] Close to three-quarters of all community college students work. Of those who do, nearly half have full-time jobs.[19] The percentage of students working is even higher among part-time students, with 82 percent employed, 59 percent of them in full-time jobs.[20] Additionally, more than 20 percent of community college students are parents.[21]

Given the extent of most students' responsibilities outside of college, class schedules that do not account for which classes students need and when they need them can greatly impede student progress. If students cannot take a required course in a sequence—either because the college is not offering it that term or because the timing conflicts with other obligations—their time to completion may be unnecessarily delayed by a semester or more. Results from the 2019 Community College Survey of Student Engagement suggest that the problem is significant: on average, 21 percent of students disagreed with the statement,

"At this college, all the courses I have needed to take have been available when and where I needed them."[22] Research on the benefits of strategic scheduling, conducted primarily by colleges and higher education software vendors, has linked scheduling inefficiencies to lower graduation rates.[23]

Failure to adopt student-centered scheduling not only hurts students but also hurts colleges. From a student perspective, traditional scheduling hinders progress, delays time to completion, and increases the likelihood of leaving college. From a college perspective, it leads to lower retention and completion rates as well as to inefficient resource management. The lack of accurate information about the number of course sections, faculty, and classrooms needed often results in cancelled classes. For students and colleges, then, student-centered scheduling is a worthwhile investment. Yet many community colleges are not aware of the connections among scheduling, the amount of time it takes to complete a credential, and student success. As a result, colleges tend to follow the status quo, with deans rolling over schedules from previous years without consulting one another to avoid scheduling conflicts for core courses. Among the fourteen practices examined in CCRC's National Science Foundation–funded evaluation of guided pathways reforms, scheduling for on-time completion was the least likely to have been implemented at scale.[24]

Building schedules that make it easier for students to complete on time requires colleges to approach course scheduling based on the needs of students. Approaches to building strategic schedules that optimize enrollment include (1) basing class schedules on students' educational plans, (2) offering condensed seven- or eight-week terms as an alternative to the standard fifteen- or sixteen-week term, and (3) increasing summer course offerings.

Class scheduling based on educational plans

Basing class schedules on students' plans helps colleges optimize resources by running more classes that are fully enrolled. This practice also helps students maximize the number of classes they can take per term. At Volunteer State Community College in Tennessee, the Office of Records & Registration streamlined scheduling processes by basing course schedules on students' educational plans and historical data rather than allowing each academic department to develop its own schedule. To move to plan-based scheduling, the college created a new full-time position to manage course schedules using data from Ad

Astra software. With this new centralized system, the college can cross-check program requirements to avoid scheduling required courses at conflicting times. In addition, the college can accommodate course demands at smaller campuses, which often do not have enough students to fill classes. For example, in-person instruction for some courses is available biweekly, alternating between the main campus and the smaller satellite campuses. On weeks when the class is held in person at the main campus, instruction is virtual at one of the satellite campuses and vice versa. This model allows students to benefit from in-person support and instruction while also enabling the college to fill courses on different campuses.

Basing class schedules on students' plans can also enable colleges to make more dramatic changes to the schedule, such as blocking off larger amounts of time to schedule multiple related classes together. Block scheduling makes it easier for students to fit college into their lives because they can enroll for all the courses they need as back-to-back courses on the same day(s) rather than taking individual courses on different days and at different times. Block scheduling is particularly impactful for working parents and students, as it gives them a more regular schedule around which to plan work and child care.[25]

Condensed-format courses

Condensed-format courses cover the same amount of material as those offered in a standard-length term, but do so in a shorter period of time (e.g., six hours a week for eight weeks rather than three hours a week for sixteen), reducing the likelihood that students will need to stop out during the middle of a term because of an unforeseen conflict. Condensed-format courses also offer students more opportunities to start taking courses, because colleges can offer two condensed terms during one standard term. A guide by Achieving the Dream notes the variety of alternative pathways available to students through condensed terms. For example, if a student fails a sixteen-week course, they can use the next semester to retake the course in a condensed format during the first eight-week term, and then take another course during the second eight-week term to catch up. If a student withdraws from a sixteen-week course during the first half of the semester, they can reenroll in a condensed version of the same course during the second eight-week term. Finally, if a student fails or withdraws from a condensed-format course during the first eight-week term, they may be able to retake the same course during the second eight-week term, if it is offered.[26]

Colleges moving to condensed terms have reported improvements across a range of student outcomes, including decreases in withdrawal rates and increases in course success rates, enrollment, full-time enrollment, and program completion.[27] For example, NWTC reported that course success and fall-to-spring persistence rates increased after it converted all courses to an eight-week format in spring 2022. From the 2021–2022 academic year to 2022–2023, the overall course success rate increased from 83.3 percent to 84.5 percent. Students who enrolled in both eight-week terms during the fall semester had the highest fall-to-spring persistence rate, 87.9 percent, and the lowest course withdrawal rate, 2.8 percent.[28]

Case Study: Giving Students the Flexibility and Support to Complete at Odessa College

Odessa College in Texas is widely recognized as a national model for adopting eight-week courses. Ten years after switching 80 percent of courses to an eight-week format in 2014, it has seen dramatic improvements in a number of outcomes, including a 60 percent increase in enrollment, a 32 percent increase in first-time-in-college enrollment, a 3 percent increase in course completion, and a 125 percent increase in credentials awarded.[29] This is but part of the story behind the better student outcomes, however. Administrators attribute these improvements to Odessa College's dedication to making a difference in the community by meeting students where they are.

When the college faced the threat of losing state funding because of low enrollment fourteen years ago, its leaders developed ambitious and wide-ranging initiatives to give more people the opportunity to attend and complete college. When much of the higher education sector was singularly focused on completion rates, Odessa College recognized that to serve its community and students, it needed to increase completion *and* improve access to the college.

A crucial first step involved appreciating students' needs for flexibility. Because the local labor market in Odessa is shaped by the oil and gas industry, employment opportunities fluctuate with the economy.[30] Transitioning from the standard sixteen-week semester to two eight-week terms per semester emerged as an important strategy for giving students more options, letting them focus on fewer courses at a time, and making it easier for them to return to work when necessary. This switch likely has had the biggest impact on increasing enrollment and completion rates and reducing time to credential, but it is just one of the innovative ways in which the college is keeping students on path to on-time completion.

Another key strategy for promoting on-time completion is automatic registration. Using the scheduling preferences students select in a survey completed during onboarding, Odessa College automatically registers students for the classes on their educational plans. In addition to removing logistical barriers to students' progression, automatic registration sends an important message: we assume you are coming back. Starting in academic year 2024–2025, the college also introduced yearlong scheduling. Half of all students who registered for fall 2024 also registered for the entire year.

Beyond modifications to scheduling and registration, Odessa College has implemented a number of other supports to improve both access and completion:

Access

- First Class Free: Anyone can take one class for free, either in-person or online, to test the waters and explore interests.
- Koonce Estate Restart Scholarship Endowment: This endowment gives former students, current students who are at risk of dropping out because of a low grade point average or outstanding debt, and potential students who may not have considered college otherwise the support they need to either start or continue their education and requalify for financial aid and Odessa College Foundation scholarships.
- Wrangler Promise: Since fall 2024, all high school graduates in the service area receive free tuition.

Academic Success

- Drop Rate Improvement Program: Faculty are trained to decrease course drop rates and keep students in class.
- Tutoring: Widely available through embedded peer tutors, this service is destigmatized by requiring it of all students in certain classes.

Wraparound Supports

- Drive to Success: This incentive program rewards student engagement in college coursework and other campus activities with opportunities to enter a drawing for a new Ford Mustang every year.
- Life Coaches: Coaches provide guidance to connect students to college resources.
- Food Pantry and Produce Garden: This support is available to students experiencing food insecurity.
- Wrangler Bucks: All full-time students receive $100 per semester to use at campus dining facilities.
- Emergency Student Aid: Originally funded through the federal Higher Education Emergency Relief Fund, aid is now supported through institutional and grant funding.

Although they are the cornerstone of Odessa College's vision for student success, eight-week courses can be understood only within the context of these additional supports. No single reform can ensure more students will complete on time. Above all, Odessa College exemplifies the impact of adopting student-centered scheduling as part of a broader commitment to college access and success.

Incentives for summer enrollment

Research suggests that students will take advantage of opportunities to enroll in more summer classes when feasible. Cuyahoga Community College in Ohio offers an innovative approach through its Summer Internship Program. Participants receive free tuition and a book stipend for one summer course as long as they have selected a program and are registered for fall courses.[31] The Alamo Colleges District in Texas provides a last-dollar scholarship covering tuition and fees for up to nine credit hours over the summer. In the first two years it offered the Summer Momentum Plan, more than one-third of the student body—seven thousand students per year—took advantage of the free credits.[32] Research by MDRC found that both an informational campaign and a campaign combined with tuition assistance increased summer enrollment, with larger increases seen with the latter. Both interventions also had statistically significant positive effects on credit accumulation, an important indicator of progress toward a credential.[33] Outcomes for students using summer Pell Grants have been similarly positive over an even longer period, including higher fall-to-spring retention rates, completion rates for associate and bachelor's degrees, and earnings gains. These results also demonstrate the significance of a focus on on-time completion as an equity issue, as Black and older students benefit most from summer Pell Grants.[34]

EMBEDDING SUPPORT FOR BASIC NEEDS

Over the past decade, higher education has become much more aware of the extent to which college students experience basic needs insecurity. Community colleges in particular are increasingly assisting students with food, housing, transportation, access to public benefits, and more. COVID-19 exacerbated these challenges, putting the impact of basic needs insecurity on student success in stark relief.

The original guided pathways framework did not explicitly address basic needs, but many colleges engaged in this type of support see it as a natural extension of efforts to keep students on path. For example, in response to findings from student focus groups and a climate survey showing a need for affordable child care and access to transportation, AAAC Pathways Project participant Broward College in Florida partnered with Lyft to help students get to and from campus and allocated $3.6 million for child care. Zane State College in Ohio, another AACC Pathways college, added questions about food, housing, and other basic needs to its intake survey for new students. Success coaches use the responses to connect students to available resources, including the campus food pantry, a clothing closet, and transportation assistance.[35]

Other guided pathways colleges outside of the AACC Pathways Project are also incorporating basic needs assistance in their student success work. Notably, California Community Colleges highlighted a number of strategies in its "Guided Pathways Playbook."[36] Examples include using applications and referral forms to identify students' needs, training faculty and staff on referring students to holistic supports, and developing basic needs centers that provide comprehensive supports.

These practices align well with the principles of the ACIP framework described in chapter 4, particularly those of *Ask* and *Connect*. Indeed, using

Ask and *Connect* practices to help students overcome nonacademic barriers may be just as important for on-time completion as addressing their academic needs. Recognizing the relationship between basic needs and student success, the National Center for Inquiry & Improvement has developed a three-strand approach to promoting students' financial stability that includes covering college costs, addressing basic needs, and using education and career planning to promote socioeconomic mobility.[37]

Although many community colleges offer case management advising and basic needs supports, Columbus State Community College in Ohio stands out for its efforts to integrate academic and nonacademic services to create a comprehensive support network. Academic advisors assigned based on program are just one of the departments represented on the college's Holistic Student Experience team, which also covers career advising, basic needs assistance, and retention. To assist with basic needs, the Student Advocacy Center offers support for food, housing, transportation, child care, mental health, referrals, and resource lists. The college also has taken multiple steps to support students' financial stability by lowering the cost of college, helping them understand the cost of college, and offering pathways to in-demand careers.[38]

TAKING ACTION ON TIMELY AND AFFORDABLE COMPLETION

Based on our guided pathways research, we believe that meaningfully advancing success for community college students requires approaching completion through the lens of timeliness and affordability. This complex process involves changing mindsets—reimagining student success based not only on the need for students to complete but also on the need to complete on schedule and at a reasonable cost. This also involves creating a vision for increasing on-time completion rates using the three core strategies plus the emerging strategy discussed in the prior section in this chapter: mandatory case management advising by field, ongoing progress monitoring, student-centered scheduling, and embedded supports for basic needs. Finally, with changed mindsets and a clear vision in place, colleges can start implementing concrete plans that increase student success and reduce time to completion. Each of these three areas—changing mindsets, creating a vision, and planning for implementation—is discussed in more detail in the following sections.

Change the definition of student success to include on-time completion

Ensuring that students complete on time requires interrogating the status quo of typical college operations. For example, colleges often assume students can complete programs in two years and that the reason more students do not do so is a matter of their personal scheduling preferences. A close look at course availability, however, often reveals that completion within two years is impossible even for students attending full time. Without knowing students' educational plans, colleges may not offer the course students need to stay on schedule or enough sections to meet demand. When departments create their own schedules, conflicting and overlapping start times may limit the number of courses a student can take in a semester. Furthermore, the challenges posed by these scheduling barriers are only exacerbated for students who attend part time because of work and family obligations. Contrary to common assumptions, it is not only older adult students who attend part time. Many young adults enrolling directly after high school also are working and caring for family members. Recognizing roadblocks and challenging long-held assumptions are the first steps toward making it possible for more students to complete on time.

Create a vision for increasing on-time completion

Next, college leaders will need to create a vision that communicates why increasing on-time completion rates is important and how to do so. Equity is a major reason why colleges are emphasizing on-time completion, because it reveals which students are left behind and how colleges can increase their rates of on-time completion.

The strategies presented in this chapter provide a framework for tackling on-time completion from multiple angles. Making advising mandatory every term and assigning advisors based on students' programs lays the foundation for getting them on a path to on-time completion from the start. Using technology to create individualized full-program educational plans and to connect students to supports enables advisors and faculty to regularly monitor student progress. Adopting a student-centered approach to course scheduling makes it logistically possible for students to complete on time. Finally, embedding basic needs supports can give students needed resources to prevent challenges outside of college from derailing their progress.

Implement plans for on-time completion

After developing a shared vision for increasing on-time completion, colleges can consider the following steps for implementation:

Mandatory Case Management Advising by Field

- **Understand program enrollment data.** Developing a strong system of case management advising by field requires having accurate program enrollment data to assign students to the appropriate advisor. The first step involves creating a process for regularly reviewing and updating lists of students by program. This process also should include closely examining course-taking patterns to check if students register for courses aligned with their programs. If the patterns do not align, advisors should confirm students' intentions and either ensure that they register for courses that apply to their program or assist them with choosing a new course.
- **Assign students an advisor in their field.** Identify which departments and advisors are responsible for which students throughout their time in college. To keep the size of advising caseloads reasonable, decide whether to assign advisors to a specific program, a set of programs within a meta-major, or an entire meta-major based on the number of students enrolled. Then provide opportunities for advisors to collaborate with program faculty on improving supports for their students to complete on time.

Ongoing Progress Monitoring

- **Use students' individualized plans developed during onboarding to monitor their progress.** Ensure that students can see their educational plans and verify time to completion. Establish processes for following up to confirm their educational plans before they register each term. Colleges that do this often require students to obtain a personal identification number from their advisor to register. Finally, identify when changes in students' plans will delay time to completion.
- **Use early alerts to prevent students from falling off plan and behind schedule.** Frame early alerts as a safety net for students rather than a punitive measure. Develop clear protocols specifying when and how faculty will submit early alerts and identify who will follow up.

Student-Centered Scheduling

- **Test how long it will take students to complete their programs using the current schedule.** Encourage deans and other staff to look at data on which programs students are enrolled in and what courses they need to identify conflicts that could prevent students from completing in three years or less. While doing so, assess how many students could move from part-time to full-time enrollment if classes were available when they needed them, including during the summer.
- **Build schedules that facilitate on-time completion.** Use students' individualized full-program plans to build course schedules.

Embedded Support for Basic Needs

- **Involve the college community in creating a network of support.** Use cross-functional teams of staff and faculty who are actively involved in monitoring students' progress to identify when nonacademic needs run the risk of derailing students from their plan. *Ask* about basic needs and *Connect* students to relevant resources as part of onboarding and as a regular part of advising check-ins.
- **Look beyond the college.** To scale support for basic needs with limited resources, *Connect* students to local nonprofits and government agencies.
- **Recognize the financial barriers to on-time completion.** Combine financial planning with educational and career planning to support on-time completion.

CHAPTER 6

Rethinking Dual Enrollment as an On-Ramp to College and Career Opportunity

In the 2010s, as guided pathways reforms were beginning to take root at community colleges across the country, another nationwide trend was unfolding: the rapid expansion of high school students enrolling at community colleges through dual enrollment programs.[1] In fall 2021, more than one million high school students were enrolled at community colleges, nearly double the number in fall 2011. Many if not most of the colleges implementing guided pathways that we have studied have large populations of dual enrollment students. In our research on implementing guided pathways at early adopter colleges, we observed colleges that have connected the dots between their guided pathways and dual enrollment strategies.[2] These exemplars use dual enrollment as an access and equity strategy by tapping into students' purposes and aspirations, and then connecting them to pathways and degree programs to draw them into college after high school. The results show how dual enrollment can counteract the decades-old system of race- and class-based tracking into vocational or college paths among high school students—and, in doing so, foster upward mobility, strengthen local economies, and grow college enrollments.

Because dual enrollment operates at such a large scale and has been shown to increase college enrollment and completion, it has great potential for increasing college access and success for Black, Hispanic, low-income, and other groups that have not been well served in the high-school-to-college transition. Yet exclusionary policies, practices, and mindsets have created barriers to entry for these marginalized groups and other potential beneficiaries of dual enrollment programs. Although their potential has not yet been fully realized, emerging and innovative models illustrate what it takes for dual enrollment to produce greater educational equity.

What have we learned from studying guided pathways adoption at community colleges with growing numbers of high school dual enrollment students? In seeking to strengthen pathways to success, a growing number of colleges have recognized the need and benefits of doing this for high school students enrolled on their campuses. They have applied guided pathways practices to dual enrollment students and offerings with the aim of creating on-ramps to career-path degree programs in high-opportunity fields for students who might not otherwise enter postsecondary education after high school. Thus, guided pathways reforms can propel colleges to restructure dual enrollment as an on-ramp to college programs for students from underserved groups, which is important for improving equity in college access and building a reliable stream of new students.

In this chapter, we unpack what we have learned studying community colleges that have linked their guided pathways reforms, their sizable dual enrollment populations, and their missions to increase college access and success.

TRANSFORMING THE HIGH-SCHOOL-TO-COLLEGE TRANSITION

Despite research we previously noted showing the strong economic value of completing postsecondary degrees, many high school students never make it to college. This transition for too many becomes a dead end that squanders talent and relegates families to poverty.[3] Among tenth graders in 2002, only 20 percent of Black and 19 percent of Hispanic students enrolled in college and earned a bachelor's degree within ten years, compared with 40 percent of white students. Only 36 percent of students from families in the lowest income quartile earned any postsecondary credential, compared with 78 percent in the top quartile.[4] Gaps in college access and attainment are products of a living legacy of race- and class-based tracking into advanced academic and vocational high school pathways, a system perpetuated by overreliance on standardized testing as a measure of student potential.[5]

Dual enrollment holds great potential for increasing college access and equity. It provides an opportunity for high school students to take actual college courses and acclimate to college-level expectations while building confidence as college learners. Dual enrollment also already operates at a very large scale across the country: some type of coursework is available at 82 percent of public high schools nationally.[6] Among the roughly fifteen million students in public high schools each year, about 1.5 million enroll in some type of dual enrollment course each fall, including about 125,000 Black high school students and 267,000 Hispanic high school students.[7] Participation in dual enrollment has expanded dramatically over the past two decades, nearly doubling in the decade preceding the pandemic (from eight hundred thousand students in fall 2009 to 1.5 million in fall 2021), and growing by more than 10 percent from 2021 to 2023.[8]

Dual enrollment encompasses a wide range of program designs, including immersive early college high schools, which have provided the strongest evidence of benefits during randomized trials.[9] The vast majority of dual enrollment students, however, experience less intensive discrete or à la carte models (i.e., taking one to two courses) either on a college campus, online, or in their high schools. Regardless of the program's form, studies consistently document that participation in dual enrollment coursework is positively associated with a range of outcomes, such as high school completion, college enrollment, and college degree completion.[10] Although some research shows mixed outcomes for low-income students and students of color (e.g., null or smaller effects for these groups compared with others), other studies suggest that dual enrollment can disproportionately benefit low-income students, Black and Hispanic students, and students who initially struggled academically in high school.[11]

Despite the abundance of dual enrollment programs and the extensive evidence showing the benefits, they are not living up to their potential for transforming the high-school-to-college transition. As these programs have grown, educators have struggled with two challenges, described by practitioners as "programs of privilege" and "random acts of dual enrollment." The phrase "programs of privilege" describes the uneven access to dual enrollment coursework and the tendency to replicate existing educational inequities. High schools serving larger proportions of lower-income students and students of color are less likely to offer dual enrollment opportunities. Nationally, low-income students, students of color, English language learners, and students with disabilities are underrepresented. The phrase "random acts of dual enrollment" refers to the typical practice of high school students selecting coursework based on instructor availability instead of on how the courses align with their education and career plans. Moreover, dual enrollment students often do not receive help exploring academic and career interests and developing an educational plan aligned with their talents and aspirations.[12] Such haphazard implementation results in missed opportunities to connect college to a student's sense of purpose, career interests, and long-term goals.

The "programs of privilege" and "random acts" approaches trace to exclusionary dual enrollment policies and practices.[13] College and high school administrators tend to take a laissez-faire approach to dual enrollment in terms of which students they encourage to enroll, which courses they offer, and what support students receive. As a result, students who are already bound for college are the ones most likely to take advantage of these opportunities. Colleges and schools also rely on standardized placement tests to determine eligibility, even though researchers question their validity as predictors of college readiness and raise concerns that they perpetuate inequities.[14]

Dual enrollment can increase equity and improve the transition from high school to college. Community colleges are best positioned to lead this transformation. Seventy percent of dual enrollment programs nationally are offered in partnership with community colleges, which enroll more than 1.7 million high school students in dual enrollment each year.[15] Some communities have successfully equalized access and expanded dual enrollment offerings. In a national analysis of school districts, researchers found that about one in five reported near zero gaps or higher rates of participation in dual enrollment among Black or Hispanic students.[16] Other researchers have documented effective practices used by community colleges and K–12 systems to achieve equity in access and success among low-income and students of color.[17] In this chapter, we describe the emerging approach for extending guided pathways to high school dual enrollment to create an on-ramp into college and career opportunities for underserved high school students. With high school dual enrollment accounting for one in five community college enrollments nationally, we also discuss incentives for colleges and K–12 schools to invest in overhauling the "programs of privilege" and "random acts" approaches.[18]

EXTENDING GUIDED PATHWAYS TO HIGH SCHOOL STUDENTS EQUITABLY

As the Community College Research Center (CCRC) studied the early implementation of guided pathways reforms at community colleges across the country, we noted the large and growing population of high school students enrolling in guided pathways colleges. In collaboration with the Aspen Institute's College Excellence Program, we first observed how guided pathways and equity-focused dual enrollment practices could transform the high-school-to-college transition in our fieldwork for the *Dual Enrollment Playbook*.[19] Five of the high-achieving dual enrollment college–school partnerships that we visited for this 2020 publication had college partners that were early adopters of guided pathways. The colleges profiled made extraordinary efforts to enhance the experience for dual enrollment students in and out of the classroom.[20] Rather than passively offering these courses to students who seek them out, these colleges actively reached out to help underserved high school students get on a path to college. They educated students and families about dual enrollment opportunities and encouraged and supported their participation. The partnerships connected students to career and college advising and other supports and promoted high-quality instruction.

CCRC used the playbook and related findings from early college high school models and our guided pathways research to develop the dual enrollment equity pathways (DEEP) framework. This framework describes how guided pathways reforms can be applied to high school dual enrollment programs to create a more equitable on-ramp to a college program that leads to career-path employment for large numbers of students. The DEEP framework includes four areas of practice that are drawn from a synthesis of related research on early college high schools, effective and equity-advancing dual enrollment practices, and guided pathways implementation. The resulting framework (figure 6.1) defines

FIGURE 6.1 DEEP framework

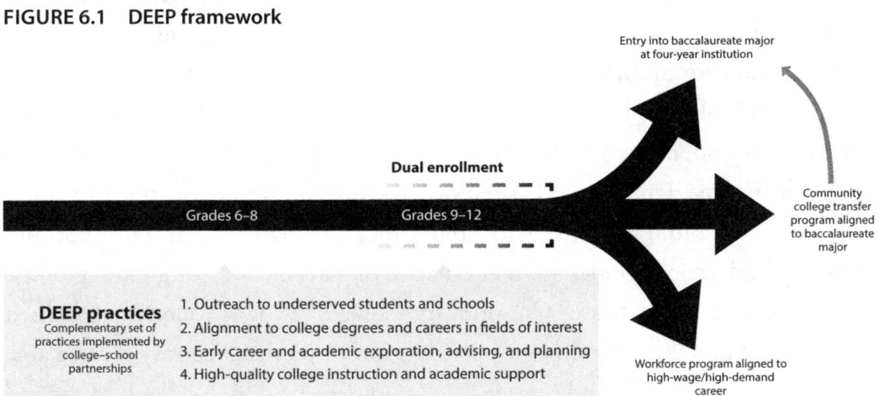

DEEP as a complementary set of practices implemented by college-led partnerships with K–12 schools with the goal of dramatically increasing the number of students entering baccalaureate degree programs (either directly at a four-year institution or through a structured community college transfer pathway aligned to the student's major) or workforce programs aligned to high-wage, high-demand careers. We outlined four areas of DEEP practice: (1) provide outreach to underserved students and schools, (2) align dual enrollment course offerings to college degrees and careers in fields of interest, (3) advise students to explore interests and develop plans, and (4) support students by delivering high-quality instruction.

To investigate the four DEEP practice areas and to understand how colleges were implementing DEEP reforms, we visited six community college–K–12 partnerships in Florida and Texas.[21] We selected colleges that were further along in implementing guided pathways reforms and that had achieved strong results using dual enrollment to expand college access and opportunities for Black, Hispanic, and low-income high school students.[22] All of the high schools are Title I schools, which serve high proportions of students from low-income families, and in most cases are "open access" because they do not use admissions tests or other screens to select students. The practices of these colleges and their K–12 partners (described in table 6.1) give a sense of what DEEP looks like in action.

DEEP outreach

One of the reasons for widespread gaps in access to dual enrollment nationally by race/ethnicity and income is that it is simply made available at many colleges without effective outreach to low-income families or communities of color. The college and high school leaders we interviewed could identify underrepresented students and communities, and they deliberately expanded access to those communities. We observed five components of DEEP outreach efforts: (1) focusing outreach on underserved high schools, students, and communities; (2) starting outreach before high school; (3) leveraging community connections to build awareness; (4) building trust with and educating parents and families; and (5) using high school grades as an alternative to placement testing for eligibility.

For example, Tallahassee Community College (TCC) in Florida examined school-by-school dual enrollment participation in its three-county service area and prioritized outreach and partnerships at underserved high schools to expand

TABLE 6.1 DEEP practices of college–K–12 partnerships in Florida and Texas

Practice area	*Component practices*
1. Provide **outreach** to underserved students and schools	• Focus outreach on underserved high schools, students, and communities • Start outreach before high school • Leverage community connections to build awareness • Build trust with and educate parents and families • Use high school grades as an alternative to placement testing for eligibility
2. **Align** dual enrollment course offerings to college degrees and careers	• Inventory dual enrollment offerings • Map dual enrollment offerings to college degree programs in fields of interest • Embed dual enrollment offerings in career-connected high school programs
3. **Advise** students to explore interests and develop plans	• Use dual enrollment to showcase college programs and support exploration • Help students develop a college educational plan and provide checkpoint advising • Coordinate advising roles across sectors
4. **Support** students by delivering high-quality instruction	• Scaffold coursework and frontload supports • Respond quickly when students are struggling • Provide additional, structured support for online classes • Support dual enrollment instructors and monitor quality

offerings.[23] TCC leaders host a regular breakfast for school guidance counselors at which they share school-level data on access to dual enrollment and course success to plan program improvements and increased outreach to underrepresented students and families. Both TCC and Florida's Miami Dade College are taking advantage of changes in state regulations to permit alternatives to standardized placement tests to determine eligibility for dual enrollment courses. The colleges instead use high school grade point averages or high school grades in related courses. Miami Dade College staff identified twelve of the most popular dual enrollment courses with the highest pass rates and broadened the grade point average threshold for those courses even further. Staff at both colleges observed a marked increase in the number of underrepresented students participating in dual enrollment without measurable declines in student success.

DEEP alignment

As we have noted, dual enrollment is sometimes referred to as "random acts" because students take courses based on availability. As a result, some students graduate with, as one practitioner called this mixture of unrelated courses, a "Franken-transcript."[24] In these cases, dual enrollment courses are less likely to help students explore career and academic interests or increase the chances they will take dual enrollment courses that do not apply to their degree. College leaders are working with their K–12 partners to backward-map dual enrollment offerings as an on-ramp to degree programs in fields students are excited to pursue, a strategy that more closely aligns dual enrollment courses with their interests in high school. We identified three component practices of DEEP alignment: (1) creating an inventory of dual enrollment offerings, (2) mapping dual enrollment offerings to college degree programs in fields of interest, and (3) embedding dual enrollment offerings in career-connected high school programs.

For example, C. E. King High School in Texas and its partner San Jacinto College (SJC) designed dual credit maps that show which dual enrollment courses students can take at each grade level, which certifications and degrees they can earn as they progress along the career pathway (from certifications through master's degrees), and the median earnings associated with each type of credential. Leaders said these maps help students and families understand how dual credit can lead to subsequent postsecondary credentials and career paths. Additionally, they serve as marketing tools for high schools to emphasize the value of their programs.

DEEP advising

Aligning dual enrollment coursework to postsecondary programs, while essential, is insufficient if students do not also have support to explore options and develop a personalized educational plan. The colleges and high schools we visited provide early career and academic exploration, advising, and planning so students can use dual enrollment courses to explore fields of interest and develop educational plans aligned to their long-term goals. We observed three component practices of DEEP advising: (1) using dual enrollment to showcase college programs and support exploration, (2) helping students develop a college program plan and providing checkpoint advising, and (3) coordinating advising roles across sectors. SJC uses checkpoint advising to help dual credit students develop full-program plans, which college advisors, high school counselors, and students can access digitally. High school counselors can view students' current and future courses on SJC's portal, which keeps them up to date on students' progress and plans. When SJC redesigned advising as a part of its guided pathways reforms, dual enrollment students were not an afterthought, but instead were included as a key constituency of the collegewide reforms.

DEEP support

Community colleges and their K–12 partners cannot broaden access to college opportunities through dual enrollment without high-quality college instruction and academic support to ensure that all students can succeed. The partnerships we visited demonstrated high expectations for student achievement and instructional quality in dual enrollment courses while providing extensive supports for student success and instructor effectiveness. We observed four component practices of DEEP support: (1) scaffolding coursework and frontloading supports, (2) responding quickly to struggling students, (3) providing additional structured support for online classes, and (4) supporting dual enrollment instructors and monitoring quality. Chipola College in Florida offers targeted support when students exhibit warning signs that they might drop or fail dual enrollment courses. The college's dual enrollment advisor monitors grades and attendance using Dropout Detective, a tool within Canvas that identifies struggling students. The advisor alerts the instructor and the Blountstown High School guidance counselor about students who need more supports and sends personal messages to students who appear to be falling behind. Crucially, this process occurs every three weeks, ensuring systematic checks on student progress and success.

Case Study: Using DEEP to Align Coursework and Share Advising at Lee College

At three thousand students (and growing) and accounting for one-third of headcount, dual credit is an increasingly important part of the student population at Lee College in Baytown, Texas. The same is true of their biggest K–12 school district partner, Goose Creek Consolidated Independent School District (GCCISD), which provides dual credit to more than a quarter of its high school graduates. The partnership with GCCISD is critical to Lee College; more than 40 percent of dual credit students return to Lee College after high school. Leaders at both organizations attribute this to efforts they have taken together to offer dual credit coursework aligned to degrees and transfer pathways at Lee College and to invest in shared advisors to help students explore options and plan their pathways.

GCCISD students can take dual credit coursework in fields aligned to their interests by design. GCCISD has built dual credit courses into related high school career academies and other career-technical education (CTE) programs. Across its five high schools, GCCISD offers ten career academy programs that include opportunities for students to complete industry-based certifications and college certificates through dual credit during high school. The default ninth- to twelfth-grade course sequences in these programs include related dual credit coursework and opportunities for students to learn about related careers and earnings in their communities and requisite associate and bachelor's degree programs offered through Lee College and university partners. For example, Stuart Career Technical High School embeds dual credit options into its CTE academies in a model in which both the high school and dual credit coursework align with the college's CTE programs. Employer advisory groups insisted on this course alignment as they weighed in on the design of the college's programs.

College leaders also have focused on reducing transfer credit loss when students earn an associate of arts in high school by encouraging them to complete the Texas Core Curriculum instead of the full associate degree and by advising them to choose core courses relevant to their intended majors.[25] To provide guidance on taking the right general education courses to promote better transferability of credits, Lee College mapped its high school partners' academies to their pathways with recommended lower division core courses by broad field of study.

Lee College and GCCISD leaders said some students and families have concerns about students selecting academic and career focus areas as early as eighth or ninth grade. To address this concern, they recommended encouraging students to simply "pick something" to try out, noting that it did not mean they were committing to a lifetime career. Leaders told students that by selecting and trying something, they were in the driver's seat—actively exploring their interests and future aspirations (and at least ruling out programs in which they have no interest).

To support students exploring and navigating their options, Lee College and GCCISD invested in advisors to work alongside high school counselors to advise dual credit students. As the offerings expanded, leaders from the two institutions recognized that shared advisors could benefit both parties. The shared advisors are Lee College employees, but GCCISD pays half of their salary. Each dual credit advisor is assigned to a specific high school, where they spend most of their week working alongside the counselors.

The dual credit advisors and counselors work collaboratively to ensure that students take the right dual credit courses to graduate and make certain that dual credit courses will apply to their intended college degree program. They look through degree program plans and show students which courses count for program requirements. They work backward, asking students, "What is your intended degree program?" and "What are your top five university destinations?" because not all universities have the same requirements even within programs. To ensure that they provide the correct information to students, they work together to develop common guides aligning high school coursework and requirements to college degree programs and major-specific transfer pathways.

The shared advisors are a worthwhile investment, according to Susan Jackson, GCCISD's deputy superintendent of curriculum and instruction: "No matter what we do, K–12 counselors are not equipped with the knowledge to understand how to adequately advise a high school student on their college courses. We have the shared advisors that are trained on the higher ed side that are now in our campuses daily working not only with our students but with our staff, so it's a huge benefit."

CREATING OPPORTUNITIES AND INCENTIVES FOR REVAMPING DUAL ENROLLMENT

Although implementing DEEP practices, such as strengthening outreach, alignment, advising, and supports, requires additional investments of time and resources, community colleges, four-year institutions, and K–12 districts have good reasons to advance the DEEP approach.

Incentives for postsecondary institutions

Community colleges, which enroll about 70 percent of dual enrollment students nationally, have experienced steep losses in enrollment among older adult students—a trend that existed for nearly a decade before 2020 and then went from bad to worse with the pandemic.[26] In other words, community colleges (and many broad-access four-year institutions serving large dual enrollment populations) have lots of open seats. Even though some colleges may generate only a fraction of the revenue per dual enrollment course than a regular course, they still have strong incentives for colleges to implement DEEP practices. When implemented well, dual enrollment can grow the pool of college-going students, including those who already have gained momentum toward pursuing a postsecondary program; who will continue at the college after high school instead of not enrolling at any college; and who, once at the college, tend to persist and complete at high rates.[27] Students with prior dual enrollment experience represent a large and growing share of students entering four-year institutions—either directly after high school or by transferring from community colleges. Four-year institutions, however, have struggled to help community college transfer students complete bachelor's degrees in a timely manner, with the outcomes particularly worrisome for Black and lower-income transfer students. Dual enrollment has the potential to substantially advance equity in the stubbornly low outcomes among community college students who transfer to four-year institutions. A national analysis of community college students entering in fall 2015 found that transfer students with prior dual enrollment transferred and completed bachelor's degrees at two to three times the rate of students with no prior dual enrollment coursework.[28] In the wake of the ban on affirmative action in college admissions, incentives are growing for leaders of selective four-year institutions to strengthen connections with community colleges and underserved high schools through dual enrollment and community college transfer programs to grow a talented and diverse pipeline of incoming students.

Incentives for K–12 schools

Encouragingly, K–12 leaders have strong incentives to prioritize the DEEP approach, particularly those at districts and schools that serve low-income students (such as Title I schools) and those working in communities where public schools compete with private and charter schools for students. The DEEP approach to dual enrollment appeals to K–12 leaders because it can help their students save money and time on their college journeys. Robust dual enrollment opportunities aligned to college degrees and careers in fields of interest to students and communities can serve as points of pride for school leaders, are a strong draw for students and families navigating high school choices, and offer a strategy for leaders of high schools with struggling enrollment to retain in-boundary students and families. Students say they appreciate earning college credits based on their performance in the course rather than on one high-stakes test, as is the case with Advanced Placement (AP).[29] K–12 leaders in states that include dual enrollment as a part of school accountability or funding models report that it is more feasible to improve performance in college readiness by expanding outreach and supports to help students succeed in dual enrollment courses than to help students improve on high-stakes standardized assessments.

TAKING ACTION ON DUAL ENROLLMENT

In our fieldwork studying DEEP practices at guided pathways early adopter colleges, leaders told us that colleges must build and sustain strong partnerships between colleges and K–12 schools to implement DEEP practices (e.g., outreach, alignment, advising, supports). We observed that effective leaders—from college presidents and dual enrollment program directors to superintendents and assistant principals—follow a common vision and work together to make offerings mutually beneficial and financially sustainable. To operate on a large scale, college and K–12 partners smoothed business operations and staffing challenges to realize the potential for dual enrollment. In this section, we draw on our fieldwork and research synthesis to outline suggested action steps for implementing DEEP practices on a large scale.

Rethink the conventional model

College and K–12 leaders can guide programmatic reforms by challenging preexisting assumptions about dual enrollment and placing greater emphasis on its potential to provide any student with a foundation for further education and career advancement after high school.

- **Expand program purpose.** Instead of making dual enrollment courses available mostly to students who are already bound for college after high school, build awareness and interest among underrepresented students and families starting in middle school.

- **Broaden school outreach.** Instead of offering dual enrollment primarily at wealthier and whiter schools, review offerings across all high schools in the college's service area and prioritize outreach and partnership development with lower-income (e.g., Title I) schools serving communities that are underrepresented in the college's dual enrollment program.
- **Don't let conventional measures of college readiness limit opportunity.** Instead of using limited measures of readiness such as standardized test scores to determine academic preparedness, cast a wider net to most or all high school students. Assume they will struggle and need additional academic supports, particularly in their first dual enrollment courses.
- **Teach for the transition to college.** Instead of only focusing on academic content standards, prioritize active teaching and learning experiences in the classroom that challenge students with the right supports to build their confidence as college learners.
- **Require college advising.** Instead of offering college advising just to students who seek it out, require that all dual enrollment students meet with college advisors to build motivation for postsecondary opportunities, with a focus on tapping into students' talents and aspirations. Help students explore interests and develop an individualized educational plan aligned to the college's degree programs and their career interests.
- **Align course offerings.** Instead of offering mostly general education courses based on instructor availability, provide courses that are foundational in their programs (including program-related general education) to introduce students to college degree programs.
- **Normalize academic supports.** Instead of offering ad hoc or by-request academic supports, prepare all students and their families for the additional challenge of dual enrollment coursework. Make academic supports unavoidable by systematically checking on every student throughout the term, and provide additional comprehensive academic supports in students' initial dual enrollment courses and in those with lower pass rates.
- **Build in connections to high school CTE.** Instead of focusing high school CTE primarily on immediate postdiploma employment with postsecondary education as a secondary goal, embed related dual enrollment courses into high school CTE programs and combine the credits with articulated high school credit so students can finish postsecondary CTE certificates and degrees faster.

- **Complement AP offerings rather than compete with them.** Instead of implementing dual enrollment in competition with AP courses for students and attention, partner with high school leaders to better weave them together. Determine how AP offerings can complement dual enrollment on-ramps to college degree programs through credit for prior learning to maximize the number of college credits students can earn in high school.
- **Develop a new business model.** Instead of a low-cost, low-revenue college business model for dual enrollment focused on university-bound students, invest in staffing and resources to implement DEEP practices and recoup these higher costs by increasing the number of students whose trajectory changes from not attending any college after high school to matriculating.

Establish a shared DEEP vision and goals with K–12 partners

In our DEEP fieldwork, college leaders told us they made large-scale DEEP reforms thanks to a shared vision and shared goals. This included agreements to the following:

- **Convene K–12 partners for strategy and vision discussion sessions.** College team participants should include senior leaders overseeing the programs (e.g., provost, dean), the program leads (e.g., director, coordinators), and advisors and instructors in dual enrollment programs. Participants from K–12 districts should include district administrators (e.g., assistant superintendent) and high school leaders (e.g., principal, assistant principal) overseeing the programs, school counselors, and high school dual enrollment instructors. Organizers may consider sharing materials for review ahead of the discussion, such as this chapter, a related CCRC publication, or a data report on dual enrollment student participation and success rates.[30]
- **Prioritize underserved communities and schools, and position dual enrollment as a pathway for upward mobility and workforce development.** College and K–12 partners can commit to focusing dual enrollment on expanding socioeconomic opportunity for their communities. Leaders at the sites we visited envision dual enrollment not only as a head start to college but also as an on-ramp to degree programs that lead to well-paying, rewarding careers.

- **Commit to doing what is best for students, even if it is not expedient.** Partnerships between colleges and K–12 schools are complex given that the various approaches to operating dual enrollment programs all come with different incentives and costs. Because of this, college and K–12 leaders emphasized the importance of sharing a common purpose and a commitment to doing what is best for students—such as in selecting between (and blending) dual enrollment, AP, and other advanced courses.
- **Believe in—and support—the potential of all students.** The college and K–12 leaders with whom we spoke expressed a shared belief that any student can be successful in dual enrollment with the right supports. The partners are committed to a policy of high expectations and to ensuring that students get the support they need to succeed.
- **Recast high school CTE as a college degree pathway to expand college and career opportunities.** Dual enrollment coursework should expand—not limit—students' options for college and career pathways after high school. By leveraging dual enrollment courses to recast high school CTE programs as a step toward a career-technical associate, apprenticeship, or bachelor's degree program, college and K–12 partners implementing DEEP practices can break down decades-old tracking into vocational or college-going paths for students after high school.

Implement and enable large-scale DEEP practices

For dual enrollment programs and DEEP practices to function smoothly on a large scale, colleges and their K–12 partners need to remove policy, practice, and other operational barriers that get in the way of DEEP practices as offerings expand. Based on our DEEP fieldwork, we recommend the following activities:

- **Assess college and partnership practices against the DEEP practice areas and subcomponents to identify and prioritize DEEP practices.** Some DEEP practices are more difficult to implement (e.g., redesigning advising) than others (e.g., expanding outreach to underserved communities and schools), and it is likely that dual enrollment partnerships will have some components of the DEEP framework in place already. Prioritize and commit to implementing at least one component of the DEEP framework that is most promising in terms of the scale and impact it will have on the least well-served high school students in the college's service area.

- **Evaluate whether dual enrollment staffing is adequate and organized effectively.** It is not uncommon for small staffs to manage dual enrollment programs at community colleges despite dramatic increases in students. As a result, staff often are spread thin sharing information and building partnerships among dozens of high school partners. Moreover, advising caseloads for dual enrollment students can be very large, which limits the amount and quality of support. The colleges we visited took different approaches to organizing and staffing dual enrollment-related functions, with some hiring more dedicated staff for programs and others integrating dual enrollment-specific responsibilities into existing positions (such as advising). Yet across the sites, leaders have invested in adequate staffing, enabling DEEP outreach, alignment, advising, and support on a large scale.
- **Strengthen back-end business processes.** Running a dual enrollment program requires complex systems to share student information and process course registration, scheduling, and billing. Without strong back-end business processes, large-scale dual enrollment can overwhelm even a well-staffed partnership. The college–K–12 partnerships we observed emphasized the importance of streamlining these processes and developing tools to share information on student registrations and outstanding requests in real time.
- **Develop a supply of qualified instructors, particularly for underserved schools.** High schools nationwide face challenges finding qualified instructors to teach dual enrollment courses, especially in rural schools and in math and science fields. To recruit and retain qualified instructors—for both academic and CTE dual enrollment courses—the schools we visited are building supplies of qualified instructors by streamlining pathways to teaching careers through grow-your-own pipeline programs. These programs have attracted and retained dual enrollment instructors by offering additional pay and other incentives.
- **Negotiate college and K–12 interests to find win-wins.** Colleges and their K–12 partners encounter a range of potential costs and incentives when running a dual enrollment program. School districts, for instance, may have to pay students' tuition and fees, but they also may want to expand dual enrollment to improve statewide accountability metrics. Colleges may be forced to offer dual enrollment courses at a steeply discounted rate,

yet they may want to expand their offerings as a strategy to recruit students after high school. The calculus of each partner's costs and incentives is specific to the local context. In our fieldwork, we observed open discussion of each side's dual enrollment-related incentives and costs as well as a concerted effort to identify strategies that benefit all parties, students included.

Implementing DEEP practices at scale requires a strong partnership and shared vision among college and K–12 leaders, but as the institutions that confer dual enrollment credit, colleges need to lead implementation. As the host institutions for the majority of dual enrollment nationally, community colleges are best positioned to lead the revamping of dual enrollment from "programs of privilege" or "random acts" to a stronger, more equitable on-ramp to college and career opportunity.

CHAPTER 7

Reorganizing Community Colleges for Student Success and Institutional Sustainability

Implementing the student outcomes- and value-focused reforms described in the previous chapters cannot be done, let alone sustained, in the siloed, functionally specialized ways community colleges are typically organized. Colleges that have found success have done so only by reorganizing staff to collaborate as they help students explore, enter, and complete programs, and by redesigning business processes and using technology to improve communication and achieve efficiencies.

Changing how colleges organize to deliver programs and supports is also crucial to funding and sustaining guided pathways. A 2020 Community College Research Center (CCRC) study of twelve diverse colleges that were early adopters of guided pathways reforms estimated the cost of starting guided pathways.[1] For an average community college (full-time equivalent enrollment of four thousand students and a $60 million annual operating budget), it amounts to about $450 per full-time equivalent student per year, or 3 percent of annual operating costs over four years.

The largest start-up cost is hiring additional advisors for individualized case management advising by field or meta-major. Other substantial costs include purchasing or upgrading information technology systems to support websites, online catalogs, individualized advising, academic planning, progress monitoring, and class scheduling. Some colleges also provide faculty and staff with stipends or release time from teaching to participate in project work groups. The estimated cost of sustaining guided pathways reforms after the initial implementation phase is somewhat lower: about $350 per full-time equivalent student per year, with advising again the priciest item.

CCRC researchers conducted two studies to examine how colleges, ranging from very large to very small, fund pathways reforms.[2] Although the colleges in both studies often used grants to fund start-up costs, they generally covered ongoing costs by reorganizing and reallocating staff and other resources and by creating efficiencies through technology rather than raising new income.

Reorganizing colleges in these ways requires a new approach to planning and budgeting, one that intentionally allocates resources for cross-college collaboration to guide students into and through high-value programs. In one sense, community colleges are financially lean institutions: many receive proportionately fewer public funds than broad-access public universities and are constrained from raising tuition by their "open-door" mission. At the same time, they are educationally inefficient because their structures often reinforce organizational silos and fragmented, unsustainable reforms. Through more strategic student outcomes–focused planning and budgeting, colleges can shift considerable resources from small, disconnected reforms to strategic, whole-college redesign based on the guided pathways model.

In this chapter, we explore how colleges are reorganizing staff and redesigning business processes and information systems to offer programs and support that produce stronger, more equitable outcomes. We also describe a new, more strategic approach to community college finance that can sustain continuous improvement at scale. We conclude with advice from college leaders who were early guided pathways adopters about how to begin redesigning college practices and organization to promote student success and institutional sustainability.

RETHINKING STAFF AND SYSTEMS TO BETTER SERVE STUDENTS

In the following sections, we examine how colleges are reorganizing staff and redesigning business systems and technology to enable implementation of the reforms described in the preceding chapters.[3]

Reorganizing program management, review, and development

Colleges cannot create the strong transfer pathways and the learning-and-earning ladder programs described in chapter 2 using the conventional approach to program organization, which creates silos between transfer and career-technical, credit and noncredit, and workforce and adult basic education offerings.

Early adopter guided pathways colleges have sought to break down organizational silos and reorganize their programs into career- and academic-focused meta-major fields. For example, each of the five separately accredited Alamo Colleges in Texas once organized programs independently. In 2015, Alamo College District leaders organized all programs across the five colleges into six career and academic fields called Alamo Institutes. They consolidated twenty-two dean positions into twelve across the five campuses, redefining their roles to oversee career-technical and academic transfer programs. The districtwide Pathways Leadership Council (PLC), made up of academic and career-technical deans from each Alamo college as well as an academic vice president and a college president, served as a steering group. To ensure that programs were aligned with workforce needs, the PLC created employer advisory boards for the institutes at the district and campus levels. The PLC coordinated transfer program review and development with the vice chancellor for academic success and six staff at the district office who were responsible for partnering with the many common transfer destination universities in the area to regularly update the transfer advising guides (TAGs) described in chapter 2. By maintaining close relationships with employer and university partners, this organization ensured that Alamo programs across colleges and fields stayed connected with changing requirements for in-demand jobs and further education.

Rethinking instructional improvement and professional development

If faculty are to be expected to teach using contextualized and active learning methods that research indicates are important for improving student learning outcomes (see chapter 3), they need support on how to do so. At most colleges, participation in professional development related to teaching is usually voluntary, meaning that not all faculty benefit, particularly part-time or adjunct instructors. A few early adopter colleges reorganized program management and professional development to support instructional improvements across programs, rather than making changes in pockets. San Jacinto College (SJC) in Texas redesigned the duties of the program chairs, who in the past were given release time from a class or two to handle departmental paperwork and procedures. Now the position is held by a full-time instructional leader who teaches only one class per year and reviews outcomes data and oversees the faculty inquiry-and-action teams working to improve instruction. The chairs also meet regularly with faculty to review disaggregated data on student performance provided by the institutional research department. Every instructor in a department has access to student performance data for their own classes and those of their colleagues. Chairs are also responsible for helping faculty develop and review mandatory annual improvement plans, which include metrics from course performance data.

To make time for these activities, the college in 2015 moved to a Monday-through-Thursday course schedule so faculty and staff (including those in front-line student services) can participate in mandatory Framework Friday meetings one or more times every month. In interviews with CCRC, SJC faculty and staff said Framework Fridays foster stronger working relationships between faculty across departments and between faculty and student services staff. SJC has continued these meetings, which one college leader describes as miniconferences at which attendees break into groups for brainstorming or discussion.

Reorganizing student program onboarding

As discussed in chapter 4, community colleges typically focus new student recruitment and onboarding on helping students enroll in the college and their first-term classes. Many if not most community colleges organize recruiting, admissions, orientation, and initial advising in functionally separate units. Inconsistent communication and collaboration across these units often result in students running from office to office as they apply, get financial aid, and enroll in classes. Career and college advising and other supports are available to help entering students explore options and choose and plan a program of study, but students must often seek out those services on their own. Although most colleges send recruiters to high schools to encourage students to enroll when they graduate, students who decide to attend are not helped through the registration and onboarding process. And few colleges actively recruit and support students to advance from noncredit workforce or adult basic education programs to college degree programs.[4]

Colleges that successfully implement program recruitment, onboarding, and ongoing advising often create cross-functional teams and train them to help students navigate the complicated application and registration process. They connect students with people and programs in fields of interest and work with students to develop educational program plans. Wake Technical Community College, the largest community college in North Carolina, established care teams for each of the thirteen career fields (meta-majors) the college created to align its programs with the regional labor market. Each team includes sector-specific advisors, success coaches, and career coaches who help students develop and follow a plan of study. Students who enroll without a clear career or program goal work with special "explore" staff and have six months to select a program and receive an assignment to a care team. The advising that the care teams provide to students in the hundreds of noncredit workforce programs the college offers focuses on helping students identify coursework that will give them footholds both to better jobs and to further education through degree or apprenticeship programs. Like many others, the college leveraged customer relationship management software to track students through admissions and enrollment and improve communication between staff and students. President Scott Ralls says this approach has improved the way faculty, advisors and success coaches, and career services staff share ideas, which better supports the students they serve.[5] By working together, colleges large and small are able to provide every student with help in exploring, choosing, and planning a program of study, not just those who seek help.

Washington State College of Ohio provides an example of how a similar reorganization can be done in a very small college.[6]

Case Study: One-Stop College and Program Onboarding at Washington State College of Ohio

Washington State College of Ohio consolidated admissions, high school outreach, financial aid, the business office, and records into a "one-stop" center located in a newly renovated space on campus. The goal was to provide prospective students with a personalized experience in which one staff member answers their questions without shuffling them around to other departments. In the past, these services were siloed, and students frequently complained about struggling to get the information they needed.

College leaders wanted frontline staff to be able to answer 80 percent of students' questions, with the remainder handled by experts beyond the counter. They also wanted staff to guide students into a program in a field of interest. That required leaders to empower frontline workers to think about their interactions with students as a conversation, not a transaction. Specialist advisors in admissions and dual enrollment became "pathways advisors" trained to answer questions from high school dual enrollment and post–high school prospects about college programs as well as course scheduling, billing, and financial aid, which increased productivity. Leaders combined the director of admissions and director of financial aid positions into a new director of enrollment services role, which reduced overall administrative costs even as it improved coordination.

Washington State conducted a survey on front-end services after the reorganization in 2021 and found high levels of student satisfaction. Leaders said that frontline staff now feel more comfortable with their newly empowered roles. According to a member of the leadership team, "[Staff] are better able to help students get the information they need, in some cases answering questions students didn't even know they had."

Of course, many students need personalized help exploring career and academic interests and developing plans. Few community colleges have sufficient staff to provide such support for every entering student who needs it before classes start. As described in chapter 4, many colleges require students to take a first-year experience or college success course to help them explore interests and develop a full-program academic plan in their first term. If well designed and taught, these courses offer a cost-effective way to provide more intensive support for students, because they are generally tuition-bearing courses.

Overhauling supports that promote on-time completion

The conventional advising model, in which generalists advise those who take the initiative to meet with them, makes it extremely difficult to provide all students with the personalized planning, guidance, and progress-monitoring assistance described in chapter 5. Most guided pathways colleges offering these supports assign advisors to a caseload of students in a particular program, such as business, technology, or allied health. This model enables advisors to develop detailed knowledge of program and transfer requirements as well as employment opportunities and also to work more closely with faculty and administrators to recruit, advise, and support students who share similar interests and goals. In some cases, faculty members receive training to carry out this work. In others, professional advisors or success coaches collaborate with faculty members who are assigned as mentors to students seeking information or professional contacts in their field of interest. Some colleges, like Wake Technical Community College described earlier in this chapter, create cross-functional teams. Bakersfield College in California established leadership teams for each meta-major that include a lead faculty member, an educational administrator, counselors, educational advisors, a job developer, a financial aid expert, and a data coach who collects and helps analyze student data. The teams report to the deans overseeing their respective meta-majors (which the college calls pathways).

Reorganizing dual enrollment and high school recruiting staffs

Most colleges rely on small groups of specialized employees to coordinate dual enrollment programs and student advising with K–12 staff. Given that dual enrollment students often account for a large segment of community college enrollment, as explained in chapter 6, colleges can no longer rely on a small but dedicated staff to advise these students. To motivate and prepare students to enter college-level degree programs after high school (and thus provide the college with an enrollment pipeline) through dual enrollment equity pathways (DEEP), colleges must take a different approach to organizing how they work with dual enrollment students.

Colleges that have implemented DEEP practices at scale often involve their "regular" academic and student services staff, who generally serve post–high school entrants, in advising and recruiting dual enrollment students. For example, since Patrick & Henry Community College in rural Virginia started offering college courses to high school students for free about a decade ago, the number of dual enrollment students has increased steadily and now accounts for more than one-third of enrollment. To better serve these students, the college hired four dual enrollment career coaches, who spend four days a week in the four local high schools and work closely with guidance counselors and other staff to educate students and families and help with enrollment. They also advise students by helping each one develop a career and college plan. These coaches also work with enrollment and advising staff on campus to help students interested in enrolling in the college after high school. Staff come to high schools on dedicated days in the spring to help register graduating seniors so they can continue in the fall. Patrick & Henry staff also ensure that once a student enrolls, there is a clear hand-off to the staff and faculty who will advise them once they are fully matriculated. By providing this seamless support for students to plan and transition to a college program, the college has increased the number of dual enrollment students who enroll directly after high school from around 40 percent to more than 55 percent. According to J. Gregory Hodges, Patrick & Henry's president, the increase in revenue has allowed the college to sustain funding for the career coaches.[7]

BUDGETING STRATEGICALLY FOR STUDENT SUCCESS

The typical way community colleges organize planning and budgeting—by department and division—does not effectively align resources toward student success. To do so, colleges must take a more strategic approach by collaborating across divisions to decide how to allocate resources to help all students, not just isolated groups, enter and complete programs of value.

Collaborative budgeting at scale

According to Sonya Christian, former president of early guided pathways adopter Bakersfield College, vice presidents and other administrators previously developed their budgets separately. After the college implemented guided pathways, they worked together using the four pillars of practice (i.e., clarifying paths to student end goals, helping students get on a path, keeping students on path, and ensuring that students are learning across their programs) as a framework to examine student success metrics, discuss what practices will improve student outcomes, and reallocate funds to those practices. Christian explained: "We draw on different buckets [of funding]. . . . No one area owns particular funds. . . . We use our common funds to invest in collegewide initiatives that will support student success, and guided pathways is the overarching model."[8]

Instead of having departments perform annual budgeting and program review, early adopter colleges develop academic budgets by field or meta-major. As part of its guided pathways reforms, Cleveland State Community College in

Tennessee conducted annual budgeting and program reviews by career community (meta-major), each of which developed budget requests based on enrollment trends and targets coupled with an analysis of local demand for program graduates. Budgeting by field also makes the funding of curricular and instructional improvements into fiscal priorities, as these are critical to students' learning and persistence in programs.

To ensure that colleges invest their limited resources in ways that advance student success, leaders must examine whether their decisions yield a return on investment in terms of improved outcomes. The largest sources of revenue for most community colleges are state funds and tuition, which typically are based on full-time equivalent enrollment. Grants from state and federal sources and, for some colleges, local tax base support account for the rest.[9] Therefore, colleges need to evaluate whether their reforms increase full-time equivalent enrollment, which will generate more state subsidies and tuition.

It is especially important that small colleges invest their scarce resources in aligning practices that benefit students. According to Vicky Wood, Washington State's former president, "raising new resources is not how we solve problems. We do it instead by creating alignment and efficiencies—making sure the right people are in the right roles, and everyone is on the same page with the goals."[10] Washington State and other small colleges have shown impressive improvements in student outcomes by strategically redefining roles and cross-training staff; using technology to improve information, communication, and coordination; and monitoring reforms to protect their limited resources. They were able to do so during a time of stagnant or declining enrollment and without tuition increases or new money from other sources.

Leaders of colleges that have implemented guided pathways reforms at scale have in effect adopted a new community college business model. Under the conventional model, colleges generate enrollment and revenue by offering diverse courses and programs at a low cost. In the new business model, colleges attract and retain students (and thus generate tuition and state subsidies) by offering affordable, high-value programs that lead to postcompletion success and by providing supports intentionally designed to enable timely completion. Colleges often talk about being student centered. Under the guided pathways approach, colleges become student outcomes focused.

Reallocating resources to support student success at scale

By shifting resources from disconnected interventions to a strategic, whole-college redesign, colleges can free up considerable resources to implement the reforms described in previous chapters. For example, Alex Johnson, former president of Cuyahoga Community College (Tri-C) in Ohio, said that roughly ninety mostly small-scale student success initiatives were absorbing a lot of staff time and resources when he came to the college. As part of its guided pathways work, the college stopped most of these efforts, reallocated staff and other resources, and invested in a case-management approach to advising organized around meta-majors and program maps. As a result, Tri-C redistributed $6.4 million in the 2020–2021 fiscal year for pathways and related student success efforts (about 2.3 percent of the college's annual operating budget of around $283 million).

Cut nonessential courses. While mapping programs to student end goals as part of the guided pathways process, leaders at Zane State College in Ohio identified numerous courses (many of them general education) with low enrollment that were not essential to program learning outcomes. The college held a speed dating–style event at which general education faculty pitched courses and explained how they contribute to specific programs. Through this process, leaders eliminated thirteen general education courses with a combined ninety-seven sections, reducing the number of adjuncts and faculty overloads needed. This freed $1 million in instructional resources to spend more productively.

Reinvest funds from increased enrollment, improved efficiencies, and performance funding. The Alamo Colleges District has for many years put 15 percent of its annual net operating fund balance into a student success fund that supports major reforms. As a result of the enrollment boom following the Great Recession and savings from automating back-office functions, the district generated a reserve of $20 million, which it used to hire new advisors, purchase systems software, and cover other costs of implementing guided pathways reforms.

In states using performance funding, many early adopter colleges have generated revenue through improvements in progression and completion rates. From the fiscal years 2017 to 2021, North Central State College in Ohio increased its allocation from the state's Student Success Initiative performance funding policy by 22 percent, compared with an average increase of 6 percent for all of Ohio's community colleges. North Central earned more points for the dramatic increase in students earning certificates, which are now embedded in associate degree programs, and for the rate at which entering students completed college-level math, because it was in the vanguard of colleges eliminating developmental math and implementing math pathways. North Central used revenue from this increase to pay for more efforts to improve student success. For example, the college receives performance funding when dual enrollment students earn college credits, complete college math and English, and reach other milestones. The college has used some of that revenue to fund tuition-free scholarships for students who earn at least eight credits through dual enrollment at North Central while in high school.

Use grant funding strategically to build capacity. Although many early adopter colleges fund the ongoing costs of guided pathways more through reorganization, reallocation, and reinvestment than new funding, many rely on grants to launch the reforms. North Central initially used a Title III grant to fund case management advisors in each of three academic divisions, but the college has since moved support for these positions to general operating funds. It also used the grant to purchase software for improved educational planning, student progress monitoring, and course scheduling and to train faculty and staff to use these tools—all one-time investments that helped build the capacity of the college to improve student outcomes.

TAKING ACTION TO LEAD AND SUSTAIN INSTITUTIONAL TRANSFORMATION

It took several years for early adopter colleges to reorganize staff, business processes, and systems and to change budgeting to allocate resources to support student outcomes. Even more colleges started down the road of guided pathways but put efforts on hold because of leadership turnover, COVID-19, or other major shocks. The growing competitive pressures on community colleges described in the introduction are motivating many to restart their reforms and are encouraging those that have not done so to begin.

Colleges should not start guided pathways reforms by reorganizing divisions and staff. Based on CCRC's research, they should initially focus on redesigning practices and then think about reorganizing staffing, processes, and systems to support them. In the following sections, we suggest strategies for starting (or restarting) and sustaining these reforms shared by leaders who have successfully implemented guided pathways.[11]

Getting started

Ensure that top-level leaders are committed. Top-level leadership is essential to launching guided pathways reforms. The colleges we studied that have made the most progress transitioning to the model generally have had stable presidential leadership. We have observed several colleges that had support for guided pathways further down in the organization or in one academic area, but reforms in those colleges typically do not have a lasting impact. A project leader at one guided pathways college said, "Pathways work has to be led at the highest level of leadership if you really want cross-divisional collaboration and engagement. Just leading from one division can be polarizing. The president and board of trustees have to be pushing and continuously talking about it."[12]

Kay McClenney, who directed the American Association of Community Colleges (AACC) Pathways Project, and who, along with Byron McClenney, has led training for community college leaders, insisted on a strong commitment to the project upfront from presidents and boards. According to Kay McClenney:

> Because local boards hire (and fire) CEOs, building their understanding of and support for the very tough nature of the work and the long time period required for successfully accomplishing needed change has proven to be critical. The key metrics provided to and discussed with the board matter greatly in shaping their policy focus; and board members can be important champions for cross-sector work (i.e., with K–12 districts, universities, and employers) in their communities. Finally, public commitment to (and resource allocation for) economic upward mobility and equitable outcomes for students is a powerful tool.[13]

Use data to highlight internal barriers to student success. One way to build awareness of the need for systemic changes is by using data to show how colleges create barriers to student success. The idea is not to cast blame—no one wants to thwart student success—but to show how removing the barriers can lead to greater student success, more revenue from retaining students, and more fulfilled college personnel.

An especially potent data point for this purpose is the median number of credits earned by associate degree graduates who started their programs at the college. As discussed in chapter 2, research by CCRC and others shows that it is not uncommon for students who graduate with associate of arts degrees in liberal arts or general studies to accumulate eighty to ninety semester-hour credits for programs that require only sixty. This suggests that colleges are not helping students develop plans to take the right courses or monitoring their progress, resulting in students spending time and money taking courses they do not need. As one AACC Pathways college leader said, "Look at what the data is telling you about what you're doing to your students. Students [at our college] were graduating with eighty-one to eighty-three credits for programs that [require] sixty to sixty-five credits. We're taking their money, their time, and their future opportunities to use financial aid."[14]

College leaders told us about other data points they have used to raise questions about barriers to student success the college itself creates:

- Number of new students who apply to the college but do not enroll in classes
- Persistence and completion rates for full- and part-time students by race/ethnicity, gender, and age
- Number of students in good standing who leave school for more than a term
- Number of students who do not have a plan for their program of study
- Rates of transfer and bachelor's completion for transfer-intending students
- Share of former high school dual enrollment students who enroll at the college—and who do not go on to any postsecondary education—after high school

Such statistics can be compelling to some, but as one AACC Pathways college leader said, "You have to appeal to people's heads and their hearts."[15] One of the most effective ways to do this is by letting students talk about their experiences. This can be done through surveys, but perhaps more compellingly in focus groups in which current (and ideally former) students describe their experiences navigating into and through programs. In general, the more college leaders can use data to illuminate students' experiences—and the barriers they face that are created by the college—the more likely stakeholders will be to see a need for change.

Build a sense of urgency about big changes to better serve students. Colleges successful in launching guided pathways reforms generally start with broad-based efforts to engage internal and sometimes external stakeholders in examining data on student outcomes, identifying barriers the college creates to student success, and building support for large-scale reform. Colleges often do this as part of their strategic planning. The key is focusing on students' experiences and their outcomes. As one AACC Pathways Project leader explained, a crucial part of the messaging when introducing guided pathways is to "always keep in the forefront doing what's best for the student." In the words of another leader, it is important to "remember why you're doing what you're doing. It's basic, but that's why we're here."[16]

Some colleges choose to design reforms explicitly focused on underserved students on the theory that other students also will benefit. The guided pathways reform leadership team at South Seattle College in Washington, which has a strong equity focus, explained that if the goal is to create structures that help more students succeed, then the college also needs to closely examine the ways structures are failing students of color. By prioritizing students of color in data analysis, feedback, and engagement, South Seattle better centered equity into course design, programming, and the student experience. This ensures that equity remains central to the guided pathways reform work.

Engage stakeholders in codesigning goals and strategies for improving student success. Leaders at many colleges have found the guided pathways framework useful for identifying barriers to student success and formulating broad goals and strategies for removing those barriers. Leaders at Laramie County Community College in Wyoming solicited campuswide input to develop "must-haves"—changes in practice to improve the experience of students that the college would commit to under each of the four pillars of the guided pathways framework. At the same time, other colleges have developed specific terminology to frame how they design reforms. For example, Tallahassee Community College in Florida successfully integrated guided pathways with other reform ideas (including Caring Campus) using a student experience–focused framework the college calls the CARE (connections, academics, resources, and engagement) model.[17] This framework has helped faculty and staff consider how their roles contribute to student success. The key is to give stakeholders a sense that they co-own reforms as opposed to reforms being foisted on them from the outside or by top leaders.

Successfully implementing systemic reforms

Use cross-functional teams to plan and implement guided pathways reforms. Guided pathways reforms are about enriching students' experience throughout their time at the college, which means all segments of the college community need to be involved in planning and implementing changes in practice. Faculty must play an integral role. Some colleges have involved faculty in mapping out programs and then have relied on student services personnel to implement reforms to onboarding, advising, and progress monitoring. They have generally come to regret this for several reasons. Faculty and academic departments need to be involved in onboarding students and helping them progress. Using a more siloed approach may also be one reason, as mentioned in chapter 3, that comparatively little attention in many colleges has been given to the fourth pillar of ensuring that students are learning across their programs. At the same time, advisors and other student services staff, as well as registrars, librarians, academic support staff, and others, have important perspectives on the student experience that faculty do not.

This is why colleges that have successfully implemented guided pathways reforms have generally relied on cross-functional teams to plan and carry out the work. These task-oriented groups are different from standing committees, although most colleges establish a steering committee to oversee teams and advise top administrators on policy changes and resources needed to support reforms. They often are led jointly by faculty and student services or support personnel. Leaders at St. Petersburg College in Florida said their "secret sauce" to guided pathways planning and implementation was appointing diverse cross-functional teams to lead the reforms. The college developed a triad model for leading each meta-major (or career and academic community). The triad team includes a faculty member, an advisor, and an academic support person, such as a librarian or tutor. Each person adds their perspective on what it takes for students to be successful. The triads train other members in the meta-major, which has helped break down silos between academic departments and student affairs. One of the benefits of this strategy, according to a college leader, is that it leads departments to change the way they work using guided pathways as a framework. Under this umbrella, the college has redesigned everything from communication with students to registration, advising, career counseling, calculating grade point averages, and monitoring progress—all with the aim of supporting students into and through their programs.

Colleges need to give teams the time and support (and, in the case of adjunct instructors, stipends) to plan and implement above their regular duties. It will take more than fall and spring professional development days to accomplish this—although those sessions do provide good opportunities to report on progress and recruit faculty and staff to participate in the following year's work. Several early adopter colleges took an approach similar to SJC's (described earlier) by scheduling classes Monday through Thursday to free Fridays for required work on collaborative professional development and improvement.

Seek students' perspectives on proposed reforms. Leaders from multiple early adopter colleges have highlighted the benefits of involving students on guided pathways design teams and in formatively evaluating progress in implementation. At Irvine Valley College in California, students participated in all guided pathways working groups, contributed to the redesign of the college's website, and shared their experiences with faculty and staff. A few years into the redesign work at South Seattle College, guided pathways leaders included students and quickly realized they should have involved them from the start. A student group, for example, used qualitative data from surveys, focus groups, events, and student mentors to assess and refine the guided pathways essential practices.

Avoid perpetual planning. On the one hand, it is essential to ensure broad support for major changes and broad engagement in planning reforms, which can take a long time. But on the other, some colleges spend years trying incrementally to pilot ideas and design the perfect plan. Laramie County Community College in Wyoming took a year to engage stakeholders and develop a plan. Joe Schaffer, the college's president, said, "Sometimes you've got to go slow to go fast," invoking the mantra of a member of the college's board of trustees who was a strong champion of the college's improvement efforts. Over that year, college leaders sought to build commitment to reform, which they did by providing opportunities for members of the college community to understand what the college was hoping to achieve by committing to guided pathways, to share their voices in the design of the reforms, and to be part of the work of change. At the next fall's convocation, Schaffer asked the audience to stand up if they were leading the reforms, if they were on one of the work teams, and if they were serving as an advisor to one of the teams. According to Schaffer, "By the time I asked my third question, nearly the entire campus community was standing in the audience. That was powerful."[18]

Once the college had built widespread commitment to change and come up with a plan, it went all in on a first round of reforms across many areas.

According to Schaffer, it can be messy to implement many changes simultaneously, but colleges will learn so much from the experience that "version 2.0" will inevitably be better than the first. Going all in also helps build confidence that big changes are possible when done collaboratively.[19]

Understand how technology will help improve student supports before buying it. As is clear from the previous sections of this chapter, information technology is key to improving recruiting and advising, helping students develop plans, and monitoring their progress to complete on time. In many colleges, acquiring or upgrading software systems was one of the largest start-up costs for guided pathways reforms and led to recurring costs for maintenance and upgrades. Systems vendors are aware of this issue and inundate college leaders with marketing for "turnkey" guided pathways solutions. Chief information technology officers we interviewed at several early adopter colleges strongly recommend that colleges not purchase new information systems before they plan and implement guided pathways reforms. They say colleges should instead assess the needs of key stakeholders in their new roles and use that as the basis for creating specifications for vendors. They argue that those who help define the use of technology are more likely to actually use it. They also point out that colleges often already own underused systems that they can redeploy to support guided pathways processes and practices.

Develop a communications plan to report progress and further plans. Leaders at colleges that have successfully implemented guided pathways reforms frequently report that regular communication is essential to sharing progress and celebrating accomplishments.

South Seattle College guided pathways team members said that having the president communicate directly with stakeholders about changes was critical to demonstrating the importance of guided pathways reforms and ensuring transparency. This energized the college's guided pathways work: people wanted to be a part of it because it came across as authentic. Leaders spoke openly about the barriers that students faced because of the college's own practices, and that openness enabled others to speak up about the barriers they saw to success.

This focus on communication also led several colleges to take fresh looks at how they share information with students. SJC hired a student communications specialist who ensures that they receive cohesive, consistent, and accurate messages. Meanwhile, Wallace State Community College in Alabama considered communication with students early in its guided pathways work and looked carefully at who was communicating with which students, when, how often, and what messages they were sharing. Leaders quickly realized that departments sent distinct messages and that students were receiving emails from many different units. The college has since streamlined its student communications.

Sustaining reforms and institutionalizing continuous improvement over time

Build leadership for guided pathways reforms throughout the institution. Although strong leadership from the president and the board are essential for launching guided pathways reforms, sustaining those reforms over time requires cultivating leaders throughout the college. CCRC's research on how early adopters managed the large-scale changes identified deans, registrars, financial aid directors, institutional researchers, and information technology directors as especially important contributors. A guided pathways leader at one AACC Pathways college noted that the institution "sets high expectations for deans and others and provides a lot of professional development for them." At another college, the guided pathways leader explained that leaders "let people be experts in their field" and emphasized the benefits of supporting people within the college: "If you have people on the team and you empower them, you will build trust and teamwork." Yet another project leader said top leaders need to empower other staff to take the lead: "It should not be top-down, but you need executive leadership who are willing to provide a platform that allows you to make change." Another college integrated more people into its guided pathways work by including them on teams for AACC Pathways institutes as well as those provided by their state associations. This college's president said taking someone to the institutes means "one more person on the campus pushing guided pathways" and that "the more people you can get involved, the easier it is to make it happen."[20]

South Seattle College developed an internal coaching model to develop shared leadership for change across the college. Coaches advise on and help coordinate parts of the guided pathways work that align with their institutional affiliation. For example, one person who works with first-year students coaches the intake and onboarding group. These coaches work collaboratively with other faculty and staff to increase involvement every year and to incorporate redesign efforts into regular college operations.

Sonya Christian, the former president at Bakersfield College, said "Guided pathways is now how we do business."[21] The college does not have an office or director of guided pathways because the reforms are everyone's responsibility. One way they ensure this is by integrating guided pathways into training for new faculty and staff. An academic dean said the college holds workshops for new faculty on how to bring guided pathways into the classroom educationally and pedagogically. The workshops help new hires understand what their responsibility is as faculty to implement the principles and tools of guided pathways.

Accept that progress is often nonlinear. Leaders at early adopter colleges say implementing whole-college reform is time-consuming and nonlinear. The provost who serves as guided pathways leader at one large AACC Pathways college said: "You need to be prepared for a lot of work that takes time. You have to be patient. I'm terribly impatient. But I've learned to be patient. One of the things that's frustrating is, with so much work, there is an expected steady upward trajectory. But there are bumps."[22] Leaders from two other AACC Pathways colleges also said leaders must be willing to try things that may not work and to change direction when a strategy fails. The first college shifted focus away from developing a new first-year experience course and toward a project that had more momentum. The second college moved from having faculty advisors to having student success coaches, which caused friction because, as the leader noted, "people have a vested interest in the way things are."[23] The faculty, however, eventually embraced this change after recognizing its benefits.

Numerous interviewees counseled patience. As one guided pathways leader said, "Just stick with it. This will take a while. The pace is sometimes frustrating to people, but don't give up—plug away." Guided pathways leaders at another college described how they persisted through some initial challenges. "There were some screwups" the first year the college hired new success coaches, one leader said, but they stuck with the strategy. Another key part of being patient is setting realistic timelines. CCRC has suggested that the process can take at least five years, but leaders at several AACC Pathways colleges said that a decade is more realistic. As an interviewee at St. Petersburg College noted, "Transforming a college on the guided pathways model is a ten-year process; it can't be done in a year or two. It is tempting to want to see results right away, but slow and steady will win the race."[24]

Reorganizing a college takes time, commitment, and involvement from staff and faculty across a college; it is also an iterative process that requires frequent assessment, adjustments, and improvements to practices. At early adopter colleges making the most progress in scaling these reforms, leadership teams have approached the work with this mindset and, even more important, have helped instill it in faculty, staff, and others involved from the start.

CHAPTER 8

Leading College Transformation Across States and Systems

In the Community College Research Center's (CCRC) National Science Foundation (NSF) evaluation of the adoption of guided pathways reforms described in chapter 1, we saw evidence that higher education agencies and college associations can help spread the adoption of innovations across colleges in their systems. The agencies in the three NSF project states adopted guided pathways (or, in the case of Tennessee, a model based on similar principles) as a framework for organizing and supporting statewide reforms. They also sponsored institutes for teams from colleges throughout their systems to learn about guided pathways reforms and formulate plans to implement them. Agencies or associations in at least sixteen other states have taken similar steps. Beyond encouraging colleges to adopt guided pathways reforms, state agencies can also play a key role in providing funding to incentivize colleges to carry out such transformational efforts.

As discussed in chapter 7, although most early adopter colleges that CCRC studied used grants to help launch guided pathways reforms, they relied more on reorganizing resources and creating efficiencies than on new revenue to cover the costs. They invested in their reforms up front, expecting a return later through the increased tuition and state subsidies they believed would come from improved student retention and success.

There are limits, however, to how much community colleges can "do more with less" through resource reallocation and efficiency measures—particularly because they often receive less funding per student than public four-year institutions to carry out their distinctive missions. Despite the popularity of performance-based funding among policy makers in many states, most studies have not found a strong positive effect on student outcomes. Additionally, performance-based funding can incentivize colleges to increase credentials of limited value and may put smaller colleges at a disadvantage. Faced with enrollment and fiscal environment challenges—and having spent their portion of the federal COVID-19 Higher Education Emergency Relief Fund—many community colleges nationally, especially small ones, face uncertain financial futures.

The next frontiers of community college reforms to improve their value and impact, which we describe in chapters 2 through 6, will likely involve costs beyond business as usual, as have earlier guided pathways reforms. Early adopters of these frontier reforms have covered the costs by "braiding" funding from grants and other sources. It is difficult, however, to sustain these reforms through funding that comes from outside the general operating support that colleges receive from state and local sources and tuition.

In this chapter, we examine how state agencies and associations can encourage colleges in their systems to adopt student reforms focused on strengthening programmatic paths to postcompletion success. We also discuss the limits of relying on colleges to "do more with less" to fund whole-college reforms and describe how states are beginning to rethink community college funding with an eye toward postcompletion student success and institutional sustainability. We conclude with suggestions for statewide agencies and associations to support whole-college reforms across their systems.

SUPPORTING INSTITUTIONAL TRANSFORMATION ACROSS SYSTEMS

Statewide efforts have been an important vehicle for community college reform since the late 2000s. One of the earliest efforts was the Ford Foundation–funded Community College Bridges to Opportunity Initiative, which included Colorado, Kentucky, Louisiana, New Mexico, Ohio, and Washington. The project focused on leveraging state policy to motivate changes in practice to support underprepared adult students into and through programs aligned with well-paying jobs. It was a precursor to statewide guided pathways reforms in its emphasis on the important role of state agencies in advocating for a statewide strategy, clarifying credentials to prepare students for the workforce, and emphasizing the organizational changes needed to achieve its goals.[1]

Another early statewide effort began in North Carolina. In 2010, the state community college system launched SuccessNC, a three-year strategy focused on developmental education, dual enrollment, workforce credentials, and other reforms.[2] Then in 2011, the Bill & Melinda Gates Foundation launched Completion by Design, which supported efforts in Florida, North Carolina, and Ohio.[3] Each state selected a small number of colleges to participate, while state system offices created statewide scaling strategies based on the lessons learned from participating colleges.

From 2012 to 2023, state agencies and college associations in seventeen states formed student success centers to improve outcomes. Their strategy centered on adopting a framework for whole-college reforms like guided pathways and on catalyzing and adopting these reforms across all colleges. The success centers serve several functions:

- **Centralized hub of information and resources.** Student success centers are a hub for collecting, analyzing, and disseminating information about effective practices. Such hubs showcase promising innovations that can be shared across campuses and regions.
- **Network of expertise and collaboration.** The centers bring together experts and practitioners from various state community colleges, creating opportunities to collaborate and exchange knowledge. The network allows participants to share experiences, challenges, and solutions, allowing colleges to adopt successful practices more quickly.
- **Professional development and training.** The centers offer professional development and training on innovative practices for faculty, staff, and administrators. Offerings range from day-long workshops to multiday statewide institutes, webinars, technical assistance programs, and coaching. These opportunities ensure that practitioners have the necessary skills and knowledge to implement new approaches effectively.
- **Data collection and analysis.** The centers can collect, analyze, and share data on student outcomes, which allows for statewide benchmarking and evaluating the effectiveness of reforms. This data-driven approach helps identify the most impactful innovations, informs future decisions, and establishes a consistent focus on the same metrics across the state over time.

- **Advocacy and policy influence.** By showcasing the positive outcomes of innovative practices, student success centers can advocate for statewide policy changes to support these initiatives, including funding mechanisms. This can lead to the broader adoption of effective strategies across a community college system.

The centers and the agencies or associations to which they are attached are, by mission, dedicated to improving outcomes of all colleges in their systems. This is especially important for small rural colleges and others that lack resources to secure grant funding or afford outside professional development and technical assistance.[4] The systemwide approach under a broad, integrated framework like guided pathways promotes cross-college learning and sharing. It builds a network of state-specific expert practitioners who have experience implementing the reforms and who can advise other colleges. It also encourages sharing at statewide meetings and professional councils (such as councils for instructional administrators, academic and student services administrators, and institutional researchers). This builds knowledge within the system, which is particularly helpful because many people who change jobs in community colleges do so within their state.

Texas and Ohio carried out statewide strategies by developing student success centers. Both centers are housed within the state community college associations that serve the fifty community college districts in Texas and the twenty-two community colleges in Ohio. In both states, the centers led statewide strategies organized around the guided pathways framework starting in 2016. The student success centers in both states supported guided pathways learning and implementation across colleges in their systems through professional development, coaching, and support for evaluation and continuous improvement.

Supporting scaled reforms through the Texas Success Center

The Texas Success Center was launched in 2013 under the umbrella of the Texas Association of Community Colleges (TACC), which serves all of the state's public community colleges. Together, the success center and TACC support statewide policy advocacy and reform. In 2016, the center kicked off a five-year strategy, Texas Pathways, to help the state's community colleges build the capacity to implement guided pathways reforms at scale. A key component of the strategy has been the Texas Pathways Institutes, a statewide learning network modeled on the American Association of Community Colleges (AACC) Pathways Project (described in chapter 1). The center also provides additional supports, including a knowledge-development agenda to inform ongoing guided pathways reforms, coaching, institutes for boards of trustees, and state policy advocacy.

From the start, the center had broad engagement statewide: in 2016, colleges from thirty-eight of the state's fifty college districts adopted the guided pathways framework. As of 2024, forty-six colleges were actively participating in statewide scaling efforts.

Broadening the framework for reforms. With support from multiple national and Texas-based funders, the Texas Success Center launched its first pathways institute series in fall 2016, which continued through spring 2019. A second series started in fall 2019, and a third in 2023. In its first five-year phase, Texas Pathways focused on supporting the implementation of guided pathways practices along the four pillars. Organizers assigned each college to one of four cadres based on their readiness and capacity to scale guided pathways reforms. Colleges could move to more advanced cadres if they made progress scaling guided pathways practices. They received customized supports based on their cadre designation. Ahead of each pathways institute, the center designed structured facilitation guides to guide colleges in examining institutional data. Although the data elements were the same for each college, those in the more advanced cadres explored data disaggregated by student characteristics and were challenged with additional guiding questions to further their understanding of barriers to moving their work forward. Additionally, the center assigned a pathways coach to support each college's redesign work during institutes and site visits.

In January 2023, the Texas Success Center launched a new five-year strategic plan, Talent Strong Texas Pathways. The new plan broadened the guided pathways framework to focus not just on increasing completion but also on increasing completion of credentials with high value for transfer and the workforce. Talent Strong Texas Pathways also emphasizes efforts to extend guided pathways practices to build on-ramps for high school students to career-path programs after graduation—consistent with the dual enrollment equity pathways (DEEP) model described in chapter 6. This broader framing was done to align college efforts with the goals of the Texas Higher Education Coordinating Board's new strategic plan and the state's anticipated community college performance-based funding model (passed in May 2023 and described later in this chapter).[5]

The Texas Success Center continues to support colleges with twice-annual institutes that bring together teams from participating colleges in intensive three-day work sessions. The institutes include pre-institute workshops, keynotes, panel discussions, and facilitated team strategy time to examine early momentum metrics, identify specific short-term goals aligned with their institutional priorities, and develop plans to share what they learned from the institutes and to make progress scaling and institutionalizing their guided pathways reforms. Between institutes, the center hosts topic-specific webinars and workshop and regional convenings. These opportunities engage a broader group of college personnel and external constituents needed to build regional talent pathways. College personnel can attend webinars and workshops and receive additional coaching.

A comprehensive knowledge-development plan. From the outset, a key feature of the Texas Success Center's statewide strategy was the knowledge development plan, which included a detailed research agenda and a steering committee.[6] One goal was to conduct action-oriented research that could support evidence-based reforms across the Texas colleges. For example, the center has administered a Texas Scale of Adoption Assessment (SOAA) approximately every eighteen months since 2016. Using CCRC's SOAA as a starting point, the center cobranded the tool, added additional questions, and customized some questions for the Texas context. After teams from each college complete the assessment, center researchers interview college pathways leads to validate the ratings across institutions and learn about emerging innovative practices. The center then publishes a detailed report on its findings with case examples and uses these results to inform the programming it provides to colleges.[7]

Professional development for trustees. As discussed in chapter 7, leadership is critical to successfully implement guided pathways reforms at scale, especially because this work takes several years and community colleges experience frequent turnover. Support from college boards is thus crucial for success. To that end, TACC aligned its longstanding professional development for trustees of the state's community colleges with the statewide guided pathways work. Since 2016, the Texas Success Center has regularly hosted multiday institutes and webinars for trustees to learn about their roles in setting strategic directions, monitoring key progress metrics, and supporting a culture of innovation to support their colleges' guided pathways reforms.[8]

Policy advocacy. A major role of statewide organizations like community college associations is state-level advocacy for policy and funding to support student success. In 2023, TACC played a lead role in formulating and lobbying for Texas House Bill 8, which revamped the fifty-plus-year-old funding model to focus on building pathways for students to high-demand jobs and efficient transfer, described in more detail later in this chapter. The passage of House Bill 8 was notable in that it received bipartisan support and had the backing of all fifty Texas community college district CEOs.

The success in scaling pathways in Texas is reflected in increases in early momentum metrics across its community colleges. A recent Talent Strong Texas Pathways report showed a statewide increase in seven of eight first-term and first-year metrics between 2015 and 2022, including completing college math, reading, and writing; earning six or more college credits in term one; and completing fifteen or more college credits in year one.[9] Moreover, for many of the metrics, African Americans, Hispanics, Pell recipients, and part-time students outperformed their peers, indicating the positive impact of the statewide strategy in addressing long-standing achievement gaps for underserved populations.

Scaling statewide innovation through the Success Center for Ohio Community Colleges

The Success Center for Ohio Community Colleges, launched in 2012, was one of the first student success centers.[10] In 2016, it kicked off the Student Success Leadership Institute (SSLI) to support adopting guided pathways and related reforms at scale across the state's twenty-three community colleges. In SSLI's first year, the center hosted six statewide institutes to start the work to develop and implement scaled guided pathways reforms. The center also has provided college teams with supports aligned with the guided pathways framework, including a knowledge-development agenda developed with CCRC and college presidents focused on implementation, student outcomes, and topics like dual enrollment and teaching and learning. The center also facilitates officers groups for senior and midlevel leaders, conducts a leadership academy for midlevel leaders, and provides coaching. The focus on student success has also led to increased student outcomes across Ohio. Since 2011, the three-year graduation rate has nearly tripled, from 9 percent to 25 percent.

Student Success Leadership Institute. Since 2016, the center has hosted statewide SSLI meetings every February and September (the twenty-third meeting was in September 2024). Colleges bring teams to hear national speakers and Ohio practitioners and to assess and plan next steps in their guided pathways work. The institutes also give teams time away from campus to focus on student success strategies and learn from colleagues at other colleges. Furthermore, SSLI provides state-level policy updates and opportunities to connect with policy makers, including the state chancellor for higher education. Another benefit is SSLI's focus on data. February institutes focus on early momentum metrics and the state performance funding formula. Colleges receive data reports showing their progress on these metrics relative to their past performance and that of other Ohio community colleges. All twenty-three of the state's community colleges have participated in SSLI from the beginning, each bringing between eight and twelve team members to each institute.

Although Ohio's success center adopted guided pathways as an overarching framework for reform—with SSLI as the cornerstone—it also has led efforts to advance specific reforms within the guided pathways framework, including developmental education, dual enrollment, holistic advising, scheduling, and teaching and learning. As CCRC learned from our research on implementing guided pathways reforms within colleges (as detailed in chapter 7), the challenge of adopting complicated reforms with many moving parts is that the parts can feel disconnected. The same thing can happen within a state effort. When colleges are pulled in too many directions, they can lose sight of the big picture. Center staff regularly engage with leadership and practitioners across the twenty-three colleges to foster statewide coherence. The center also hosts regular workshops and webinars and provides coaching to colleges on topics like advising and holistic student support.

Expanding participation in statewide officers groups. One of the center's strategies for promoting coherence is regular and frequent engagement with statewide groups of presidents and officers. Across the state's community colleges, the chief student affairs officers, chief academic affairs officers, and chief financial officers have met for more than a decade. Starting in 2014, the Ohio Association of Community Colleges (OACC) brought these groups together for meetings to help plan and coordinate their efforts to improve student learning and success. Requests from additional college practitioners led OACC to create groups for institutional researchers and workforce development personnel in 2013 and 2019, respectively. These groups each meet monthly and a member of the staff of OACC attends each one to provide updates, share reminders about upcoming events, and keep up with discussions and concerns. The officers groups also meet before each SSLI. These pre-institute meetings initially involved only chief academic and financial officers but have expanded to include leaders in student affairs, institutional research, and workforce programs. Additionally, the executive director of the success center joins the college presidents' monthly meeting to share SSLI updates and early copies of any data reports that will be distributed at the next institute. The broad involvement of practitioners in multiple roles encourages cross-college collaboration among cabinet-level leaders. The frequent interaction among groups helps maintain alignment and engagement and ensures that support from OACC and the success center remains relevant to state policies and the colleges' needs.

Preparing leaders for their next roles. In 2019, the success center started the Ohio Leadership Academy for Student Success, a new initiative to develop midlevel leaders like directors and deans to manage and lead guided pathways reforms effectively. The impetus was frequent turnover in senior leadership positions, and the goal was to build a pipeline of leaders to lead reforms from their current roles and prepare them to do so when they move into cabinet-level positions. The success center codesigned the academy's curriculum with the Aspen Institute's College Excellence Program based on its successful presidential fellowship program and with the National Center for Inquiry & Improvement, which provides technical assistance on guided pathways implementation to colleges nationally. The curriculum focuses on student success, leadership, and external partnerships and includes an applied guided pathways–based group project. In the 2024–2025 academic year, the academy supported its fifth cohort. In all, nearly two hundred fellows in Ohio have completed the academy, one-third of whom have since been promoted. The academy's success led Michigan, New York, and Texas to replicate this strategy.

FUNDING FOR TRANSFORMATION AND SUSTAINABILITY

The next frontiers of community college reforms described in chapters 2 through 6, which we argue are needed to improve the colleges' value and impact, likely involve costs above those needed for guided pathways reforms to date.

For example, the pre-major transfer pathways and learning-and-earning career ladder programs described in chapter 2 are particularly challenging to fund. Both require dedicated staff to coordinate outreach with employers and universities and to manage program development, review, and improvements. Building career ladders that lead to high-demand jobs offering good pay and career advancement prospects typically requires offering programs that are expensive and serve relatively small numbers of students. As described in chapter 3, high-quality workforce and transfer programs also require extensive professional development for faculty.

The efforts discussed in chapters 4 and 5—recruiting, onboarding, and supporting students, particularly those from underserved groups, to enter and complete high-value programs—require retraining student services staff and, in some cases, hiring new personnel. Similarly, providing a greater level of outreach and support to expand access and effectiveness for a growing number of dual enrollment students, as described in chapter 6, is especially challenging to fund in states where colleges offer dual enrollment at a discount or, in some cases, for free.[11]

Systemic reforms require more than grants

Colleges implementing systemic reforms like those described in previous chapters typically combine grant funding from various sources to support the added costs. There are limits, however, to this approach's sustainability.

Probably the most reliable source of funding for community college workforce programs is through the federal Carl D. Perkins Career and Technical Education Act of 2006, which in fiscal year 2023 provided $1.43 billion for career-technical education and training in K–12 schools and colleges nationally. To receive Perkins funding, colleges must apply through their states every four years and report student outcomes annually. How much Perkins funding goes to colleges versus K–12 schools varies, but in all states, both sectors compete for a declining pot of funds. Although there have been some increases in recent years to account for inflation, Perkins funding is well below 1990s levels.[12]

Under the Biden administration, the federal government enacted more than $1 trillion dollars in investments over ten years through the Bipartisan Infrastructure Law, the Inflation Reduction Act, and the CHIPS and Science Act of 2022, which are projected to create many new, well-paying jobs. These federal initiatives all include funding to support education and training for these new jobs, and many states have also enacted additional funding.[13]

To tap into the new workforce funding, colleges must apply for grants from an array of agencies that many have not dealt with before, such as federal and state energy departments. To pursue this funding, they often need to expand their grant-writing operations, which is challenging for most community colleges but especially smaller ones. In other cases, colleges must negotiate with employers to receive pass-throughs from companies that receive federal or state incentives. Colleges also need to leverage relationships with employers to purchase or use expensive technology for instruction, create opportunities for internships and other work-based learning for students, and identify employees who can teach part-time. Here again, it takes dedicated staff to build these relationships with employers.

Even when colleges are successful, grant funding and employer cost sharing generally help launch programs, build facilities, and buy equipment. To operate programs over time, however, colleges must rely on core operating revenue from state and local subsidies and tuition. It is particularly challenging to fund high-cost programs in states that do not provide extra money for more expensive programs and in colleges that lack substantial funding from local taxes. Colleges must subsidize expensive programs in nursing, allied health, and other advanced technology fields with enrollments in lower-cost liberal arts and sciences courses, even in states with variable program funding or local tax base support.[14]

It is relatively rare to find grant funding to help colleges launch whole-college redesigns like those described in this book. Notable exceptions are the Title IV and Title V grants from the US Department of Education, designed for colleges serving underrepresented groups to strengthen organization and infrastructure for improved student outcomes. Many colleges have used guided pathways as the framework for successful Title IV or Title V grant proposals. As mentioned in the introduction, California and Washington provided categorical funding to support guided pathways reforms. Like most grant and categorical programs, these programs provide funding for a limited time period and the innovations they support will not be sustained unless colleges can find ongoing resources to fund them.

Operating funds are often inadequate to support high-value programs and supports

Even when community colleges reallocate resources and create efficiencies to better support student success, they have historically received less state support than public four-year institutions.[15] The gap has narrowed in recent years, in part because of declines in community college enrollment. Indeed, in twelve states, average funding per student is higher at community colleges than at public four-year institutions.[16] Even so, compared with public regional universities, community colleges serve a higher proportion of students who are more likely to have experienced substandard education before college and to face substantial barriers to completion—all of which make these students more challenging and expensive to serve well.[17] This is reflected in the higher share of resources that public two-year colleges devote to student supports than public four-year institutions. That support includes 36 percent of expenditures on instruction (versus 35 percent for public four-years), 11 percent on student services (versus 5 percent), and 14 percent on scholarships and discounts (versus 5 percent).[18] Moreover, community colleges are less able to raise revenue from tuition than public broad-access four-year institutions.

Community colleges in more than two dozen states rely on performance-based funding (PBF) for at least some of their state allocation. Despite its popularity among policy makers, research shows this type of funding is generally associated with null or modest positive effects on retention and graduation.[19] Moreover, especially in states where PBF accounts for a high proportion of state funding, these policies can also have unintended consequences, including poorer student outcomes and lower funding per full-time equivalent student, particularly for colleges that serve an above-average share of underrepresented students.[20] Such colleges generally lack the staff of better-resourced institutions to manage large-scale change and raise grant funds to support it, and smaller colleges cannot produce economies of scale from reforms. PBF policies that include equity provisions for colleges that enroll or graduate underserved student groups can offset some of these unintended consequences.[21] PBF policies can also incentivize community colleges to push students into short-term certificates at the expense of longer-term associate degrees that bring greater labor market returns.[22] In such cases, the policies mitigate efforts described in this book to guide underserved students into high-value programs.

By last count, thirty states offer tuition-free college programs for qualified students to enroll at a community college.[23] Often referred to as "college promise" or "free-college" programs, most of these offer "last-dollar" support to cover tuition costs that remain after other grants and scholarships have been awarded.[24]

A growing body of rigorous research finds positive effects of providing free college and other types of financial aid on college completion.[25] A randomized study of a program offering $12,000 to attend college to first-time ninth graders in half of Milwaukee public high schools who attended class 90 percent of the time, maintained a 2.5 grade point average, and graduated on time found that the graduation rate from two-year colleges among such students was three percentage points higher than among students in the control group. Given that the study group was composed of low-income ninth graders and that a third of the control group did not graduate from high school, this seemingly small effect amounted to a 25 percent increase in two-year degrees.

This research suggests that the financial support offered by free college and similar scholarship programs helps students defray some of the costs of college and thus increases their chances of graduating. Although students who attend colleges through such programs generate more tuition and state subsidy income for colleges, these programs do not increase per-student funding for colleges. Therefore, they do not provide the added revenue that colleges need to provide high-quality programs and support services. Moreover, the introduction of free-college programs does not seem to have substantially made up for the long-term declines in community college enrollment in many states.

Faced with continuing enrollment challenges—and having already spent their federal COVID-19 Higher Education Emergency Relief Fund—many community colleges nationally, especially small ones, face an uncertain financial future.[26]

Rethinking community college funding with student outcomes and sustainability in mind

To incentivize whole-college efforts to improve programs and student supports while also ensuring that colleges remain financially sound, states need to rethink how they provide core operational funding to community colleges. A handful of states are beginning to move in this direction.

Under a model that had prevailed for more than fifty years, state funding for community colleges in Texas was provided through a formula based primarily on enrollment. A patchwork of local taxing districts also provided local funding for some colleges, with colleges in urban locations more likely to receive tax revenue than those in rural areas. Many colleges, however, served areas with no local taxing authority.

In 2023, Texas shifted away from its previous enrollment-based model. The new policy, established through House Bill 8, aligns funding with the state's higher education goals and workforce needs. State funding of colleges is now based on their performance measured as much on the postcompletion success of their students as on their success while at the college. At the same time, the new policy helps adequately fund colleges, especially small rural ones.

The policy seeks to accomplish these goals through four key features. First, the model rewards community colleges on measurable outcomes. The three most important are

- the number of credentials of value awarded that offer purpose in the economy, value in the labor market, and opportunities for good jobs and meaningful careers;
- the number of students who transfer successfully to public four-year universities after completing fifteen semester credit hours at a community college or in a structured coenrollment program; and
- the number of high school students who complete fifteen semester credit hours in dual credit or dual enrollment courses at a community college.

The outcomes are weighted to recognize the higher costs of educating adult learners and students from economically and academically disadvantaged backgrounds. Colleges will also qualify for bonuses when they deliver credentials of value at a lower cost than other providers of the same credentials statewide.

Second, the model incentivizes colleges to offer programs that align with regional and state workforce needs, ensuring graduates have in-demand skills. This model has led colleges to review existing programs and develop new ones, including creating career ladder programs in well-paying, high-demand fields.

Third, the model increases state funding for community colleges, providing them with additional resources to support their mission. Every college receives a base level of support, which is important to smaller colleges in rural parts of the state hobbled by enrollment declines and limited local tax funding.

Fourth and finally, House Bill 8 establishes the Financial Aid for Swift Transfer program, which provides scholarships for high school students from low-income backgrounds to take dual enrollment courses at no cost. Colleges must offer courses that align with a workforce or transfer program offered by the college, again with an emphasis on high-demand fields in Texas. Thus, the program gives students a head start earning college credits, exploring potential career paths, and developing the skills and knowledge needed for high-demand jobs.

North Carolina is also rethinking how it funds community colleges. Three major changes are under consideration. First, although the state has for some time funded community college courses according to "tiers" based on their cost, under the proposed policy, courses in high-demand fields such as healthcare, engineering, industrial technology and trades, public safety, and information technology would be funded at even higher levels than is currently the case. The idea is to shift the focus from course tiers to careers by providing incentives and resources for colleges to offer programs aligned to labor market needs.

Second, the new model would fund high-demand courses at the same level whether they are credit or noncredit, meaning that colleges would have sufficient support to offer short-term training as well as degree training to help students get into a field and more rapidly meet employer needs. The North Carolina Community College System office is using the statewide course library to map pathways that show students how they can use credit and noncredit offerings to enter and advance career ladders in high-demand fields—along the lines of the learning-and-earning career ladder approach described in chapter 2.

Third, the current formula, which was established in the 1980s, does provide base funding to all colleges, but the levels are based on prior-year enrollments and have not kept up with inflation. The new policy would provide enhanced base funding to enable colleges to expand existing programs and develop new ones in response to increased demand.

Although the General Assembly had not at the time of this writing passed a budget based on this new funding model, it was reflected in the budgets proposed by the state's House, Senate, and governor. This suggests that North Carolina policy makers support an approach to funding community colleges that both provides an adequate level of funding for colleges to provide high-quality programs and prioritizes resources for programs that meet the workforce needs of communities and the state.

TAKING ACTION TO SCALE WHOLE-COLLEGE REFORMS ACROSS SYSTEMS

Statewide agencies can play a pivotal role in advancing student success. In addition to those featured in this chapter, success centers in California, Michigan,

New York, Oregon, Wisconsin, and elsewhere have played similar roles organizing and supporting statewide guided pathways reforms at scale. Based on our work with these and other states, we recommend the following actions to support scaling innovation across a state.

Adopt a framework for organizing the work

A common feature of every state that has made progress spreading whole-college reforms is the use of an organizing framework. A guiding framework can help ensure that colleges across a system are working toward the same goals. It also helps facilitate cross-college collaboration, because many colleges want to learn from similar institutions, especially those in their state. Guided pathways has proved effective as such a framework because it is not overly prescriptive about what practices colleges should implement and how, but rather allows colleges to adapt the model's design principles to their local contexts and priorities.

Establish a regular cadence of activities

As we have seen in Ohio and Texas, regular statewide meetings are essential to keep colleges engaged in systemic reform work. The regular schedule allows colleges to plan so they can have new practitioners attend and learn about reforms, thus bringing more people into the work.

Include all colleges and provide universal and customized support

In Ohio and Texas, all community colleges engage in the institutes and other learning opportunities. But this does not mean all colleges receive the same supports or professional development. In Texas, the cadres allow for more tailored support based on each college's progress and needs. Rural or smaller colleges may need additional support or technical assistance, as they may struggle to pay for this on their own. As colleges continue this journey, the supports they need may diverge further. As we learned in our evaluation of the AACC Pathways Project, progress implementing systemic reforms is not usually linear—some colleges pause or slow down reforms and resume or speed them up later, with every college proceeding at its own pace. To provide support tailored to each college, state agencies should establish mechanisms for checking in with colleges to assess their progress and needs regularly.

Codevelop an applied research agenda

A systemwide applied research agenda benefits state agencies and colleges by providing a strategy for regularly collecting data on each college's progress adopting reforms, including successes and challenges, and for sharing quantitative data on key student outcome measures. The agenda needs must be developed and implemented jointly with colleges. Engaging them to understand the questions and challenges they face provides practitioners with useful and actionable guidance.

Align the work with state policy priorities and initiatives

All states—as well as the federal government and private foundations—provide categorical grant funding beyond operating support to colleges for projects that improve student success. One challenge is that discrete funding too often leads to efforts focused on one aspect of the student experience or one group of students. Those efforts typically are not sustained when the funding ends. Thus, such funding tends not to change the programs that colleges offer and how they serve students generally. As mentioned earlier in this chapter and in the advice from leaders of early adopter colleges in chapter 7, colleges often must braid funding from multiple sources to pay for innovations in programs and practices. They do this by applying for grants that fit within the larger vision, goals, and strategies for reforming programs and practices at scale. Leaders assess changes in practice to see if they lead to improved student recruitment and retention and, if so, sustain them by integrating support into general operating budgets.

Use statewide reform frameworks to advocate for increased funding

State agencies and associations can help colleges scale innovation across a system by presenting a larger framework for reform to help them integrate the funding they are receiving from multiple sources to support systemic reforms, not just boutique innovations. At the same time, state agencies and associations can use this framework to help change mindsets of policy makers and to advocate for adequate funding to support changes in practice that lead to improved success for large numbers of students. This is what college and state leaders did in Texas, and what those in North Carolina and other states are trying to do.

Conclusion

In the decade since *Redesigning America's Community Colleges* was published, we have had the privilege of studying the efforts by community colleges nationwide to implement whole-college reforms based on the guided pathways model it proposed. We know from this research that enacting these reforms is multifaceted, challenging, and time-consuming. Why, then, should community colleges and state systems commit to the considerable investment of time and resources to make these reforms?

First, the need for the education and training opportunities that community colleges provide continues to grow across the country. Although the public at large is markedly skeptical about the value of a college degree, research shows that education beyond high school is essential for securing good jobs that pay living wages and offer real prospects for career advancement. Short-term skills training is important to help underemployed workers gain a foothold in a field and keep incumbent workers current with new technologies. But broader education is still essential. It is as valuable as ever in today's workplace to teach students to communicate effectively, to think critically and creatively, and to adapt to changing technology over the long term. As discussed in chapter 2, public and private investments in infrastructure, a reduced-carbon economy, advanced manufacturing, and technology more generally are projected to create strong demand for skilled technicians—jobs that tend to provide living wages and a good future career path. To prepare workers for these jobs, community colleges must expand and diversify career-technical associate and bachelor's degree, apprenticeship, and prebaccalaureate transfer programs, particularly in healthcare, information technology, engineering, and industrial and construction technologies. To meet other needs of their communities, colleges also need to expand programs in education, public safety, and social services.

Second, community colleges are well positioned to meet this demand. Although they face strong competition from public four-year colleges and online education providers, community colleges have long offered small classes taught by faculty dedicated to excellent teaching and supported by staff committed to providing the added supports often needed by students poorly served by their previous education. Community colleges also have the competitive advantage of being able to work closely with local employers, universities, and economic development groups to develop and offer programs that lead to good jobs in demand in their regions and to partner with K–12 schools and community groups to recruit current and future workers into those programs.

Third, in an otherwise divisive political environment, state and national policy makers continue to show strong bipartisan support for affordable education and training that enables students to secure career-path employment and that supplies talent to meet workforce needs.

Fourth, and finally, since *Redesigning* first outlined the guided pathways framework for community colleges in 2015, we and the field have learned a great deal from early adopter colleges and state systems about how to more effectively and efficiently implement these reforms for the benefit of students.

The Community College Research Center (CCRC) has developed an array of guidance materials and tools based on our research to help colleges implement guided pathways reforms. We frequently offer conference presentations, webinars, and online and in-person workshops on implementing various aspects of the reforms supported by our research. Nationally, numerous other organizations not only conduct applied research but also provide technical assistance to colleges and state systems and advocate for policies that improve student outcomes. We are fortunate to have partnered with many of them, as we indicate in the acknowledgments.

Some of the most useful guidance comes from experienced practitioners. CCRC frequently receives requests for examples of colleges that have implemented various aspects of guided pathways reforms. The national guided pathways reform movement has created a cadre of expert practitioners who have led successful reforms in their colleges and states. This is the realization of the guided pathways learning community envisioned by *Redesigning*'s authors. CCRC has learned so much from these practitioners and appreciates their willingness to share their expertise with other colleges and states.

As described in chapter 8, state community college agencies and associations also have been effective in building and maintaining their own learning communities of practitioners through ongoing professional development activities, leadership academies, and coaching using guided pathways as a shared framework for reform. CCRC has participated in numerous institutes and workshops organized by these statewide entities that connect teams from colleges across their systems to share ideas and approaches that they take back with them to their institutions. Several of these entities also provide their colleges with regular institutional data on important leading indicators, which gives colleges and systems a way to measure the early effects of reforms and inform continuous improvement efforts. A statewide approach to knowledge development and sharing, professional enrichment, and technical assistance benefits all colleges in a state, especially small and underresourced institutions that may have a limited ability to pay for outside support or travel to conferences to learn from others.

No educational institutions in the country offer such a diverse array of educational programs and services to their localities as community colleges. These institutions are essential for promoting social mobility and supplying talent to foster the economic and social well-being of their communities and states. In our research on colleges implementing guided pathways and in our applied learning field education to guide adoption of these reforms, we have encountered thousands of dedicated professionals who—often with limited resources—have worked together to rethink their programs and practices to better serve students and communities. The work of these student success champions provides us with considerable optimism about the future of community colleges and their capacity to continue to perform their vital missions. We look forward to learning how these individuals and other innovative educators will further redesign the community college experience to strengthen pathways to educational and career success and thereby expand opportunity for students, families, and communities.

Notes

Foreword

1. Judith Scott-Clayton, "The Shapeless River: Does a Lack of Structure Inhibit Students' Progress at Community Colleges?," working paper (Community College Research Center, January 2011), abstract, https://ccrc.tc.columbia.edu/publications/lack-of-structure-students-progress.html.

Introduction

1. National Student Clearinghouse Research Center, "Current Term Enrollment Estimates (CTEE) Expanded Edition: Fall 2023 Enrollment Overview," January 11, 2024, https://public.tableau.com/app/profile/researchcenter/viz/CTEEFall2023dashboard/CTEEFall2023.
2. National Student Clearinghouse Research Center, "Current Term Enrollment Estimates (CTEE)."
3. Davis Jenkins and John Fink, "How Will COVID-19 Affect Community College Enrollment? Looking to the Great Recession for Clues," *The Mixed Methods Blog*, Community College Research Center, April 30, 2020, https://ccrc.tc.columbia.edu/easyblog/covid-community-college-enrollment.html.
4. Bridget Terry Long, "The Financial Crisis and College Enrollment: How Have Students and Their Families Responded?," in *How the Financial Crisis and Great Recession Affected Higher Education*, ed. Jeffrey R. Brown and Caroline M. Hoxby (University of Chicago Press, 2014), 209–33, https://scholar.harvard.edu/files/btl/files/blong_-_the_financial_crisis_and_college_enrollment_-_july_2013.pdf.
5. Jeff Strohl, Artem Gulish, and Catherine Morris, *The Future of Good Jobs: Projections Through 2031* (Georgetown University Center on Education and the Workforce, 2024), https://cew.georgetown.edu/wp-content/uploads/cew-the_future_of_good_jobs-fr.pdf.
6. Veronica Minaya and Judith Scott-Clayton, "Labor Market Trajectories for Community College Graduates: How Returns to Certificates and Associate Degrees Evolve Over Time," *Education Finance and Policy* 17, no. 1 (2022): 53–80, https://doi.org/10.1162/edfp_a_00325.
7. Jenkins and Fink, "How Will COVID-19 Affect Community College Enrollment?"
8. *Understanding Community College Practitioners' Perspectives on Student Customer Service Survey Results and Five Strategies to Improve the Student Experience* (EAB, 2023), https://www.luminafoundation.org/wp-content/uploads/2023/07/Understanding-Community-College-Practitioners-Customer-Service.pdf.
9. National Center for Education Statistics, "Number and Percentage of Students Enrolled in Degree-granting Postsecondary Institutions, by Distance Education Participation, Location of Student, Level of Enrollment, and Control and Level of Institution: Fall 2021 and Fall 2022," 2023, https://nces.ed.gov/programs/digest/d23/tables/dt23_311.15.asp.
10. Clive Belfield and Thomas Brock, "Behind the Enrollment Numbers: How COVID Has Changed Students' Plans for Community College," *The Mixed Methods Blog*, Community

College Research Center, November 19, 2020, https://ccrc.tc.columbia.edu/easyblog/covid-enrollment-community-college-plans.html.

11. Serena C. Klempin et al., *Pandemic Relief Spending and Recovery Strategies: Findings from a Survey of Community Colleges in Six States* (Accelerating Recovery in Community Colleges Network and Community College Research Center, June 2024), https://ccrc.tc.columbia.edu/publications/pandemic-relief-spending-recovery-strategies-survey-six-states.html.
12. *Completing College: National and State Reports* (National Student Clearinghouse Research Center, November 2023), https://nscresearchcenter.org/completing-college/.
13. *Persistence and Retention: Fall 2022 Beginning Postsecondary Student Cohort* (National Student Clearinghouse Research Center, July 3, 2024), https://nscresearchcenter.org/persistence-retention/.
14. Elizabeth Zachry Rutschow et al., *Turning the Tide: Five Years of Achieving the Dream in Community Colleges* (MDRC, January 2011), https://www.mdrc.org/publication/turning-tide. ATD (achievingthedream.org) has since developed into an important organization supporting innovation and transformation at more than three hundred community colleges nationwide.
15. Thomas R. Bailey, Shanna Smith Jaggars, and Davis Jenkins, *Redesigning America's Community Colleges: A Clearer Path to Student Success* (Harvard University Press, 2015).
16. Davis Jenkins and Lauren Pellegrino, *Collaborating to Break Down Barriers to Student Success: Guided Pathways Reforms at San Jacinto College* (Community College Research Center, September 2019), https://files.eric.ed.gov/fulltext/ED598447.pdf.
17. "Understanding Dual Enrollment" (Community College Research Center, April 2024), https://ccrc.tc.columbia.edu/publications/understanding-dual-enrollment.html.

Chapter 1

1. Thomas R. Bailey, Shanna Smith Jaggars, and Davis Jenkins, *Redesigning America's Community Colleges: A Clearer Path to Student Success* (Harvard University Press, 2015).
2. Bailey at al., *Redesigning*, 3.
3. Bailey at al., *Redesigning*, 4.
4. Bailey et al., *Redesigning*, 20.
5. Bailey et al., *Redesigning*, 20.
6. For a detailed discussion of how our thinking about the guided pathways model has evolved, see Davis Jenkins, Hana Lahr, and Amy Mazzariello, *How to Achieve More Equitable Community College Student Outcomes: Lessons from Six Years of CCRC Research on Guided Pathways* (Community College Research Center, September 2021), https://ccrc.tc.columbia.edu/media/k2/attachments/equitable-community-college-student-outcomes-guided-pathways.pdf.
7. For a review of the research behind this set of model practices, see Davis Jenkins, Taylor Myers, and Farzana Matin, *Whole-College Guided Pathways Reform: Scale of Adoption by Community Colleges in Three States* (Community College Research Center, September 2023), https://ccrc.tc.columbia.edu/publications/whole-college-guided-pathways-reform.html.
8. *Persistence and Retention: Fall 2022 Beginning Postsecondary Student Cohort* (National Student Clearinghouse Research Center, June 2024), https://nscresearchcenter.org/persistence-retention/.
9. For a literature review, see Amy E. Brown, Veronica Minaya, and Hana Lahr, *A Strategy for Estimating the Effects of Whole-College Guided Pathways Reforms in Community Colleges*, working paper (Community College Research Center, July 2022), https://ccrc.tc.columbia.edu/publications/estimating-effects-whole-college-guided-pathways-reforms.html.

10. Davis Jenkins et al., *Funding Guided Pathways: A Guide for Community College Leaders* (Community College Research Center, October 2020), https://ccrc.tc.columbia.edu/publications/funding-guided-pathways-guide.html.
11. In its 2012 report, AACC's 21st-Century Commission on the Future of Community Colleges argued for a new model that met the needs of contemporary students and communities. See *Reclaiming the American Dream: Community Colleges and the Nation's Future: A Report from the 21st-Century Commission on the Future of Community Colleges* (American Association of Community Colleges, 2012), http://www.aacc21stcenturycenter.org/wp-content/uploads/2014/03/21stCenturyReport.pdf.
12. For more, see "AACC Pathways Project," American Association of Community Colleges, https://www.aacc.nche.edu/programs/aacc-pathways-project/.
13. For specific practices implemented, see Jenkins et al., *What We're Learning About Guided Pathways* (Community College Research Center, 2018), https://ccrc.tc.columbia.edu/publications/what-we-are-learning-guided-pathways.html. For how colleges are managing the large-scale organizational changes involved, see Davis Jenkins et al., *Redesigning Your College Through Guided Pathways: Lessons on Managing Whole-College Reform from the AACC Pathways Project* (Community College Research Center, 2019), https://ccrc.tc.columbia.edu/publications/redesigning-your-college-guided-pathways.html. For how much the reforms cost and how colleges paid for them, see Jenkins et al., *Funding Guided Pathways.*
14. For details on the design, administration, and analysis of the survey, see Jenkins et al., *Whole-College Guided Pathways Reform.*
15. For the effects of early momentum on success by students generally, see Clive Belfield, Davis Jenkins, and John Fink, *Early Momentum Metrics: Leading Indicators for Community College Improvement* (Community College Research Center, 2019), https://ccrc.tc.columbia.edu/publications/early-momentum-metrics-leading-indicators.html. For the effects on students of color and low-income students, see Yuxin Lin, Maggie P. Fay, and John Fink, "Stratified Trajectories: Charting Equity Gaps in Program Pathways Among Community College Students," *Research in Higher Education* 64 (2023): 547–73, https://eric.ed.gov/?id=ED610667.
16. To ensure objectivity, the CCRC researchers who led the evaluation were experts in quantitative analysis and had not been involved in guided pathways research. Additionally, experts in the quantitative evaluation of education reforms reviewed the methodology, which we documented in the Registry of Efficacy and Effectiveness Studies (https://sreereg.icpsr.umich.edu/sreereg/index).
17. Only one college, at which leadership could not convince faculty and others of the value of guided pathways, had not scaled practices in at least one of the four practice areas shown in figure 1.1.
18. For details on the findings of the AACC study, see Hana Lahr, Serena C. Klempin, and Davis Jenkins, *Innovating at Scale: Guided Pathways Adoption and Early Student Momentum Among the AACC Pathways Colleges* (Community College Research Center, September 2023), https://ccrc.tc.columbia.edu/publications/guided-pathways-aacc-colleges.html.
19. For details on the findings of the NSF study, see Jenkins et al., *Whole-College Guided Pathways Reform.*
20. Implementing ongoing advising models (3a), developing schedules based on students' program plans (3c), and investing in teaching and learning in core programmatic courses (4b) generally require meta-majors and support for students' early progress (practice areas 1 and 2).
21. In particular, Tennessee widely adopted corequisite math in 2015 and 2016, when it was strongly recommended by the Tennessee Board of Regents. Adoption of corequisite math

also increased in Ohio in 2018, when the Ohio Association of Community Colleges and the Ohio Department of Higher Education launched a statewide effort to scale corequisite reforms in math and English through Strong Start to Finish (https://strongstart.org/). In comparison, relatively few Washington community colleges had adopted corequisite math with math pathways by 2022.

22. Jenkins et al., *Redesigning Your College.*
23. "Washington Guided Pathways," Washington State Board for Community and Technical Colleges, https://www.sbctc.edu/colleges-staff/programs-services/student-success-center/guided-pathways.
24. For details on the findings of the AACC Pathways evaluation, see Lahr et al., *Innovating at Scale.*
25. Judith Scott-Clayton and Olga Rodriguez, "Development, Discouragement, or Diversion? New Evidence on the Effects of College Remediation," working paper (Community College Research Center, August 2012), https://ccrc.tc.columbia.edu/publications/development-discouragement-diversion.html.
26. Peter M. Crosta, "Intensity and Attachment: How the Chaotic Enrollment Patterns of Community College Students Relate to Educational Outcomes," *Community College Review* 42, no. 2 (April 2014): 118–42, https://journals.sagepub.com/doi/abs/10.1177/0091552113518233.
27. For details on the NSF effects study, see Veronica Minaya and Nicolas Acevedo, *Whole-College Reforms in Community Colleges: Guided Pathways Practices and Early Academic Success in Three States* (Community College Research Center, 2024), https://ccrc.tc.columbia.edu/publications/guided-pathways-practices-early-academic-success-three-states.html.
28. Yet there was a positive association in Ohio with college-level math credits earned when practices in areas 1 and 3 were adopted together.
29. Florence Xiaotao Ran and Yuxin Lin, "The Effects of Corequisite Remediation: Evidence from a Statewide Reform in Tennessee," *Educational Evaluation and Policy Analysis* 44, no. 3 (2022): 355–79, https://journals.sagepub.com/doi/10.3102/01623737211070836.

Chapter 2

1. *The Value of Community College: Recent Students' Motivation and Outcomes* (Strada Education Foundation, September 7, 2023), https://stradaeducation.org/wp-content/uploads/2023/09/090723-PV_report.pdf.
2. Jeff Strohl, Artem Gulish, and Catherine Morris, *The Future of Good Jobs: Projections Through 2031* (Georgetown University Center on Education and the Workforce, 2024), https://cew.georgetown.edu/cew-reports/goodjobsprojections2031/.
3. For data from a survey of a nationally representative sample of community college students, see Laura Horn and Paul Skomsvold, *Community College Student Outcomes: 1994–2009* (National Center for Education Statistics, November 2011), https://nces.ed.gov/pubsearch/pubsinfo.asp?pubid=2012253. For data from a more recent survey, see *Helping Community College Students Climb the Transfer Ladder* (Center for Community College Student Engagement, 2023), https://cccse.org/NR2023.
4. Tatiana Velasco et al., *Tracking Transfer: Community College Effectiveness in Broadening Bachelor's Degree Attainment* (Community College Research Center, Aspen Institute College Excellence Program, and National Student Clearinghouse Research Center, February 2024), https://ccrc.tc.columbia.edu/publications/Tracking-Transfer-Community-College-and-Four-Year-Institutional-Effectiveness-in-Broadening-Bachelors-Degree-Attainment.html.

5. Kerstin Gentsch et al., "The Vertical Transfer Pipeline and Its Leaks: Tracking Students from Associate Degree Programs to Bachelor's Degrees," *Journal of Postsecondary Student Success* 3, no. 2 (2023): 18–55, https://journals.flvc.org/jpss/article/view/134267.
6. Government Accountability Office, "Students Need More Information to Help Reduce Challenges Transferring Credits," August 2017, https://www.gao.gov/assets/gao-17-574.pdf.
7. John Fink et al., "Using Data Mining to Explore Why Community College Transfer Students Earn Bachelor's Degrees with Excess Credits," working paper (Community College Research Center, February 2018), https://ccrc.tc.columbia.edu/publications/using-data-mining-explore-why-community-college-transfer-students-earn-bachelors-degrees-excess-credits.html.
8. David B. Monaghan and Paul Attewell, "The Community College Route to the Bachelor's Degree," *Educational Evaluation and Policy Analysis* 37, no. 1 (2015): 70–91, https://journals.sagepub.com/doi/abs/10.3102/0162373714521865; and Government Accountability Office, "Higher Education: Students Need More Information to Help Reduce Challenges Transferring Credits," August 14, 2017, https://www.gao.gov/products/gao-17-574.
9. Di Xu et al., "Are Community College Transfer Students a Good Bet for 4-Year Admissions? Comparing Academic and Labor-Market Outcomes Between Transfer and Native 4-Year College Students," *Journal of Higher Education* 89, no. 4 (2018): 478–502, https://www.tandfonline.com/doi/abs/10.1080/00221546.2018.1434280.
10. Associate of arts degrees in liberal arts or general studies correspond to Classification of Instructional Program or CIP code 24.01. They are distinct from associate degrees in English, history, sociology, or other liberal arts and sciences subjects. For a discussion of near-term earnings, see Ben Backes, Harry J. Holzer, and Erin Dunlop Velez, "Is It Worth It? Postsecondary Education and Labor Market Outcomes for the Disadvantaged," *IZA Journal of Labor Policy* 4, no. 1 (2015), https://izajolp.springeropen.com/articles/10.1186/s40173-014-0027-0. An analysis by the authors of award data from the Integrated Postsecondary Education Data System matched to College Scorecard Data on earnings of students who received Title IV financial aid indicates that the average median earnings two years after completion among such students who had earned an associate of general or liberal studies and were not still enrolled in college was $24,095, inflation-adjusted to 2019 dollars. Similarly, the median earnings two years after completion associated with associate degrees in general business and management was $29,797. Both figures are well below the average living wage for an individual nationally in 2019, according to the Massachusetts Institute of Technology Living Wage Calculator's estimate of $35,000.
11. Fink et al., "Using Data Mining."
12. John Fink et al., "Toward a Practical Set of STEM Transfer Program Momentum Metrics," *Research in Higher Education* 65 (2023): 259–82, https://link.springer.com/article/10.1007/s11162-023-09759-2#citeas.
13. Velasco et al., *Tracking Transfer.*
14. John Fink, "Visualizing the Many Routes Community College Students Take to Complete a Bachelor's Degree," *The Mixed Methods Blog*, Community College Research Center, March 8, 2017, https://ccrc.tc.columbia.edu/easyblog/visualizing-many-routes-bachelors-degree.html.
15. Douglas L. Robertson and Martha Pelaez, "Behavior Analytic Concepts and Change in a Large Metropolitan Research University: The Graduation Success Initiative," *Journal of Organizational Behavior Management* 36, no. 2–3 (2016): 123–53, https://doi.org/10.1080/01608061.2016.1200513.
16. Velasco et al., *Tracking Transfer.*

17. Lauren Schudde et al., "Students' Sense Making of Higher Education Policies During the Vertical Transfer Process," *American Educational Research Journal* 58, no. 5 (2021): 921–53, https://journals.sagepub.com/doi/abs/10.3102/00028312211003050.
18. *Improving Transfer at Scale* (Aspen Institute College Excellence Program, 2017), https://collegeexcellencecurriculum.aspeninstitute.org/wp-content/uploads/2017/03/ImprovingTransferAtScale_Complete_WithHandouts4.18.pdf.
19. Information for this case study came from site visits to the Alamo Colleges conducted in spring of 2020 as part of our research on how early adopter colleges are funding guided pathways reforms. Data and the graphic in figure 2.2 taken from a March 2023 PowerPoint presentation by George Railey Jr. and Angela Gaudian-Mendez to the annual American Association of Collegiate Registrars and Admissions Officers conference, "Seamless Transfer Pathways: Transfer Advising Guides (TAGs) and the Impact on Student Success."
20. *Texas Public Higher Education Almanac* (Texas Higher Education Coordinating Board), accessed July 21, 2024, http://www.txhighereddata.org/index.cfm?objectid=3A948B80-8B79-11EC-98D60050560100A9.
21. A quasi-experimental study of reverse transfer in Tennessee found some small short-term gains in grade point average and employment but no longer-term benefits for bachelor's completion or earnings. Taylor Odle and Lauren C. Russell, *Giving Credit Where Credit Is Due: Causal Impacts of Reverse Transfer Associate Degrees on Education and Labor Market Outcomes*, working paper (Annenberg Institute at Brown University, April 2022), https://doi.org/10.26300/dmvn-d795.
22. Anthony P. Carnevale et al., *After Everything: Projections of Jobs, Education and Training Requirements Through 2031* (Georgetown University Center on Education and the Workforce, 2023) https://cew.georgetown.edu/cew-reports/projections2031/.
23. Velasco et al., *Tracking Transfer.*
24. Elizabeth Meza and Ivy Love, "Community College Baccalaureate Programs as an Equity Strategy: Student Access and Outcomes Data," New America, March 3, 2022, https://www.newamerica.org/education-policy/briefs/community-college-baccalaureate-programs-as-an-equity-strategy-student-access-and-outcomes-data/.
25. Carnevale et al., *After Everything.*
26. An analysis of community college bachelor's degrees in Florida, which produces the largest number of such degrees nationally, found students of color were underrepresented among graduates of these programs. Thus, colleges need to take steps to ensure that these programs reflect the makeup of the communities they serve and help increase diversity in high-opportunity fields. See Tiffany Thai and Ivy Love, "Community College Bachelor's Degrees in Florida: An Update on Enrollment and Labor Market Outcomes," New America, May 21, 2024, https://www.newamerica.org/education-policy/briefs/community-college-bachelors-degrees-in-florida/.
27. This categorization of jobs and earnings levels associated with community college workforce associate degrees is a rough approximation based on an analysis by the authors of earnings data from the College Scorecard matched to awards data from the Integrated Postsecondary Education Data System from 2021 to 2022 on 916 community colleges in the fifty states and US Territories. The College Scorecard earnings data for particular awards are based on tax records of awardees who received federal financial aid and were not still enrolled in a postsecondary institution during the measurement period. Scorecard data here are median earnings during the 2017 and 2018 calendar years for federal financial aid recipient awardees who completed a community college workforce award in the given field in the 2014–2015 and 2015–2016 academic years and were not enrolled in an institution of

higher education during the measurement years, inflation-adjusted to 2019 dollars. In 2019, according to Massachusetts Institute of Technology's Living Wage Calculator, the living wage for an individual with no children was around $35,000. As such, the earnings data reported here are based on the historical earnings of awardees who earned the same credential. We have averaged the median earnings data for particular programs by field across all community colleges nationally. Given that the College Scorecard sample consists of students who received federal financial aid and were thus low-income earners, combined with the fact that community college career-technical associate degrees are generally designed to enable students to secure jobs they would not be able to without a degree, we believe that examining the earnings of low-income awardees nationally by field two years after completion gives a reasonable rough approximation of the level of earnings associate degree graduates in these fields could earn relative to a living wage.

28. Zachary Mabel et al., *Missed Opportunities: Credential Shortages in Programs Aligned with High-Paying Middle-Skills Jobs in 55 US Metro Areas* (Georgetown University Center on Education and the Workforce, 2024), https://cew.georgetown.edu/wp-content/uploads/cew-missed_opportunities-fr.pdf.
29. Veronica Minaya and Judith Scott-Clayton, "Labor Market Trajectories for Community College Graduates: How Returns to Certificates and Associate's Degrees Evolve Over Time," *Education Finance and Policy* 17, no. 1 (2022): 53–80, https://doi.org/10.1162/edfp_a_00325.
30. Lindsay Daugherty et al., *Stackable Credential Pipelines and Equity for Low-Income Individuals: Evidence from Colorado and Ohio* (RAND Corporation, 2023), https://www.rand.org/pubs/research_reports/RRA2484-1.html.
31. Daugherty et al., *Stackable Credentials.*
32. For a review of the literature on short-term credentials, see Monique O. Ositelu, Clare McCann, and Amy Laitinen, "The Short-Term Credentials Landscape: What We See and What Remains Unseen," New America, 2021, https://www.newamerica.org/education-policy/reports/the-short-term-credentials-landscape/.
33. These features are drawn from interviews by CCRC researchers with staff and faculty at colleges that are developing learning-and-earning ladders. The text also draws from a white paper produced by Wake Technical Community College in North Carolina, which is a leader in creating such programs. "Ladder Economics," white paper (Wake Technical Community College in North Carolina, updated March 13, 2023), https://www.waketech.edu/sites/default/files/page-file-uploads/Ladder%20Economics%20White%20Paper.pdf.
34. For a guide on how to use this taxonomy, see Davis Jenkins, Konrad Mugglestone, and Josh Wyner, *Classifying Community College Programs by Post-Completion Success in Transfer and Workforce* (Aspen Institute College Excellence Program and Community College Research Center, August 2024), https://highered.aspeninstitute.org/wp-content/uploads/2024/08/Aspen-CEP-CCRC-Program-Classification-Guide-Classifying-Programs-by-Post-Completion-8.22.24.pdf.

Chapter 3

1. Anthony P. Carnevale et al., *Workplace Basics: The Competencies Employers Want 2020* (Georgetown University Center on Education and the Workforce, 2020), https://cew.georgetown.edu/wp-content/uploads/cew-workplace-basics-fr.pdf.
2. Brent Orrell and David Veldran, *Perspectives on Opportunity: The Value of a Bachelor's Degree* (American Enterprise Institute for Public Policy Research, January 2024), https://www.aei.org/wp-content/uploads/2024/01/The-Value-of-a-Bachelors-Degree-3.pdf?x85095.

3. *Building Momentum: Using Guided Pathways to Redesign the Student Experience* (Center for Community College Student Engagement, 2020) 19–22, https://cccse.org/sites/default/files/BuildingMomentum.pdf.
4. Elizabeth Kopko, Hollie Daniels, and Dan Cullinan, *The Long-Term Effectiveness of Multiple Measures Assessment: Evidence from a Randomized Controlled Trial* (Center for the Analysis of Postsecondary Education, October 2023), https://postsecondaryreadiness.org/long-term-effects-multiple-measures-assessment/. See also A. W. Logue, Daniel Douglas, and Mari Watanabe-Rose, "Corequisite Mathematics Remediation: Results Over Time and in Different Contexts," *Educational Evaluation and Policy Analysis* 41, no. 3 (May 2019): 294–315, https://doi.org/10.3102/0162373719848777; A. W. Logue, Mari Watanabe-Rose, and Daniel Douglas, "Should Students Assessed as Needing Remedial Mathematics Take College-Level Quantitative Courses Instead? A Randomized Controlled Trial," *Educational Evaluation and Policy Analysis* 38, no. 3 (July 2016): 578–98, https://journals.sagepub.com/doi/10.3102/0162373716649056; and Trey Miller et al., "Assessing the Effect of Corequisite English Instruction Using a Randomized Controlled Trial," *Journal of Research on Educational Effectiveness* 15, no. 1 (2022): 78–102, https://www.tandfonline.com/doi/full/10.1080/19345747.2021.1932000.
5. Thomas J. Kane et al., "Is College Remediation a Barrier or a Boost? Evidence from the Tennessee SAILS Program," *Journal of Policy Analysis and Management* 40, no. 3 (2021): 883–913, https://www.researchgate.net/publication/351073042_Is_College_Remediation_a_Barrier_or_a_Boost_Evidence_from_the_Tennessee_SAILS_Program.
6. Florence Xiaotao Ran and Yuxin Lin, "The Effects of Corequisite Remediation: Evidence from a Statewide Reform on Tennessee," *Educational Evaluation and Policy Analysis* 44, no. 3 (2022): 458–84, https://journals.sagepub.com/doi/10.3102/01623737211070836. A ten-year follow-up analysis had similar findings; see Florence Xiaotao Ran and Hojung Lee, "Does Corequisite Remediation Work for Everyone? An Exploration of Heterogeneous Effects and Mechanisms," EdWorkingPaper 24-928 (Annenberg Institute at Brown University, 2024), https://doi.org/10.26300/h26j-2484.
7. Kane et al., "Is College Remediation a Barrier or a Boost?"
8. Susan Bickerstaff et al., *Five Principles of Reforming Developmental Education: A Review of the Evidence* (Center for the Analysis of Postsecondary Readiness, October 2022), https://ccrc.tc.columbia.edu/publications/five-principles-reforming-developmental-education.html.
9. This case study was based on *Leading the Way: Cuyamaca College Transforms Math Remediation* (California Acceleration Project, September 2017), https://accelerationproject.org/wp-content/uploads/documents/Cap_Leading_the_Way_Web_Final.pdf. Cuyamaca participated in two phases of institutes and coaching provided by the California Community College Chancellor's Office and the National Institute for Inquiry and Improvement to help the state's community colleges adopt guided pathways reforms; see "Guided Pathways," California Community Colleges, accessed August 13, 2024, https://www.cccco.edu/College-Professionals/Guided-Pathways.
10. Elizabeth Zachry Rutschow et al., *The Changing Landscape of Developmental Education Practices: Findings from a National Survey and Interviews with Postsecondary Institutions* (Center for the Analysis of Postsecondary Readiness, 2019), https://postsecondaryreadiness.org/wp-content/uploads/2019/11/changing-landscape-developmental-education-practices.pdf. See also Anne Kim, *Incomplete: The Unfinished Revolution in College Remedial Education* (FutureEd, June 2024), https://www.future-ed.org/wp-content/uploads/2024/06/FutureEd-Dev-Ed-Reform-Report.pdf.

11. Matthew Zeidenberg, Davis Jenkins, and Marc Scott, "Not Just Math and English: Courses That Pose Obstacles to Community College Completion," working paper (Community College Research Center, November 2012), https://ccrc.tc.columbia.edu/publications/obstacle-courses-community-college-completion.html.
12. Xueli Wang et al., "Exploring the Relationship Between Community College Students' Exposure to Math Contextualization and Educational Outcomes," *Research in Higher Education* 63 (2022): 309–36, https://ideas.repec.org/a/spr/reihed/v63y2022i2d10.1007_s11162-021-09644-w.html. See also Dolores Perin, *Facilitating Student Learning Through Contextualization: A Review of Evidence*, working paper (Community College Research Center, February 2011), https://files.eric.ed.gov/fulltext/ED516783.pdf.
13. Amy E. Brown and Hana Lahr, *Approaching Institutional Change with Clarity and Commitment: Guided Pathways at Wallace State Community College* (Community College Research Center, September 2019), https://ccrc.tc.columbia.edu/publications/redesigning-your-college-guided-pathways.html.
14. Steve Olson and Donna Gerardi Riordan, *Report to the President: Engage to Excel: Producing One Million Additional College Graduates with Degrees in Science, Technology, Engineering, and Mathematics* (Executive Office of the President and President's Council of Advisors on Science and Technology, 2012), 86, https://eric.ed.gov/?id=ED541511.
15. Elli J. Theobald et al., "Active Learning Narrows Achievement Gaps for Underrepresented Students in Undergraduate Science, Technology, Engineering, and Math," *Proceedings of the National Academy of Sciences of the United States of America* 117, no. 12 (2020): 6476–83, https://doi.org/10.1073/pnas.1916903117.
16. Nancy Kober, *Reaching Students: What Research Says About Effective Instruction in Undergraduate Science and Engineering* (National Academies Press, 2015), https://www.nap.edu/catalog/18687/reaching-students-what-research-says-about-effective-instruction-in-undergraduate.
17. Theobald et al., "Active Learning Narrows Achievement Gaps."
18. Xueli Wang et al., "Does Active Learning Contribute to Transfer Intent Among 2-Year College Students Beginning in STEM?," *Journal of Higher Education* 88, no. 4 (2017): 593–618, https://www.tandfonline.com/doi/abs/10.1080/00221546.2016.1272090. For a fuller discussion of the evidence, see Xueli Wang, *On My Own: The Challenge and Promise of Building Equitable STEM Transfer Pathways* (Harvard Education Press, 2020).
19. Cynthia Brame, *Active Learning* (Vanderbilt Center for Teaching and Learning, 2016), https://cft.vanderbilt.edu/guides-sub-pages/active-learning/.
20. Leilani A. Arthurs and Bailey Zo Kreager, "An Integrative Review of In-Class Activities That Enable Active Learning in College Science Classroom Settings," *International Journal of Science Education* 39, no. 15 (2017): 2073–91, https://www.researchgate.net/publication/319411641_An_integrative_review_of_in-class_activities_that_enable_active_learning_in_college_science_classroom_settings.
21. Robin Dahman and Aaron Weiss, telephone interview with Davis Jenkins, September 6, 2024.
22. For online course data, see "Number and Percentage of Students Enrolled in Degree-Granting Postsecondary Institutions, by Distance Education Participation, Location of Student, Level of Enrollment, and Control and Level of Institution: Fall 2020 and Fall 2021" (National Center for Education Statistics, 2022), https://nces.ed.gov/programs/digest/d22/tables/dt22_311.15.asp. For growth during the pandemic, see Richard Garrett et al., *CHLOE 8: Student Demand Moves Higher Ed Toward a Multi-Modal Future: The Changing*

Landscape of Online Education 2023: Quality Matters and Eduventures Survey of Chief Online Officers (Quality Matters and Encoura Eduventures Research, 2023), https://qualitymatters.org/sites/default/files/research-docs-pdfs/QM-Eduventures-CHLOE-8-Report-2023.pdf.

23. *The Online Student: Impact of Course Modality on Engagement* (Center for Community College Student Engagement, 2023), https://files.eric.ed.gov/fulltext/ED629498.pdf.
24. Di Xu and Shanna Smith Jaggars, "The Impact of Online Learning on Students' Course Outcomes: Evidence from a Large Community and Technical College System," *Economics of Education Review* 37 (2013): 46–57, https://www.sciencedirect.com/science/article/abs/pii/S0272775713001039.
25. Justin C. Ortagus, "The Relationship Between Varying Levels of Online Enrollment and Degree Completion," *Educational Researcher* 52, no. 3 (2023): 170–73, https://journals.sagepub.com/doi/abs/10.3102/0013189X221147522#:~:text=Using%20institutional%20transcript%20data%20from,students%2C%20but%20enrolling%20in%20all.
26. *Online Student.*
27. Amy E. Brown, Susan Bickerstaff, and Nikki Edgecombe, *Supporting Learning Online: Perspectives of Faculty and Staff at Broad-Access Institutions During COVID-19* (Community College Research Center, 2024), https://ccrc.tc.columbia.edu/media/k2/attachments/supporting-learning-online-perspectives-faculty-staff.pdf.
28. Brown et al., *Supporting Learning Online.*
29. *Using Technology to Support Postsecondary Student Learning: A Practice Guide for College and University Administrators, Advisors, and Faculty* (What Works Clearinghouse, May 2019), https://ies.ed.gov/ncee/wwc/practiceguide/25.
30. Peter Strelan, Amanda J. Osborn, and Edward J. Palmer, "The Flipped Classroom: A Meta-Analysis of Effects on Student Performance Across Disciplines and Education Levels," *Educational Research Review* 30 (2020): 100314, https://www.researchgate.net/publication/339681032_The_flipped_classroom_A_metaanalysis_of_effects_on_student_performance_across_disciplines_and_education_levels.
31. Sarah Ryan et al. "The Effectiveness of Blended Online Learning Courses at the Community College Level," *Community College Journal of Research and Practice* 40, no. 4 (2016): 285–98, https://www.researchgate.net/publication/282998772_The_effectiveness_of_blended_online_learning_courses_at_the_community_college_level.
32. Strelan et al., "Flipped Classroom."
33. Brown et al., "Effectiveness of Blended Online Learning Courses."
34. Anthony P. Carnevale, Nicole Smith, Michelle Melton, and Eric W. Price, *Learning While Earning: The New Normal* (Georgetown University Center on Education and the Workforce, 2015), https://cew.georgetown.edu/wp-content/uploads/Working-Learners-Report.pdf.
35. *National Survey of College Internships 2023 Report* (Strada Education Foundation, June 2024), https://stradaeducation.org/wp-content/uploads/2024/06/Building-Better-Internships-NSCI-Descriptive-Report-June-2024.pdf.
36. Peter Cappelli, "Skill Gaps, Skill Shortages and Skill Mismatches: Evidence for the U.S.," working paper (National Bureau of Economic Research, August 2014), https://www.nber.org/papers/w20382.
37. John M. Nunley et al., "College Major, Internship Experience, and Employment Opportunities: Estimates from a Résumé Audit," *Labour Economics* 38 (2016): 37–46, https://www.sciencedirect.com/science/article/abs/pii/S0927537115001207.
38. Matthew T. Hora et al., *What Are the Longitudinal Impacts of a College Internship During a Pandemic? Findings from the College Internship Study on Program Participation, Quality, Equitable Access, and Student Outcomes* (Center for Research on College-Work Transitions,

March 2023), https://ccwt.wisc.edu/wp-content/uploads/2023/04/20230330-Research-Brief-T3-Internship-Study-Hora-Thompson-Jang-Tucci-Pasqualone-Akram-Wolfgram-Lee-1.pdf.

39. *The 2022 Student Survey Report: Attitudes, Preferences, and Outcomes of Bachelor's Degree Students at Four-Year Schools* (National Association of Colleges and Employers, September 2022), https://www.naceweb.org/store/2022/2022-nace-student-survey-report-and-dashboard-4-year.
40. Carnevale et al., *Learning While Earning.*
41. Carnevale et al., *Learning While Earning*; see also Hora et al., *What Are the Longitudinal Impacts of a College Internship?*
42. Hora et al., *What Are the Longitudinal Impacts of a College Internship?*
43. These data on student performance were provided by SPSCC college leaders.
44. Margaret Prothero, interview with Al Solano, Continuous Learning Institute, Student Success Podcast, podcast audio, https://www.continuous-learning-institute.com/blog/student-success-equity-with-margaret-prothero; and Rebecca Kaminsky, interview with Al Solano, Student Success Podcast, podcast audio, https://www.continuous-learning-institute.com/blog/student-success-equity-with-rebecca-kaminsky.

Chapter 4

1. Sophie Litschwartz et al., *Multiple Measures Assessment and Corequisite Courses: Alternate Ways to Place and Prepare New College Students* (Center for the Analysis of Postsecondary Readiness, November 2023), https://postsecondaryreadiness.org/wp-content/uploads/2023/11/multiple-measures-corequisite-alternate-ways-place-prepare.pdf.
2. *Persistence and Retention: Fall 2022 Beginning Postsecondary Student Cohort* (National Student Clearinghouse Research Center, June 27, 2024), https://nscresearchcenter.org/persistence-retention/.
3. Benjamin L. Castleman and Lindsay C. Page, "A Trickle or a Torrent? Understanding the Extent of Summer Melt Among College-Intending High School Graduates," *Social Science Quarterly* 95, no. 1 (2014): 202–20, https://www.jstor.org/stable/26612158.
4. Hana Lahr, Davis Jenkins, and Brad Phillips, "Engage Students Early or Lose Them: Here's How to Do It," *Diverse Education*, November 22, 2022, https://www.diverseeducation.com/opinion/article/15303487/engage-new-students-early-or-lose-them-heres-how-to-do-it.
5. For more details on the research supporting the ACIP framework, see Davis Jenkins and Hana Lahr, *Research Evidence on Community College Ask-Connect-Inspire-Plan Onboarding Practices* (Community College Research Center, May 2022), https://ccrc.tc.columbia.edu/publications/ask-connect-inspire-plan-onboarding.html.
6. Jeff Allen and Steve Robbins, "Effects of Interest-Major Congruence, Motivation, and Academic Performance on Timely Degree Attainment," *Journal of Counseling Psychology* 57, no. 1 (2010): 23–35, https://psycnet.apa.org/doiLanding?doi=10.1037%2Fa0017267.
7. Among entering students, 44 percent of students got advice on academic goal setting, educational planning, course recommendations, and graduation requirements from family, friends, or other students; 43 percent got this information from college faculty or staff. *Building Momentum: Using Guided Pathways to Redesign the Student Experience* (Center for Community College Engagement, 2020), https://cccse.org/sites/default/files/BuildingMomentum.pdf.
8. Elizabeth Kopko and Sarah Griffin, *Redesigning Community College Student Onboarding Through Guided Pathways. Part 2: Student Perspectives on Reformed Practices at Two Florida*

Colleges (Community College Research Center, May 2020), https://ccrc.tc.columbia.edu/publications/redesigning-community-college-onboarding-guided-pathways.html.

9. *A Mind at Work: Maximizing the Relationship Between Mindset and Student Success* (Center for Community College Student Engagement, 2019), https://cccse.org/sites/default/files/Mindset.pdf.
10. Peter Felten and Leo M. Lambert, *Relationship Rich Education: How Human Connections Drive Success in College* (Johns Hopkins University Press, November 2020).
11. Maggie P. Fay, Shanna S. Jaggars, and Negar Farakish, "'Lost in the Shuffle': How Relationships and Personalized Advisement Shape Transfer Aspirations and Outcomes for Community College Students," *Community College Review* 50, no. 4 (2022): 366–90, https://doi.org/10.1177/00915521221111468.
12. Felten and Lambert, *Relationship Rich Education*.
13. Serena C. Klempin et al., "A Framework for Advising Reform," working paper (Community College Research Center, July 2019), https://ccrc.tc.columbia.edu/publications/framework-advising-reform.html.
14. Hana Lahr, Serena C. Klempin, and Davis Jenkins, *Innovating at Scale: Guided Pathways Adoption and Early Student Momentum Among the AACC Pathways Colleges* (Community College Research Center, 2023), https://ccrc.tc.columbia.edu/publications/guided-pathways-aacc-colleges.html.
15. Colleen Flaherty, "Survey: Half of College Students with Mental Health Issues Haven't Accessed Care," *Inside Higher Ed*, May 23, 2023, https://www.insidehighered.com/news/student-success/health-wellness/2023/05/26/gaps-mental-health-care-college-students.
16. Prerana Bharadwaj et al., "Driving Toward a Degree 2023" (Tyton Partners, July 19, 2023), https://tytonpartners.com/driving-toward-a-degree-2023-awareness-belonging-and-coordination/.
17. Xueli Wang, *On My Own: The Challenge and Promise of Building Equitable STEM Transfer Pathways* (Harvard Education Press, 2020).
18. Selena Cho et al., *A Foundation and a Fire: Strengthening Humanities Education in Community Colleges* (Community College Research Center, 2023), https://ccrc.tc.columbia.edu/media/k2/attachments/foundation-fire-strengthening-humanities-education.pdf.
19. *Building Momentum*.
20. Colleen Flaherty, "Nearly Half of Students Lack Key Academic Guidance," *Inside Higher Ed*, February 28, 2023, https://www.insidehighered.com/news/2023/03/01/student-survey-reveals-gaps-core-academic-advising-functions#.
21. Rachel Fishman and Olivia Cheche, "Why Didn't the Community College Students Come Back?," New America, February 22, 2023, https://www.newamerica.org/education-policy/edcentral/why-didnt-the-community-college-students-come-back/.
22. Serena Klempin and Hana Lahr, *How Guided Pathways Reforms Can Improve Support for Adult Students: Lessons from Three Tennessee Community Colleges* (Community College Research Center, January 2021), https://ccrc.tc.columbia.edu/publications/guided-pathways-adults-tennessee.html.
23. TCC's associate of science in healthcare management is awaiting state approval; the college hopes to offer the program in the fall 2025 term.
24. Amy E. Brown and Hana Lahr, *Approaching Institutional Change with Clarity and Commitment: Guided Pathways at Wallace State Community College* (Community College Research Center, September 2019), https://ccrc.tc.columbia.edu/media/k2/attachments/guided-pathways-case-study-5-wallace-state.pdf.

25. Davis Jenkins, Konrad Mugglestone, and Josh Wyner, *Classifying Community College Programs by Post-Completion Success in Transfer and Workforce* (Aspen Institute College Excellence Program; Community College Research Center, August 2024), https://ccrc.tc.columbia.edu/media/k2/attachments/program-classification-guide.pdf.

Chapter 5

1. Doug Shapiro et al., *Time to Degree: A National View of the Time Enrolled and Elapsed for Associate and Bachelor's Degree Earners* (National Student Clearinghouse Research Center, 2016), https://eric.ed.gov/?id=ED580231.
2. "Understanding College Affordability: Time to Degree," Urban Institute, https://collegeaffordability.urban.org/covering-expenses/time-to-degree/.
3. *Building Momentum: Using Guided Pathways to Redesign the Student Experience* (Center for Community College Student Engagement, 2020), https://cccse.org/sites/default/files/BuildingMomentum.pdf.
4. Rachel Fishman and Olivia Cheche, "Why Didn't the Community College Students Come Back?," New America, February 22, 2023, http://newamerica.org/education-policy/edcentral/why-didnt-the-community-college-students-come-back/.
5. Eric P. Bettinger and Rachel Baker, "The Effects of Student Coaching: An Evaluation of a Randomized Experiment in Student Advising," *Educational Evaluation and Policy Analysis* 36, no. 1 (2014): 3–19, https://cepa.stanford.edu/content/effects-student-coaching-evaluation-randomized-experiment-student-advising.
6. Melinda Karp et al., *Effective Advising for Postsecondary Students: A Practice Guide for Educators* (Institute of Education Sciences, October 2021), https://ies.ed.gov/ncee/wwc/Docs/PracticeGuide/WWC-practice-guide-advising-full-text.pdf.
7. Himani Gupta, *The Power of Fully Supporting Community College Students: The Effects of the City University of New York's Accelerated Study in Associate Programs After Six Years* (MDRC, October 2017), https://www.mdrc.org/work/publications/power-fully-supporting-community-college-students; and Colin Hill, Colleen Sommo, and Kayla Warner, *From Degrees to Dollars: Six-Year Findings from the ASAP Ohio Demonstration* (MDRC, April 2023), https://www.mdrc.org/work/publications/degrees-dollars.
8. Rachel Fulcher Dawson, Melissa S. Kearney, and James X. Sullivan, *Comprehensive Approaches to Increasing Student Completion in Higher Education: A Survey of the Landscape* (Wilson Sheehan Lab for Economic Opportunities, August 2020), https://leo.nd.edu/assets/411401/comprehensive_approaches_to_increasing_student_completion_in_higher_education_fulcher_dawson_sullivan.pdf.
9. Hana Lahr, Serena C. Klempin, and Davis Jenkins, *Innovating at Scale: Guided Pathways Adoption and Early Student Momentum Among the AACC Pathways Colleges* (Community College Research Center, September 2023), https://ccrc.tc.columbia.edu/media/k2/attachments/guided-pathways-aacc-colleges.pdf.
10. Melinda Mechur Karp et al., "How Colleges Use Integrated Planning and Advising for Student Success (iPASS) to Transform Student Support," working paper (Community College Research Center, July 2016), https://files.eric.ed.gov/fulltext/ED568156.pdf.
11. *Building Momentum.*
12. Serena Klempin et al., "A Framework for Advising Reform," in *Academic Advising in the Community College*, ed. Terry U. O'Banion (Rowman & Littlefield, 2019), 29–50.
13. Lahr et al., *Innovating at Scale.*

14. The authors based their calculations on data from the SOAAs of the AACC Pathways colleges.
15. "Faculty Mentoring" (Northeast Wisconsin Technical College, n.d.).
16. "Dream Core Data Preview: Early Alert and Equity" (Northeast Wisconsin Technical College, n.d.).
17. "Faculty Mentoring."
18. John Hamman and Monica Trent, "Course Scheduling Through an Equity Lens," *Community College Daily*, July 12, 2023, https://www.ccdaily.com/2023/07/course-scheduling-through-an-equity-lens/; and Shayne Spaulding, Teresa Derrick-Mills, and Thomas Callan, *Supporting Parents Who Work and Go to School: A Portrait of Low-Income Students Who Are Employed* (Urban Institute, January 12, 2016), https://www.urban.org/research/publication/supporting-parents-who-work-and-go-school-portrait-low-income-students-who-are-employed.
19. Nearly three-quarters of public two-year college students had a job while enrolled, with 46 percent working full time, according to a CCRC analysis of federal data from 2019 to 2020. For more information, see the National Center for Education Statistics, "National Postsecondary Student Aid Study," https://nces.ed.gov/surveys/npsas/; and "Community College FAQs," Community College Research Center, https://ccrc.tc.columbia.edu/community-college-faqs.html.
20. National Center for Education Statistics, "2019–20 National Postsecondary Student Aid Study," American Association of Community Colleges, https://www.aacc.nche.edu/research-trends/fast-facts/.
21. Leon Mait, "To Support Student Parents, Colleges Need to Know Who They Are," New America, October 2, 2023, https://www.newamerica.org/education-policy/edcentral/student-parents-data/.
22. *Building Momentum.*
23. John Barnshaw, *Bending the Curve: How Colleges and Universities Can Rethink the Course Schedule to Graduate More Students Faster* (Ad Astra Information Systems, September 2018), https://cdn2.hubspot.net/hubfs/4523134/HESI/BendingTheCurve-RELEASE.pdf.
24. Davis Jenkins, Taylor Myers, and Farzana Matin, *Whole-College Guided Pathways Reform: Scale of Adoption by Community Colleges in Three States* (Community College Research Center, September 2023), https://ccrc.tc.columbia.edu/publications/whole-college-guided-pathways-reform.html.
25. Shayne Spaulding, Teresa Derrick-Mills, and Thomas Callan, *Supporting Parents Who Work and Go to School: A Portrait of Low-Income Students Who Are Employed* (Urban Institute, January 12, 2016), https://www.urban.org/research/publication/supporting-parents-who-work-and-go-school-portrait-low-income-students-who-are-employed.
26. *Preparing for Shortened Academic Terms: Guide, Workbook, and Spotlights* (Achieving the Dream, May 24, 2021), https://achievingthedream.org/preparing-for-shortened-academic-terms-guide-workbook-and-spotlights/.
27. *Preparing for Shortened Academic Terms.*
28. "8-Week Advantage AY2022 Data" (Northeast Wisconsin Technical College, n.d.).
29. *Preparing for Shortened Academic Terms*; Odessa College provided the authors with data for this report.
30. *Preparing for Shortened Academic Terms.*
31. "Summer Internship Program," Cuyahoga Community College, https://www.tri-c.edu/career-services/student-career-services/summer-internship-program/index.html.

32. "Summer Momentum Plan," Alamo College District, https://www.alamo.edu/admission–aid/paying-for-college/tuition-and-fees/summer-momentum-plan/; and Ashley A. Smith, "Summer Gains in Alamo," *Inside Higher Ed*, September 18, 2018, https://www.insidehighered.com/news/2018/09/19/alamo-colleges-see-improvement-summer-momentum-experiment.
33. Camielle Headlam, Caitlin Anzelone, and Michael J. Weiss, *Making Summer Pay Off: Using Behavioral Science to Encourage Postsecondary Summer Enrollment* (MDRC, 2018), https://www.mdrc.org/work/publications/making-summer-pay.
34. Vivian Yuen Ting Liu, Rachel Yang Zhou, and Jordan Matsudaira, "Six Years Later: Examining the Academic and Employment Outcomes of the Original and Reinstated Summer Pell," working paper (Community College Research Center, February 2023), https://direct.mit.edu/edfp/article-abstract/doi/10.1162/edfp_a_00423/119134/Six-Years-Later-Examining-the-Academic-and?redirectedFrom=fulltext.
35. Lahr et al., *Innovating at Scale.*
36. "Guided Pathways Playbook: Connecting Students to Programs of Study," California Community Colleges, https://www.cccco.edu/College-Professionals/Guided-Pathways/ca-guided-pathways-playbook; and "Guided Pathways Playbook: Developing a Structure to Provide Holistic Supports," California Community Colleges, https://www.cccco.edu/-/media/CCCCO-Website/docs/gp-playbook/CAGP-Institute-Insights-Structure-to-Provide-Holistic-Student-Supports-Brief.pdf.
37. "Student Financial Stability," National Center for Inquiry & Improvement, 2024, https://ncii-improve.com/student-financial-stability/.
38. "Student Financial Stability."

Chapter 6

1. We use *dual enrollment* as a broad term throughout this chapter to refer to the numerous ways through which a student completes college coursework in partnership with a college before high school graduation. This includes models commonly described as concurrent enrollment, dual credit, articulated credit, early or middle college, early college high schools, and pathways to technology early college high schools (P-TECHs).
2. Sarah Griffin, Serena Klempin, and Davis Jenkins, *Using Guided Pathways to Build Cross-Sector Pathways Partnerships* (Community College Research Center, 2021), https://ccrc.tc.columbia.edu/publications/guided-pathways-cross-sector-partnerships.html.
3. Caroline M. Hoxby and Christopher Avery, "The Missing 'One-Offs': The Hidden Supply of High-Achieving, Low Income Students," working paper (National Bureau of Economic Research, December 2012), https://www.nber.org/system/files/working_papers/w18586/w18586.pdf.
4. Erich Lauff and Steven J. Ingels, *Education Longitudinal Study of 2002 (ELS:2002): A First Look at 2002 High School Sophomores 10 Years Later* (National Center for Education Statistics, US Department of Education, 2014), https://nces.ed.gov/pubs2014/2014363.pdf.
5. Karen Levesque et al., *Career and Technical Education in the United States: 1990 to 2005* (National Center for Education Statistics, US Department of Education, July 22, 2008), https://nces.ed.gov/pubs2008/2008035.pdf.
6. Soheyla Taie and Laurie Lewis, *Dual or Concurrent Enrollment in Public Schools in the United States* (National Center for Education Statistics, US Department of Education, 2020), https://nces.ed.gov/pubsearch/pubsinfo.asp?pubid=2020125.

7. John Fink, "How Equitable Is Access to AP and Dual Enrollment Across States and School Districts?," *The Mixed Methods Blog*, Community College Research Center, January 14, 2021, https://ccrc.tc.columbia.edu/easyblog/ap-dual-enrollment-access-update.html.
8. Benjamin Berg et al., "Current Term Enrollment Estimates: Spring 2023" (National Student Clearinghouse Research Center, May 2023), https://nscresearchcenter.org/wp-content/uploads/CTEE_Report_Spring_2023.pdf.
9. *Dual Enrollment Programs* (Institute of Education Sciences, 2017), https://ies.ed.gov/ncee/wwc/Intervention/1043.
10. Jason L. Taylor et al., *Research Priorities for Advancing Equitable Dual Enrollment Policy and Practice* (Collaborative for Higher Education Research and Policy, 2022), https://cherp.utah.edu/publications/research_priorities_for_advancing_equitable_dual_enrollment_policy_and_practice.php; and Tracey King Schaller et al., "A Systematic Review and Meta-Analysis of Dual Enrollment Research," *Journal of College Student Retention: Research, Theory and Practice* (2023), https://journals.sagepub.com/doi/10.1177/15210251231170331?icid=int.sj-abstract.citing-articles.4.
11. For mixed outcomes, see Steven W. Hemelt, Nathaniel L. Schwartz, and Susan M. Dynarski, "Dual-Credit Courses and the Road to College: Experimental Evidence from Tennessee," *Journal of Policy Analysis and Management* 39, no. 3 (2019): 686–719, https://doi.org/10.1002/pam.22180; and Ben Struhl and Joel Vargas, *Taking College Courses in High School: A Strategy for College Readiness* (Jobs for the Future, October 2012), https://eric.ed.gov/?id=ED537253. For a review of the benefits for underrepresented students, see appendix A3 in Taylor et al., *Research Priorities for Advancing Equitable Dual Enrollment Policy and Practice*; Vivian Yuen Ting Liu, Veronica Minaya, and Di Xu, *The Impact of Dual Enrollment on College Application Choice and Admission Success*, working paper (Community College Research Center, December 2022), https://ccrc.tc.columbia.edu/publications/impact-dual-enrollment-application-choice-admission-success.html; and Veronica Minaya, *Can Dual Enrollment Algebra Reduce Racial/Ethnic Gaps in Early STEM Outcomes? Evidence from Florida* (Community College Research Center, February 2021), https://ccrc.tc.columbia.edu/publications/dual-enrollment-algebra-stem-outcomes.html. For students who struggle academically in high school, see Han Bum Lee and Michael U. Villarreal, "Should Students Falling Behind in School Take Dual Enrollment Courses?," *Journal of Education for Students Placed at Risk* 28, no. 4 (2022): 439–73, https://eric.ed.gov/?id=ED618071.
12. M. Allison Kanny, "Dual Enrollment Participation from the Student Perspective," *New Directions for Community Colleges* 2015, no. 169 (2015): 59–70, https://doi.org/10.1002/cc.20133.
13. Taylor et al., *Research Priorities for Advancing Equitable Dual Enrollment Policy and Practice.*
14. Judith Scott-Clayton, Peter M. Crosta, and Clive R. Belfield, "Improving the Targeting of Treatment: Evidence from College Remediation," *Educational Evaluation and Policy Analysis* 36, no. 3 (2014): 371–93, https://ccrc.tc.columbia.edu/publications/improving-the-targeting-of-treatment.html.
15. John Fink, "How Many Students Are Taking Dual Enrollment Courses in High School? New National, State, and College-Level Data," *The Mixed Methods Blog*, Community College Research Center, August 26, 2024, https://ccrc.tc.columbia.edu/easyblog/how-many-students-are-taking-dual-enrollment-courses-in-high-school-new-national-state-and-college-level-data.html.
16. Di Xu, Sabrina Solanki, and John Fink, "College Acceleration for All? Mapping Racial Gaps in Advanced Placement and Dual Enrollment Participation," *American*

Educational Research Journal 58, no. 5 (2021): 954–99, https://journals.sagepub.com/doi/10.3102/0002831221991138.

17. Gelsey Mehl et al., *The Dual Enrollment Playbook: A Guide to Equitable Acceleration for Students* (Aspen Institute and Community College Research Center, October 2020), https://ccrc.tc.columbia.edu/publications/dual-enrollment-playbook-equitable-acceleration.html; and John Fink et al., *DEEP Insights: Redesigning Dual Enrollment as a Purposeful Pathway to College and Career Opportunity* (Community College Research Center, October 2023), https://ccrc.tc.columbia.edu/publications/deep-insights-redesigning-dual-enrollment.html.
18. Fink, "How Many Students Are Taking Dual Enrollment Courses?"
19. Mehl et al., *Dual Enrollment Playbook.*
20. Three of the other four partnerships were anchored by colleges that began implementing guided pathways reforms more recently.
21. For more details on the methodology and findings from this study, see Fink et al., *DEEP Insights.*
22. The researchers selected sites using results from SOAAs organized by state student success centers, as described in chapter 1, as well as statewide administrative student records, to identify dual enrollment partnerships with colleges more advanced in their guided pathways implementation and with the strongest results for access to and success in dual enrollment courses and high rates of post–high school college enrollment and persistence among Black, Hispanic, and low-income students.
23. For more detail on the examples presented in this chapter from Tallahassee Community College, Miami Dade College, C. E. King High School, San Jacinto College, Chipola College, Blountstown High School, Lee College, and Goose Creek Consolidated Independent School District, see Fink et al., *DEEP Insights.*
24. Mehl et al., *Dual Enrollment Playbook,* 31.
25. For evidence that students who earn an associate degree through dual enrollment in Texas are unable to apply many of the credits earned to a bachelor's degree in their field of study, see Thomas R. Bailey et al., *Policy Levers to Strengthen Community College Transfer Student Success in Texas* (Community College Research Center and Greater Texas Foundation, January 2017), 19, https://ccrc.tc.columbia.edu/publications/policy-levers-to-strengthen-community-college-transfer-student-success-in-texas.html. The Texas Core Curriculum is a list of the general education courses that state universities are required to accept for credit toward a bachelor's degree. Texas Higher Education Coordinating Board, "Texas Core Curriculum," accessed July 17, 2024, https://www.highered.texas.gov/new-program-development/texas-core-curriculum/.
26. John Fink, "What Happened to Community College Enrollment During the First Years of the Pandemic? It Depends on the Students' Age," *The Mixed Methods Blog,* Community College Research Center, January 9, 2023, https://ccrc.tc.columbia.edu/easyblog/what-happened-to-community-college-enrollment-depends-students-age.html.
27. Clive Belfield, Davis Jenkins, and John Fink, *Early Momentum Metrics: Leading Indicators for Community College Improvement* (Community College Research Center, 2019), https://ccrc.tc.columbia.edu/publications/early-momentum-metrics-leading-indicators.html.
28. Tatiana Velasco et al., *Tracking Transfer: Community College and Four-Year Institutional Effectiveness in Broadening Bachelor's Degree Attainment* (Community College Research Center, February 2024), https://ccrc.tc.columbia.edu/media/k2/attachments/tracking-transfer-community-college-effectiveness.pdf.
29. Mehl et al., *Dual Enrollment Playbook.*

30. For a shorter summary of the DEEP framework, see John Fink and Davis Jenkins, "Introducing DEEP: A Research-Based Framework for Broadening the Benefits of Dual Enrollment," *The Mixed Methods Blog*, Community College Research Center, October 10, 2023, https://ccrc.tc.columbia.edu/easyblog/introducing-deep-research-based-framework.html. Data for discussion may be available from the college; for sample data templates, see Mehl et al., *Dual Enrollment Playbook.*

Chapter 7

1. Clive Belfield, "The Economics of Guided Pathways: Costs, Funding and Value," working paper (Community College Research Center, October 2020), https://ccrc.tc.columbia.edu/publications/economics-guided-pathways-cost-funding-value.html.
2. Davis Jenkins et al., *Funding Guided Pathways: A Guide for Community College Leaders* (Community College Research Center, October 2020), https://ccrc.tc.columbia.edu/publications/funding-guided-pathways-guide.html; and Davis Jenkins, Serena C. Klempin, and Hana Lahr, *Funding Guided Pathways Reforms at Small Colleges: Three Ohio Community Colleges Show How to Do It* (Community College Research Center, September 2022), https://ccrc.tc.columbia.edu/publications/funding-guided-pathways-reforms-small-colleges.html.
3. The examples mentioned in this section and the next are drawn from Jenkins et al., *Funding Guided Pathways*, and Jenkins et al., *Funding Guided Pathways Reforms at Small Colleges.*
4. Benjamin L. Castleman and Lindsay C. Page, *Summer Melt Supporting Low-Income Students Through the Transition to College* (Harvard Education Press, 2014).
5. Scott Ralls, email communication with Davis Jenkins, December 5, 2023.
6. This case study is drawn from Jenkins et al., *Funding Guided Pathways Reforms at Small Colleges.*
7. J. Gregory Hodges, telephone interview with Davis Jenkins and John Fink, July 8, 2024.
8. Jenkins et al., *Funding Guided Pathways Reforms at Small Colleges.*
9. Clive Belfield et al., "Aftershocks: How the Pandemic Affected Community College Finances," *The Mixed Methods Blog*, Community College Research Center, February 14, 2024, https://ccrc.tc.columbia.edu/easyblog/aftershocks-how-pandemic-affected-community-college-finances.html.
10. Jenkins et al., *Funding Guided Pathways Reforms at Small Colleges.*
11. Examples in this section are drawn from Hana Lahr, *Engaging the College Community in Guided Pathways Reforms: Advice from Leaders at AACC Pathways Colleges* (Community College Research Center, September 2023), accessed July 17, 2024, https://ccrc.tc.columbia.edu/publications/engaging-college-community-guided-pathways.html.
12. Lahr, *Engaging the College Community in Guided Pathways Reforms.*
13. Kay McClenney made these comments in an April 2023 review of a proposal for this book.
14. Lahr, *Engaging the College Community in Guided Pathways Reforms.*
15. Lahr, *Engaging the College Community in Guided Pathways Reforms.*
16. Lahr, *Engaging the College Community in Guided Pathways Reforms.*
17. "Caring Campus: Improving Student Retention and Success," Institute for Evidence-Based Change, https://www.iebcnow.org/caring-campus/.
18. Joe Schaffer, interview with Davis Jenkins and Hana Lahr, September 27, 2024.
19. Joe Schaffer, interview with Davis Jenkins and Hana Lahr, September 27, 2024.
20. Lahr, *Engaging the College Community in Guided Pathways Reforms.*
21. Jenkins et al., *Funding Guided Pathways.*
22. The quotes in this paragraph are from Lahr, *Engaging the College Community in Guided Pathways Reforms.*
23. Lahr, *Engaging the College Community in Guided Pathways Reforms.*
24. Lahr, *Engaging the College Community in Guided Pathways Reforms.*

Chapter 8

1. *Bridges to Opportunity for Underemployed Adults: A State Policy Guide for Community College Leaders* (Community College Research Center, 2008), https://ccrc.tc.columbia.edu/publications/underprepared-adults-state-policy-guide.html.
2. R. Edward Bowling, Sharon Morrissey, and George M. Fouts, "State-Level Reforms That Support College-Level Program Changes in North Carolina," *New Directions in Community Colleges*, no. 127 (2014): 73–86, https://onlinelibrary.wiley.com/doi/abs/10.1002/cc.20112.
3. "Completion by Design," Completion by Design, https://www.completionbydesign.org/s/.
4. In CCRC's study of how three small and rural colleges in Ohio funded guided pathways reforms, we found that the Ohio Center for Student Success provided critical resources through professional development and technical assistance to help the colleges adopt guided pathways reforms that they would otherwise struggle to afford. Read more in Davis Jenkins, Serena C. Klempin, and Hana Lahr, *Funding Guided Pathways Reforms at Small Colleges: Three Ohio Community Colleges Show How to Do It* (Community College Research Center, September 2022), https://ccrc.tc.columbia.edu/publications/funding-guided-pathways-reforms-small-colleges.html.
5. The Texas Higher Education Coordinating Board launched the Talent Strong Texas strategic plan for all higher education institutions in the state in 2022. For more information, see "Building a Talent Strong Texas," Texas Higher Education Coordinating Board, https://www.highered.texas.gov/our-work/talent-strong-texas/.
6. To learn more about the detailed research agenda, see "Knowledge Development," Texas Success Center, https://tacc.org/tsc/knowledge-development. CCRC researchers have participated on the Knowledge Development Steering Committee since 2016.
7. Following the 2023 administration of the scale of adoption assessment, the Texas Success Center released detailed reports about pillars 1 and 2. For more on pillar 1, see Kristina Flores, Stacy Ybarra, and Jo-Carol Fabianke, *Progress Scaling Texas Pathways: Results of the 2023 Scale of Adoption Assessment, Pillar 1: Mapping Pathways to Student End Goals* (Texas Association of Community Colleges, December 2023), https://tacc.org/sites/default/files/2024-01/pillar_1-mapping_pathways_to_student_end_goals.pdf.
8. To read more about the Texas Association of Community Colleges' Trustee Institute, see "Board of Trustees Institute," Texas Success Center, https://tacc.org/tsc/board-trustees-institute.
9. Kristina Flores, *Talent Strong Texas Pathways: Early Momentum Metrics Overview* (Texas Association of Community Colleges, 2024), https://tacc.org/sites/default/files/2024-09/emm_overview_08.23.2024.pdf. See chapter 1 for a discussion of early momentum metrics and their use as leading indicators in evaluating the effects of guided pathways reforms on student progression and success.
10. The Ohio Student Success Center is part of the Ohio Association of Community Colleges, https://ohiocommunitycolleges.org/success-center/.
11. Clive Belfield, Peter M. Crosta, and Davis Jenkins, "Can Community Colleges Afford to Improve Completion? Measuring the Cost and Efficiency Consequences of Reform," *Educational Evaluation and Policy Analysis* 36, no. 3 (2014): 327–45, https://doi.org/10.3102/0162373713517293.
12. "Investing in Career Technical Education: An American Imperative," Advance CTE, https://careertech.org/document/investing-in-cte-an-american-imperative/.
13. *State Policies Impacting CTE: 2023 Year in Review* (Advance CTE, 2024), https://careertech.org/wp-content/uploads/2024/02/CTE_2023YIR_021324.pdf. Efforts by the Trump administration in its first few weeks to enact draconian cuts to government programs raise

questions about whether funding appropriated under the Biden administration for workforce education and training to support infrastructure and economic transition will be sustained.

14. Belfield et al., "Can Community Colleges Afford to Improve Completion?"
15. Richard D. Kahlenberg et al., *Policy Strategies for Pursuing Adequate Funding of Community Colleges* (The Century Foundation, October 25, 2018), https://tcf.org/content/report/policy-strategies-pursuing-adequate-funding-community-colleges/.
16. *SHEF: State Higher Education Finance, FY 2022*, State Higher Education Executive Officers Association, 2023, https://shef.sheeo.org/wp-content/uploads/2023/05/SHEEO_SHEF_FY22_Report.pdf.
17. Victoria Yuen, "The $78 Billion Community College Funding Shortfall," Center for American Progress, October 7, 2020, https://www.americanprogress.org/article/78-billion-community-college-funding-shortfall/.
18. National Center for Education Statistics, "Table 05. Amount and percentage distribution of revenues and expenses of Title IV institutions and administrative offices, by level and control of institution or administrative office, accounting standards utilized, and source of funds and type of expense: United States, fiscal year 2022," https://nces.ed.gov/ipeds/search?query=&query2=&resultType=table&page=1&sortBy=date_desc&surveyComponents=Fall%20Enrollment%20(EF)&surveyComponents=Finance%20(F)&surveyComponents=Academic%20Libraries%20(AL)&surveyComponents=Human%20Resources%20(HR)&collectionYears=2022-23&sources=Tables%20Library&overlayTableId=36100.
19. Justin C. Ortagus, Robert Kelchen, and Nicholas Voorhees, "Performance-Based Funding in American Higher Education: A Systematic Synthesis of the Intended and Unintended Consequences," *Educational Evaluation and Policy Analysis* 42, no. 4 (2000): 520–50, https://journals.sagepub.com/doi/10.3102/0162373720953128.
20. Justin C. Ortagus et al., "The Unequal Impacts of Performance-Based Funding on Institutional Resources in Higher Education," *Research in Higher Education* 64 (2023): 705–39, https://static1.squarespace.com/static/5d9f9fae6a122515ee074363/t/61f42ff33d2a6053c9889514/1643393013933/InformedStates_Paper_UnequalImpactsofPBFinResources.pdf.
21. Ortagus et al., "Performance-Based Funding in American Higher Education."
22. Amy Y. Li and Alec I. Kennedy, "Performance Funding Policy Effects on Community College Outcomes: Are Short-Term Certificates on the Rise?," *Community College Review* 46, no. 1 (2019): 3–39, https://tacc.org/sites/default/files/documents/2018-07/performance_funding_policy_effects.pdf; and Amy Y. Li and Justin C. Ortagus, "Raising the Stakes: Impacts of the Complete College Tennessee Act on Underserved Student Enrollment and Sub-baccalaureate Credentials," *Review of Higher Education* 43, no. 1 (2019): 295–333, https://eric.ed.gov/?q=source%3A%22review+of+education%22&ff1=eduAdult+Education&pg=8&id=EJ1229948.
23. Hanneh Bareham, "States with Free College Tuition," *Bankrate*, March 4, 2024, https://www.bankrate.com/loans/student-loans/states-with-free-college-tuition/.
24. Douglas N. Harris and Jonathan Mills, *Optimal College Financial Aid: Theory and Evidence on Free College, Early Commitment, and Merit Aid from an Eight-Year Randomized Trial* (Annenberg Institute, May 2021), 21–393, https://edworkingpapers.com/sites/default/files/ai21-393_0.pdf.
25. For a review of the literature, see Harris et al., *Optimal College Financial Aid*.
26. Clive Belfield et al., "Aftershocks: How the Pandemic Affected Community College Finances," *The Mixed Methods Blog*, Community College Research Center, February 14, 2024, https://ccrc.tc.columbia.edu/arccnetwork/2024/02/14/aftershocks-how-the-pandemic-affected-community-college-finances/.

Acknowledgments

Our work on guided pathways would not have been possible without the courage and commitment of colleges willing to embrace the model. We are especially grateful to the faculty, staff, and administrators at the more than one hundred community colleges nationally that served as sites for our research and at scores more who participated in our applied learning field engagement activities. We have learned so much from you and are inspired by your continuing commitment to finding ways to better serve your students and communities. We also want to thank the students we spoke with at many of these colleges who shared stories with us about their educational experiences and about their lives. We appreciate their time, insight, and candor. They have helped us to understand how community colleges can better support future students to realize their educational and career goals.

We have also learned a great deal from our partnerships with community college agencies and associations in many states that have led efforts to promote the scaling of guided pathways reforms across colleges in their systems. These include Arkansas Community Colleges, Arizona Community Colleges, California Community College Chancellor's Office and the Foundation for California Community Colleges, Connecticut State Colleges and Universities, Florida State Department of Education State Colleges Division, University System of Georgia, Indiana Commission for Higher Education, Iowa Department of Education, Kentucky Community and Technical College System, Maine Community College System, Michigan Community College Association, Community College System of New Hampshire, New Jersey Council of County Colleges, State University of New York System, North Carolina Community College System, Ohio Association of Community Colleges and Ohio Department of Higher Education, Oregon Community College Association, Tennessee Board of Regents, Texas Association of Community Colleges, Washington State Board for Community and Technical Colleges, and Wisconsin Technical College System.

We are fortunate to have collaborated with and learned alongside many insightful and dedicated people who work at other organizations that conduct applied research, provide technical assistance to colleges and state systems, and advocate for policies to support efforts to improve outcomes for community college students. The organizational partners in our work on guided pathways and related reforms have included Achieving the Dream, American Association of Community Colleges, The Aspen Institute's College Excellence Program, Career Ladders Project, Center for Community College Student Engagement, Complete College America, Continuous Learning Institute, Institute for Evidence-Based Change, Jobs for the Future, National Alliance of Concurrent Enrollment Partnerships, National Center for Inquiry & Improvement, National Student Clearinghouse, Sova Solutions, and WestEd. Individual researchers we have worked closely with include Shanna Jaggars at The Ohio State University, Lauren Schudde at University of Texas at Austin, and Di Xu at University of California, Irvine.

We could not have produced this book without the support of our colleagues at the Community College Research Center (CCRC). We are particularly indebted to CCRC Director Thomas Brock for encouraging us to write it, helping raise the funds to do so, and providing helpful advice on its main themes and structure. Megan Anderson at CCRC assisted with preparing and organizing several of the case studies that aim to flesh out the ideas in the book. We also thank CCRC's communications team. Doug Slater provided feedback that helped us to clarify our arguments. Juliette Isaacs and Stacie Long contributed their artistic talents to designing the graphics that appear in the book. Elizabeth Ganga has been instrumental in helping us to disseminate our research and guidance on guided pathways to the field. We also appreciate the ongoing support from CCRC's administration and finance team, in particular Corinne Herlihy, Mathilda Lombos, and Sandra Spady. And we thank CCRC research colleagues Susan Bickerstaff, Nikki Edgecombe, and Hoori Kalamkarian for providing helpful comments on an outline for the book. We feel fortunate to have conducted and published research on which this book is based with CCRC's founding director, Thomas Bailey, and with other talented current and former CCRC researchers, including Elisabeth Barnett, Mariel Bedoya-Guevara, Clive Belfield, Amy E. Brown, Aurely Garcia Tulloch, Sarah Griffin, Shanna Jaggars, Melinda Karp, Elizabeth M. Kopko, Vivian Yuen Ting Liu,

Farzana Matin, Amy Mazzariello, Veronica Minaya, Taylor Myers, Lauren Pellegrino, Florence Xiaotao Ran, Daniel Sparks, Jessica Steiger, Tatiana Velasco, and Takeshi Yanagiura.

Shanna Jaggars, Kay McClenney, and Xueli Wang—highly influential researchers in the field—provided us with feedback on early drafts of this book. We thank them for their valuable insights. We also thank Margaret Moffett, who did a masterful job editing the manuscript that became this book. Margaret helped us sharpen our ideas and transform our sometimes stilted academic prose into a much easier and more impactful read. Jayne Fargnoli of Harvard Education Press encouraged us to write the book and helped us develop a successful proposal for it. Her colleague Molly Cerrone shepherded us through editing and publication.

Many philanthropies have supported our work on guided pathways; they have also served as important thought partners on strategies for improving community college success at scale, connected us to others working on similar issues, and helped us disseminate our findings and guidance to the field. Ascendium Education Group supported the writing of this book, and it has invested in other efforts we have taken to help the field translate research into action. The Bill & Melinda Gates Foundation was an important funder of research that led to CCRC's 2015 book, *Redesigning America's Community Colleges*, and it has continued to support our guided pathways work since then. The Gates Foundation and the National Science Foundation (Grant No. 1915191) each provided funding for separate multiyear evaluations of guided pathways, both of which are discussed in this book. We thank these and other funders of our guided pathways work, which include The Belk Foundation, College Futures Foundation, ECMC Foundation, Greater Texas Foundation, The Joyce Foundation, JPMorgan Global Philanthropy, The Kresge Foundation, Lumina Foundation, Strada Education Foundation, and The Teagle Foundation. The findings and conclusions contained in this book are those of the authors and do not necessarily reflect positions or policies of these funders.

About the Authors

Davis Jenkins is a senior research scholar at the Community College Research Center (CCRC) at Teachers College, Columbia University, where he is also a research professor in education and social policy.

Hana Lahr is assistant director of research and director of applied learning at CCRC.

John Fink is a senior research associate and director of transitions research at CCRC.

Serena C. Klempin is a CCRC research associate.

Maggie P. Fay is a CCRC senior research associate.

Index